TEACHING GUIDE AND RESOURCES

PEARSON

REALITY CENTRAL

PEARSON

GRADE **10**

Upper Saddle River, New Jersey • Boston, Massachusetts
Chandler, Arizona • Glenview, Illinois • Shoreview, Minnesota

S0-BFA-658

ISBN-13: 978-0-13-367445-3

ISBN-10: 0-13-367445-2

10 V036 14

TABLE OF CONTENTS

Philosophy and Purpose

Reality Central consists of an anthology of accessible nonfiction articles on edgy and often debatable topics for struggling readers in grades 6 through 10. The *Real World Writing Journal* and the *Teaching Guide and Resources* are companions to the student anthologies. The topics in the student anthology are relevant to students' experiences and serve as motivating factors for reading and discussion.

Program Materials

The *Reality Central* student anthology brings real-life topics to readers with scaffolded support throughout each lesson.

The *Real World Writing Journal* supports your students as they write about topics related to the student anthology and deeply explore vocabulary words. A handbook of grammar, usage, and mechanics is a ready reference for student writers and a practice tool to lift each writer's skills.

The *Teaching Guide and Resources* provides a systematic and explicit approach to teaching with the student anthology and writing journal. Innovative think-alouds, teaching tips, and suggestions for making the content accessible for all readers allow you to differentiate instruction and reach learners of varying proficiency levels.

Who benefits from *Reality Central*?

The materials in *Reality Central* are specially crafted for readers who may need extra support.

Struggling Readers

All components of *Reality Central* provide practice and support for struggling readers by addressing the following critical elements:

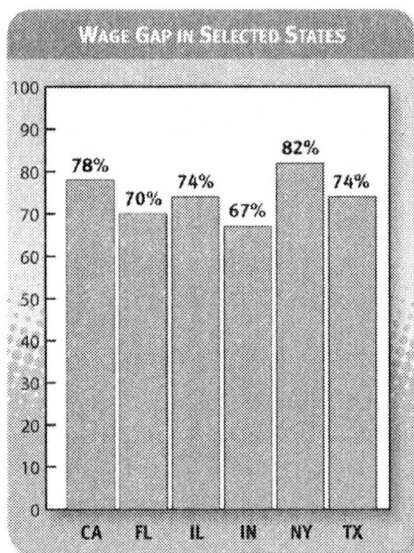

- **Vocabulary Development** Multiple exposure to content and academic vocabulary is developed throughout the anthology articles. Each unit focuses on a small number of crucial words, repeating words in various forms throughout the unit. The *Real World Writing Journal* provides opportunities for further practice in various contexts.
- **Connection to Background Knowledge** Each article begins with a Real-Life Connection that allows students to connect what they already know with what they will learn.
- **Targeted Writing Instruction** Writing instruction that includes pre-writing, drafting, and revision is explicit and systematic.
- **Discussion** Numerous opportunities for discussion support the reading and provide practice in critical thinking and oral language skills.

English Learners

The student anthology in *Reality Central* is appropriate not only for struggling readers, but also for ELs (English Learners). Pedagogy important for ELs included in *Reality Central* includes:

WAGE GAP IN SELECTED STATES

State	Percentage
CA	78%
FL	70%
IL	74%
IN	67%
NY	82%
TX	74%

Information is from the Current Population Survey, American Association of University Women.

- **Pre-reading Support** A controlled number of vocabulary words are systematically introduced before reading. Students connect what they already know to article topics. In some cases, topics may be new to students. Relevant background information is provided to help readers get the most out of the articles.
- **Support During Reading** Selections have been carefully written at Lexile levels appropriate for ELs. In addition, articles include limited use of idioms and other language that may be difficult for ELs. Graphic sources in the articles provide other methods for students to access information.
- **Post-reading Support** Comprehension of text is scaffolded by beginning with literal questions after reading. These questions support students as they "find it on the page." As students' confidence and ability to navigate text grow, questions invite them to use their critical thinking and problem-solving skills.

What features are important to *Reality Central*?

Big Questions anchor units.

- A Big Question appears on the unit opener for each unit. Opening activities use the Big Question as an anchor for the other activities in the unit.
- Each article has its own Big Question, carefully related to the Unit Big Question.
- A closing activity allows for students to solidify their thinking about the Big Questions. In a creative format, such as a debate, television show, or poster, students demonstrate the depth of their understanding of the Big Question.

Careful consideration of leveling cultivates students' success.

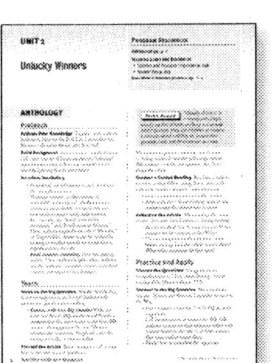

- Articles are typically one to two reading levels below the targeted grade-level audience.
- The articles are written with accessible language in a student-friendly tone.
- Visuals such as graphs and charts support students' informational literacy.

Multiple readings foster growth in skills.

- Lesson plans outline a multiple-reading strategy that builds fluency and the use of comprehension strategies.
- On a first reading, the teacher may read to students and guide their thinking.
- On repeated readings, students own the reading process by looking for clues that help them answer questions.
- As students delve into writing, they are encouraged to revisit the article for details that support their ideas.

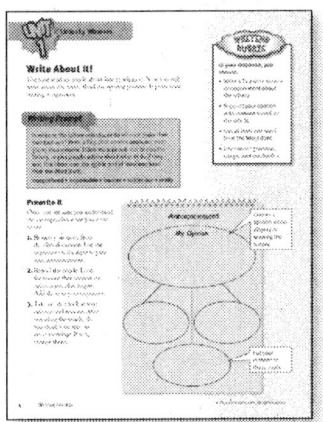

Opportunities for direct instruction in writing, vocabulary, and grammar lift students' achievement.

- Writing instruction follows a mediated approach, in which students receive instruction in all phases of the writing process. Modeling by the teacher enhances student understanding.
- Direct instruction in vocabulary focuses on the idea that multiple exposures to words in various contexts provide not just familiarity, but the ability to use a growing vocabulary.
- A handbook of grammar, usage, and mechanics provides exercises that focus on "real-life" writings. The handbook approach treats editing as an ongoing strategy.

Reality Central **Student Anthology**

Unit Opener

❶ Use the illustration to engage students and prompt their thinking.

❷ Set the stage and provide a purpose for reading by sharing the Big Question.

The teaching plan includes suggestions for creating a visual anchor for the unit focused on the Big Question.

Article

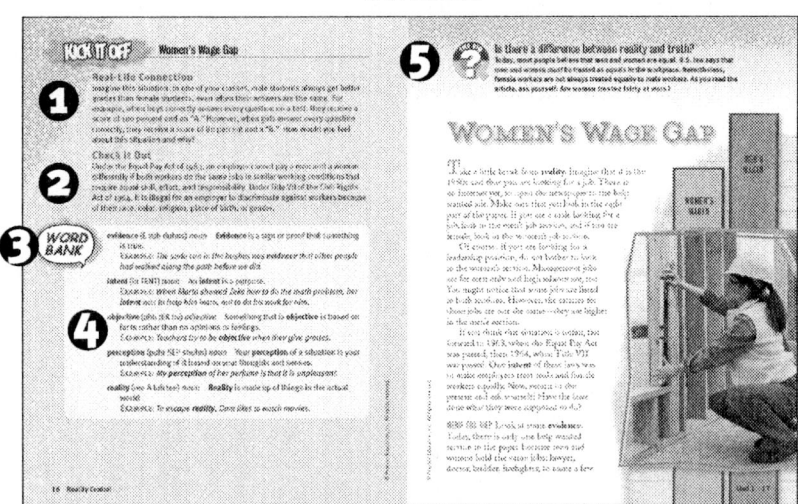

❶ Use the Real-Life Connection to link the article topic to students' experiences, providing a connection and engaging readers.

❷ Read the Check It Out features with students to share information that they will need to access ideas in the text.

❸ Introduce the Word Bank. Many of these words appear multiple times throughout the unit, introducing a controlled vocabulary.

❹ Highlight the example section in the Word Bank to put each word into a meaningful context for students.

❺ Read through the introduction with students to prompt their thinking about the topic and the Article Big Question. Discuss how the Article Big Question and the Unit Big Question are connected.

Article

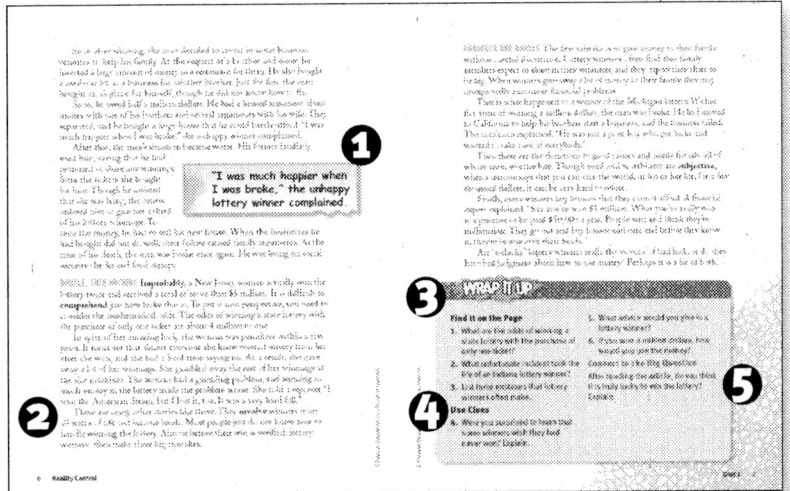

❶ Draw attention to graphics, charts, and other visuals to boost students' nonfiction literacy skills.

❷ Point out the boldface vocabulary words. These words are variations of the Word Bank words.

❸ Use the "Find It on the Page" questions to key students directly to lesson content.

❹ Prompt deeper thinking with the "Use Clues" questions after a second reading.

❺ Bring students back to the Big Question to provide closure.

Unit Closer

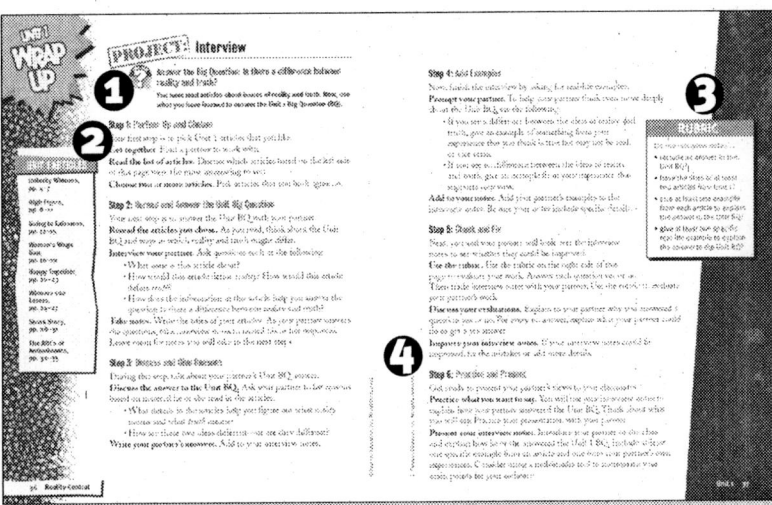

❶ Introduce the product students will create.

❷ Follow the instructions to guide students in creating a product that answers the Unit Big Question and uses information from the articles.

❸ Prompt students to use the rubric in order to assess and make changes to their work.

❹ Encourage students to share their work.

Reality Central **Real World Writing Journal**

Write About It!

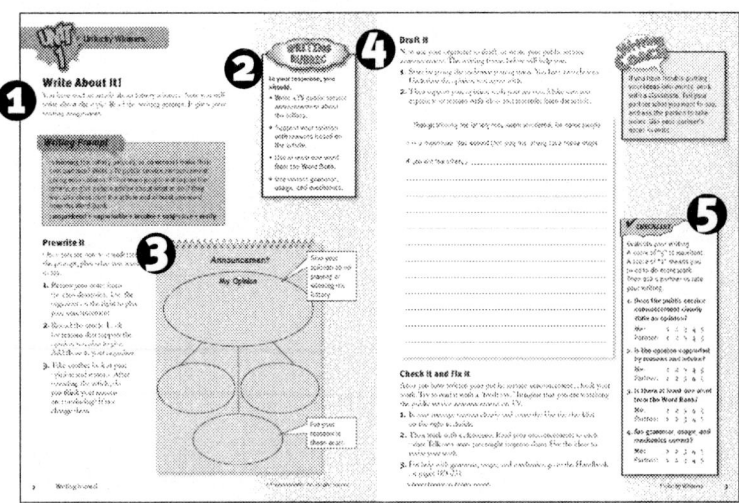

1 Introduce the topic with the writing prompt.

2 Point out the rubric before students begin to write to help them focus their writing goals.

3 Model how to use the graphic organizer. Assist students as they gather their thoughts.

4 Prompt students to use a mediated approach for their writing as they follow the steps in organizing their finished work.

5 Draw attention to the checklist as a way for students to evaluate—and then to make changes—to improve their writing.

Vocabulary Workshop

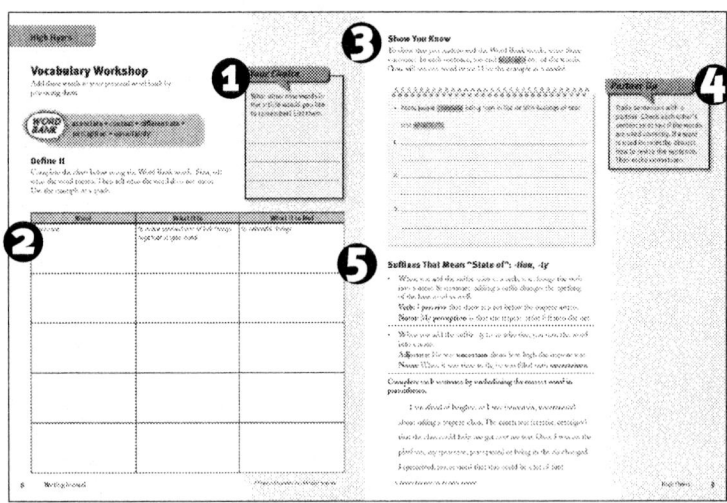

1 After revisiting the Word Bank words, encourage students to record other words from the article. These words can be recorded in the personal word bank in the back of the journal.

2 Help students use words in various contexts as they complete graphic organizers.

3 Encourage students to demonstrate their understanding using the Show You Know activities.

4 Pair students and use the Partner Up suggestions to guide their work.

5 A culminating activity allows students to use word parts, sort words, or investigate multiple-meaning words.

Grammar, Usage, and Mechanics Handbook

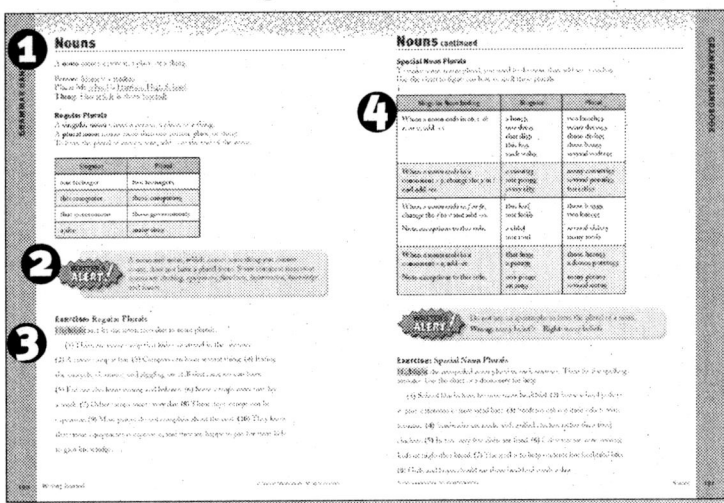

❶ Introduce the topic in a direct, easy-to-understand way.

❷ Point out the Writer's Alerts, demonstrating how these alerts help students avoid common mistakes.

❸ Discuss the exercises, which provide explicit strategy practice.

❹ Draw attention to the charts that organize useful information about grammar, usage, and mechanics for an at-a-glance reference.

Checklist and Word Bank

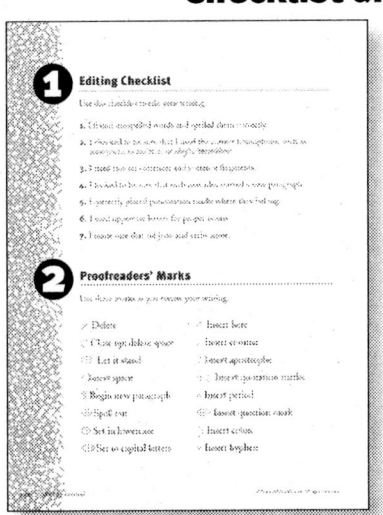

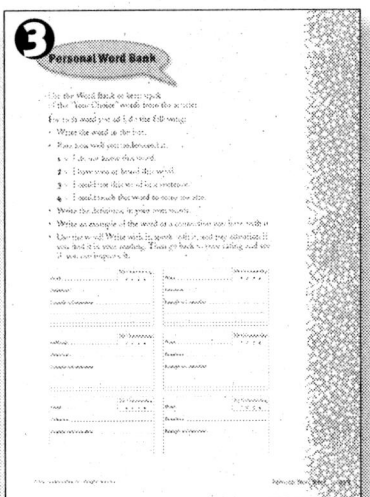

❶ Encourage students to add their own goals to an editing checklist.

❷ Demonstrate how to use proofreaders' marks to perform a thorough edit and revision to create a polished piece of writing.

❸ Have students add the "Your Choice" words to the personal word bank. Encourage them to rate their knowledge, use the words, and then rate their knowledge again.

Reality Central **Teaching Guide and Resources**

Unit Opener Lesson

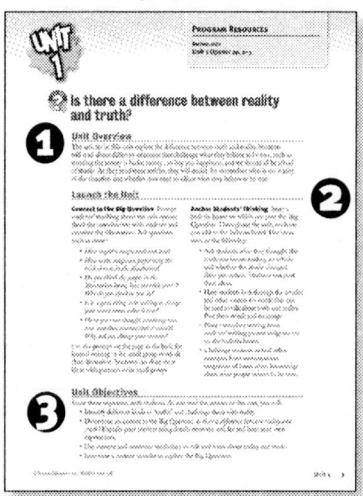

❶ Set the stage for the unit by discussing the unit opener in the anthology.

❷ Begin a visual anchor to guide students' thinking as they read the unit selections.

❸ State objectives for the unit to prepare students for reading, writing, and discussion.

Article Lesson: Student Anthology and Writing Journal

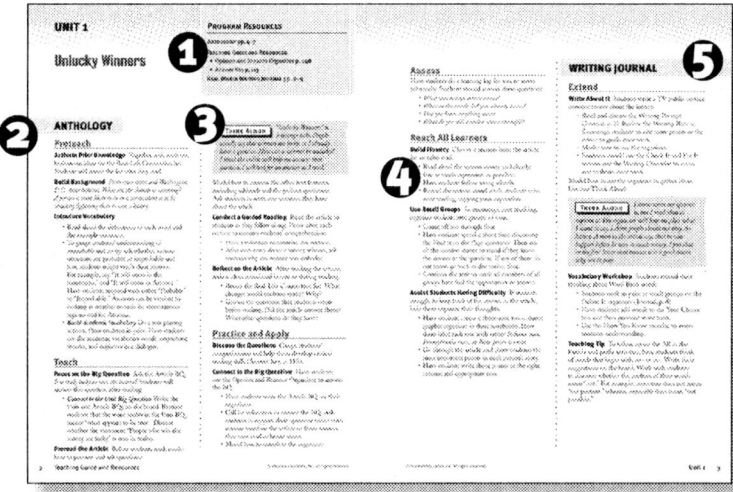

❶ The Resources box assists you in gathering and organizing needed materials.

❷ Each part of the lesson includes directions to help your students get the most out of the student anthology articles.

❸ Think Alouds prompt explicit modeling. Modeling gives a window to your thinking as students follow your lead.

❹ Tips for building fluency, assisting students who are struggling, and using small groups allow you to reach all your learners.

❺ Teaching Tips and Think Alouds provide deeper instruction for the *Real World Writing Journal*.

Unit Closer Lesson

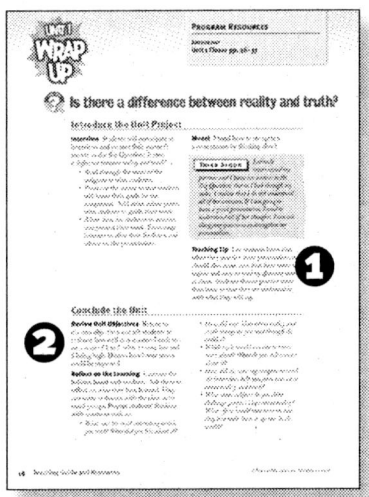

❶ Use the Think Aloud and Teaching Tip to deepen the instruction of the unit closer activity.

❷ Wrap up the visual anchor for the unit and link it back to the Big Question to bring the unit to a close.

Additional Instructional Support

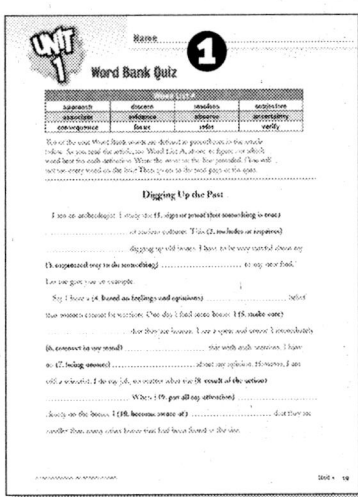

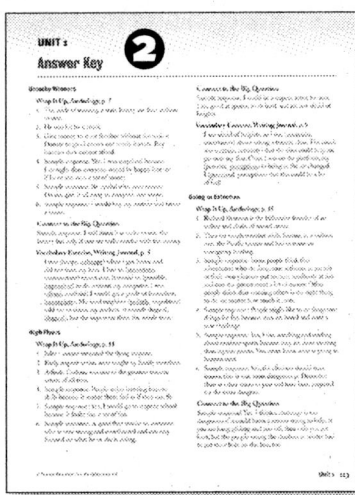

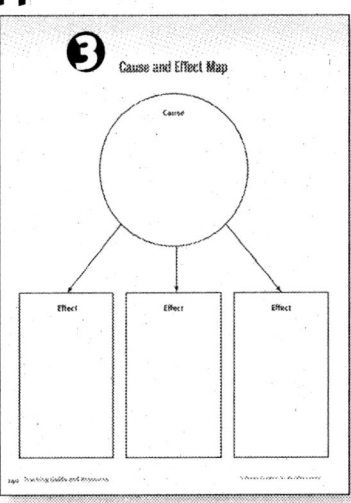

❶ The Word Bank Quiz assesses students' understanding of vocabulary by providing context clues in a passage.

❷ Answer Keys are provided for the student anthology questions, vocabulary exercises from the *Real World Writing Journal*, the unit Word Bank Quiz, and the Grammar, Usage, and Mechanics Handbook.

❸ Graphic organizers key into instruction in comprehension and vocabulary, allow students to gather thoughts about Big Questions, and assist students who need to make further connections.

Correlations to Prentice Hall *Literature*

Each unit in *Reality Central* has a corresponding unit in Prentice Hall *Literature*. The units in both anthologies have identical Big Questions. Each selection in the *Reality Central* Student Anthology is linked to a reading selection in Prentice Hall *Literature*. Individual selections may be linked by topic or by theme.

As a supplement to Prentice Hall *Literature*, *Reality Central* allows you to:

- build students' background knowledge of a topic with related nonfiction.
- support struggling readers by presenting a related selection at a reading level that matches students' levels of proficiency.
- explore the various treatments of ideas and themes across genres.

- expand students' strategy use to multiple genres with varying text features.
- allow students multiple opportunities to think about the Big Questions as they read selections in different genres with different treatments of topics and themes.
- provide multiple exposure to vocabulary words in different contexts.

Reality Central can be used effectively on its own, but it also provides strong links to Prentice Hall *Literature*.

With identical Big Questions, both resources allow for exploration across genres and topics.

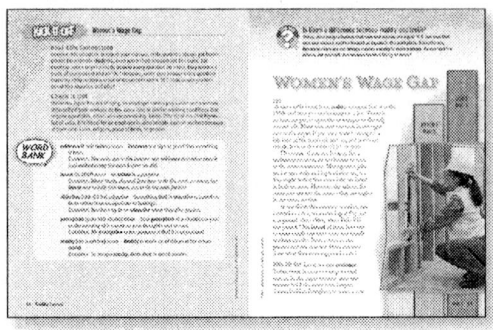 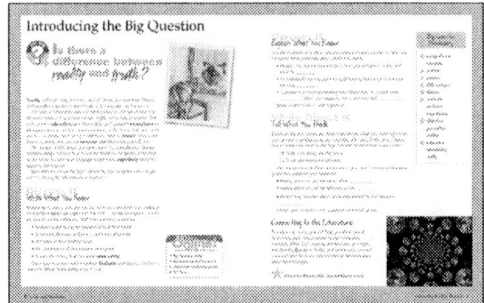

Strong links between selections allow *Reality Central* to be used in conjunction with Prentice Hall *Literature*.

Unit 1: Is there a difference between reality and truth?

Reality Central Title	Page	Prentice Hall Literature Title	Page
Unlucky Winners	4	The Monkey's Paw	32
High Flyers	8	The Leap	46
Going to Extremes	12	from Swimming to Antarctica	68
Women's Wage Gap	16	Occupation: Conductorette from I Know Why the Caged Bird Sings	78
Happy Together	20	Contents of the Dead Man's Pocket	118
Winners and Losers	24	Games at Twilight	138
Shark Story	28	The Marginal World	156
The ABCs of Antioxidants	32	Making History With Vitamin C	168

Unit 2: Can progress be made without conflict?

Reality Central Title	Page	Prentice Hall Literature Title	Page
Sibling Strife	40	A Visit to Grandmother	243
Holding Parents Responsible	44	A Problem	256
Identity Theft	48	The Street of the Cañon	272
Tracking Teen Drivers	52	There Will Come Soft Rains	284
The Greed Game	56	How Much Land Does a Man Need?	338
Learning from Crime Victims	60	Civil Peace	358
Preparing for the Flu	64	The Masque of the Red Death	372
The Development Debate	68	The Garden of Stubborn Cats	384

Unit 3: What kind of knowledge changes our lives?

Reality Central Title	Page	Prentice Hall Literature Title	Page
Sixth Sense Survival	76	The Spider and the Wasp	464
Looking over Your Shoulder	80	from Longitude	474
Dressing by the Book	84	The Sun Parlor	490
Textbook Technology	88	from In Commemoration: One Million Volumes	500
The Witness Dilemma	92	Keep Memory Alive	542
Instant Friends	96	from Nobel Lecture	548
The Newest Newcomers	100	The American Idea	560
Hip-Hop: Keeping It Real	104	What Makes a Degas a Degas?	568

Unit 4: Does all communication serve a positive purpose?

Reality Central Title	Page	Prentice Hall Literature Title	Page
Ooooh, Scary!	112	The Bridegroom	642
		The Guitar	648
		The Fish	650
		Danny Deever	652
Up a Tree	116	Mowing	658
		A Tree Telling of Orpheus	659
		Making a Fist	664
		Spring and All	665
As Big As All Outdoors	120	My City	677
		Do Not Go Gentle into That Good Night	679
		The clustering clouds	680
		When I went to visit…	680
Put Me In, Coach!	124	The Waking	685
		Sonnet 18	687
		One cannot ask loneliness…	688
		Was it that I went to sleep…	688
Longing to be Like Mike	128	The Wind—tapped like a tired Man	718
		Glory	720
		Metaphor	722
Time to Serve	132	Conscientious Objector	726
		Pride	727
		Tell all the Truth but tell it slant	728
Hip-Hop into Hall of Fame	136	The Weary Blues	736
		In Flanders Fields	738
		Jazz Fantasia	739
Texting on Trial	140	Meeting at night	744
		The Kraken	745
		Reapers	746

Unit 5: To what extent does experience determine what we perceive?

Reality Central Title	Page	Prentice Hall *Literature* Title	Page
Pros and Cons of Protest	148	Antigone, Part 1	814
Royal Rights to Privacy	152	Antigone, Part 2	839
In or Out of the In Crowd	156	The Tragedy of Julius Caesar, Acts I-III	892
The *Titanic* Tragedy	160	The Tragedy of Julius Caesar, Acts IV-V	966

Unit 6: Can anyone be a hero?

Reality Central Title	Page	Prentice Hall *Literature* Title	Page
Science's Double-Edged Swords	168	Prometheus and the First People	1066
Buffalo Battles	172	The Orphan Boy and the Elk Dog	1076
The Youngest Heroes	176	*from* Sundiata: An Epic of Old Mali	1094
Equality on the Playing Field	180	Rama's Initiation *from* Ramayana	1108
Our Hero!	184	Arthur Becomes King of Britain *from* The Once and Future King	1156
Peacekeepers	188	Morte d'Arthur	1174
Leaping into the Fire	192	*from* A Connecticut Yankee in King Arthur's Court	1192
The Sport Entertainment Hero	196	*from* Don Quixote	1208

Supporting Struggling Readers

The materials in *Reality Central* are designed especially with struggling readers in mind. As you read through the lessons in the *Teaching Guide and Resources*, you will notice strategies designed to allow students to improve their comprehension and build fluency. Small group activities will engage readers and prompt deeper thinking.

There are many strategies that encourage and support vocabulary development. The following are suggestions you may want to use or adapt for your students. The *Reality Central Teaching Guide and Resources* use many of these activities, supporting the growth of your readers.

Read aloud to students.

Read aloud to students on a "first run" of the text. Your readaloud serves multiple purposes. You model fluent reading for students, focusing on correct phrasing, attention to punctuation, emphasizing meaning, and so on. Use your readaloud as a time to model your use of reading strategies. Provide a window into your thinking, telling students what you are doing before you read the text and pausing occasionally to model strategy use. Your thinkaloud should be "in the moment," showing the strategies that you are using as a proficient reader. If you are summarizing, for example, summarize naturally, showing students that strategies are helpful for navigating text, not simply "one more thing to do."

Model by thinking aloud.

Pause to "fix up" as you go so that students see first-hand what good readers do when they encounter unknown words or difficult ideas. Some of the many strategies you might model in a think aloud include:

- *determining word meanings*
- *applying background knowledge to text*
- *making predictions based on text features*
- *changing predictions during reading*
- *thinking about opinions and reactions*

- *summarizing*
- *differentiating between important ideas and irrelevant details*
- *making mental pictures*
- *rereading, reading on*

Focus on pre-reading tasks.

With the articles in *Reality Central*, the pre-reading process can include examining graphics, captions, pull-out quotes, headings, and so on. Share a routine for pre-reading:

- **Read the title:** What clues does it give you about the topic and the author's focus?
- **Read the introduction:** The introduction is a lead-in. What does it tell you about the rest of the article?
- **Read the boldface headings:** The heads are labels for the sections. Use the headings to predict article content and set purposes for reading.
- **Look for boldface words:** Word Bank Words are boldface in the articles. What do these words tell you about the content of the article?
- **Look over visual aids:** *Reality Central* articles showcase photographs, charts, and graphs. What information can you glean from these graphic sources?
- **Read through the questions at the end:** How does reading these questions help you set purposes for reading?

Use graphic organizers.

Graphic organizers help students organize ideas before, during, and after reading. Use the graphic organizers on pages 140–157 of this resource as starting points for assisting your students with exploring Big Questions and thinking more deeply about their comprehension. A Table of Contents on page 139 describes each graphic organizer and offers hints on how each might be used with your students.

. . . .

Teach fix-up strategies.

Struggling readers often work through the text with the idea of getting to the end. Work with students to have them monitor their thinking and "fix-up" their problems.

As students read, they can mark trouble spots with sticky notes. As students revisit or navigate through parts of the text that confuse them, offer these strategies as tools:

Make a Prediction: Think about what is coming next to set purposes for reading and look for "answers."

Make a Connection: Think about what you already know to better understand what you are reading.

Ask Questions: Stop and ask questions as you read. You may or may not find the answers in the text, but you are setting the stage for purposeful reading.

Stop and Think About What You Have Read: Rather than read on, stop and think. What do you already know about this? What have you learned so far? What do you still wonder about?

Adjust Your Rate: Adjust the reading rate depending on how hard the material is to read, what you already know about it, and the purpose you have for reading.

Visualize: Create images in your head that will help you make sense of the words on the page.

Retell: Can you retell the main ideas in your own words and not the author's words? Tell a partner about what you have read. See if you include all the important words.

. . . .

Focus on fluency.

The lessons in the *Teaching Guide and Resources* include strategies for building fluency with your readers. Strategies such as these help students focus on all aspects of fluency—speed, accuracy, and expression.

Echo Reading You read a portion of the text, modeling phrasing, accuracy, and so on. Then students, individually or in small groups, echo after you. You can pair readers for this activity.

Choral Reading Choral reading is reading done in a group, with or without your lead. Students should choral read only text that is familiar to them.

Partner Reading Students read aloud for each other as partners listen and perhaps take notes. They offer tips to partners on the reading. Carefully model this process and how to offer helpful feedback.

Tape Recordings Have students tape record their readings. They can listen, identify areas for improvement, and read again to assess their growth. You can also save tape recordings for "readalongs."

Supporting Struggling Writers

All writers, even proficient ones, struggle at times during the writing process. Writing instruction in *Reality Central* provides scaffolds for students who need them, with the goal of eventually removing supports as writers gain confidence and proficiency.

There are many strategies that encourage and support development of struggling writers. The following are suggestions you may want to use or adapt for your students. The *Reality Central Real World Writing Journal* uses many of these activities, supporting the growth of your writers.

Help students diagnose their own difficulties.

Remind students that all writers struggle sometimes, and one strategy to become more proficient at writing is to figure out the exact causes of writing problems. Prompt writers with questions such as:

- Do you understand the writing form and what your product should look like?
- Do you understand the topic well enough to write about it? If not, what can you do to learn more?
- What needs to be clearer in the directions?
- Do you know how to begin the piece?

Once you start asking questions focused on the writing process and product, you'll begin to know which questions are best for prompting which students. Soon, students will begin to identify their own problems.

Hold writing conferences.

Confer often with individuals as they write. Conferences can be a "formal" scheduled time, but consider incorporating on-the-run assessment. Use the information you gather to pinpoint individual students' needs as you work with them. If a small group of students face the same problem with their writing, pull them together for a mini lesson focused on their particular challenge, such as not knowing how to write a powerful beginning. Use these informal conferences as a way to assist with particular problems that you diagnose.

Use graphic organizers.

Organizers can help students as they are forming their ideas for writing. Students can also use graphic organizers as they write, moving ideas from one place to another, trying out different combinations of ideas, and so on. Have students' graphic organizers on hand as you conference with them, pointing out how they might better organize or beef up their writing. The graphic organizers on pages 140–157 of this resource provide starting points for writers. The *Reality Central Real World Writing Journal* provides a graphic organizer for each writing assignment, but students may find other organizers helpful as well.

Provide writing models.

Provide two types of models for students:

Teacher Models Model writing for students. When you model, do the writing yourself. As students gain more proficiency, invite them to share their ideas for writing. But on a first modeling, explicitly share your thinking as you write. Write the way that you would write, rather than writing as a student would write, to show students how to lift their writing to the next level. As you create modeled writing pieces, save them for students' reference in the future.

Student Models Displaying and discussing student models is one way to showcase great work, but those student models also can help students see what they are trying to accomplish. You might give small groups student models (removing student identifiers or using pieces from past classes) and ask groups to assess those models. They can identify the positive points of the writing they examine and discuss how to incorporate those traits into their own pieces of writing.

Build background.

Beginning a writing piece "cold" is difficult even for the most seasoned writers. Provide background for students before they write to help them become more comfortable with the writing process and assignment. Use ideas such as the following:

- Model how to begin the process with graphic organizers.
- Prompt discussion in pairs, small groups, or with the whole class.
- Share readings, images, or video about writing topics.
- Have students "quick write," not as a final product, but to have ideas to begin their writing.

Provide tools for writers.

Steep your classroom in tools that students that can use to elevate their writing:

- Show students self-assessment tools and checklists and model their use. You can use the tools in the back of this resource or devise your own (or have students devise them).
- Provide checklists such as the editing checklist and proofreaders' marks in the *Reality Central Real World Writing Journal*. Having students design checklists helps them focus on the traits of good writing.
- Create posters as visual reminders, such as appropriate vocabulary to use for different types of writing.
- Have students create word banks of words useful for different types of writing. Students, for example, could create a word bank of transitions or a word bank of words that are effective in persuasive writing.

Supporting Vocabulary Development

Vocabulary instruction has a profound effect on students' comprehension of academic content. Systematic instruction of vocabulary words allows students to approach text with a higher probability of understanding important ideas.

Vocabulary instruction in *Reality Central* focuses on words that students will see frequently, academic vocabulary, and words that may be difficult. Vocabulary words are provided in several different forms in the articles in the student anthology.

In general, you can help support students' vocabulary development by:

- activating prior knowledge about vocabulary words.
- defining words in multiple contexts.
- assisting students in using context clues to determine word meanings.
- explicitly teaching word parts (prefixes, roots, and suffixes) as clues to word meaning.
- providing opportunities for students to integrate new vocabulary into their speaking and writing.
- giving multiple exposures to new words.
- focusing on a small number of important words.
- relating words to concepts to increase depth of content knowledge.

There are many strategies that encourage and support vocabulary development. The following are suggestions you may want to use or adapt for your students.

Introduce and activate the meanings of words.

When you introduce word meaning, provide meaningful real-life context.

EXAMPLE

Endurance is the ability to handle pain or hardship for a long time. We hear about people who have endurance and tasks that require it. Think about athletes who run marathons. Running a marathon might be painful after a while. It takes a lot of endurance to run for so long. Can you think of someone who has shown a lot of endurance, who was able to put up with hardship or pain? In what situations is endurance useful?

Provide a sentence completion activity.

Provide a sentence frame that encourages students to stretch their thinking about vocabulary words. As students complete these sentences, you can further clarify word meanings.

EXAMPLE

Restrict: to limit; to confine; to control
Some things that I know about that are restricted are _____

Present cloze activities.

Present words in different contexts by writing sentences that use the words, then removing the words and leaving "blanks" in the sentences for students to fill in. Encourage discussion as students begin filling in the blanks, especially if more than one word might make sense.

A paragraph cloze provides an opportunity for students to practice using context. Model for students how to skip over choices that are difficult, cross out words as they are used, and "try out" possibilities to find the best fit. Guide students with questions such as "Is this the only word that fits?" and "What makes this choice the best?"

Provide multiple ways for students to define and explore words graphically.

Graphic organizers prompt students to think about and describe the meanings of words and concepts. Use the graphic organizers throughout the *Real World Writing Journal* and on pages 140–157 of this resource as starting points for assisting your students with exploration of vocabulary words. Graphic organizers might include such elements as definitions, characteristics, examples, non-examples, similar words, and so on.

Use word analogy exercises.

Students explain the relationship between words and use that relationship to create new pairs.

Types of analogies include:

Part to whole:	bulb : flashlight :: petal : flower
Person to situation:	fisherman : rod :: artist : brush
Synonym:	graceful : elegant :: loud : noisy
Antonym:	graceful : clumsy :: loud : quiet
Geography:	Chicago : Illinois :: Los Angeles : California
Measurement:	inch : foot :: centimeter : meter

Sort words.

Word sorting is a simple activity for students to do independently or in groups. You can provide categories to students and then ask students to sort vocabulary words into these categories, such as parts of speech. Alternatively, provide students a list of words and challenge them to sort these words into categories after discerning the common features and describing the categories.

 # Is there a difference between reality and truth?

Unit Overview

The articles in this unit explore the difference between truth and reality. Students will read about different situations that challenge what they believe to be true, such as winning the lottery is lucky, money can buy you happiness, and we should all be afraid of sharks. As they read these articles, they will decide for themselves what is the reality of the situation and whether they need to adjust what they believe to be true.

Launch the Unit

Connect to the Big Question Prompt students' thinking about the unit opener. Read the introduction with students and examine the illustration. Ask questions such as these:

- *How might a magic trick look true?*
- *How is the magician performing the trick shown in the illustration?*
- *Do you think the people in the illustration know how the trick works? Why do you think as you do?*
- *Is it a good thing to be willing to change your mind about what is true?*
- *Have you ever thought something was true and then learned that it wasn't? Why did you change your opinion?*

Use the prompt on the page as the basis for journal writing or for small group or whole class discussion. Students can share their ideas with partners or in small groups.

Anchor Students' Thinking Start a bulletin board on which you post the Big Question. Throughout the unit, students can add to the bulletin board. Use ideas such as the following:

- Ask students what they thought the truth was before reading an article and whether the article changed their perception. Students can post their ideas.
- Have students look through the articles and other sources for words that can be used to talk about truth and reality. Post these words and meanings.
- Place exemplary writing from students' writing journal assignments on the bulletin board.
- Challenge students to find other examples from newspapers or magazines of times when knowledge alters what people believe to be true.

Unit Objectives

Share these objectives with students. As you read the articles in this unit, you will:

- Identify different kinds of "truths" and challenge them with reality.
- Determine an answer to the Big Question: *Is there a difference between reality and truth?* Explain your answers using details from the articles and from your own experiences.
- Use content and academic vocabulary to talk and write about reality and truth.
- Interview a partner in order to explore the Big Question.

UNIT 1

Unlucky Winners

PROGRAM RESOURCES

ANTHOLOGY pp. 4–7

TEACHING GUIDE AND RESOURCES
- Opinion and Reasons Organizer p. 148
- Answer Key p. 113

REAL WORLD WRITING JOURNAL pp. 2–5

ANTHOLOGY

Preteach

Activate Prior Knowledge Together with students, brainstorm ideas for the Real-Life Connection list. Students will revisit the list after they read.

Build Background *Forty-two states and Washington, D.C., have lotteries. What are the chances of winning? A person is more likely to be in a car accident or to be struck by lightning than to win a lottery.*

Introduce Vocabulary

- Read aloud the definitions of each word and the example sentences.
- To gauge students' understanding of *improbable* and *verify*, ask whether various situations are probable or improbable and how students might verify their answers. For example, say, "It will snow in the mountains," and "It will snow in Arizona." Have students respond with either "Probable" or "Improbable." Answers can be verified by looking at weather records for mountainous regions and for Arizona.
- *Build Academic Vocabulary* Do a role playing activity. Place students in pairs. Have students use the academic vocabulary words *comprehend, involve,* and *subjective* in a dialogue.

Teach

Focus on the Big Question Ask the Article BQ, *Is it truly lucky to win the lottery?* Students will answer this question after reading.

- *Connect to the Unit Big Question* Write the Unit and Article BQs on the board. Remind students that the word *reality* in the Unit BQ means "what appears to be true." Discuss whether the statement "People who win the lottery are lucky" is true in reality.

Preread the Article Before students read, model how to preview and ask questions:

> **THINK ALOUD** *"Unlucky Winners" is a strange title. People usually say that winners are lucky, so I already have a question: How can a winner be unlucky? I think the article will help me answer that question. I will look for an answer as I read.*

Model how to preview the other text features, including subheads and the pullout quotation. Ask students to write one question they have about the article.

Conduct a Guided Reading Read the article to students as they follow along. Pause after each section to monitor students' comprehension.

- Have a volunteer summarize the section.
- After each story about a lottery winner, ask students why the winner was unlucky.

Reflect on the Article After reading the article, review ideas introduced before or during reading.

- Revisit the Real-Life Connection list. What changes would students make? Why?
- Discuss the questions that students wrote before reading. Did the article answer them? What other questions do they have?

Practice and Apply

Discuss the Questions Gauge students' comprehension and help them develop critical reading skills (Answer Key, p. 113).

Connect to the Big Question Have students use the Opinion and Reasons Organizer to answer the BQ.

- Have students write the Article BQ on their organizers.
- Call for volunteers to answer the BQ. Ask students to support their opinions either with reasons based on the article or from sources they have read or heard about.
- Model how to complete the organizer.

Assess

Have students do a learning log for you to assess informally. Students should answer these questions:

- *What was today's article about?*
- *What in the article did you already know?*
- *Did you learn anything new?*
- *What do you still wonder about the topic?*

Reach All Learners

Build Fluency Choose a section from the article for an echo read.

- Read aloud the section slowly and clearly. Use as much expression as possible.
- Have students follow along silently.
- Reread the section aloud while students echo your reading, copying your expression.

Use Small Groups To encourage peer teaching, organize students into groups of four.

- Count off one through four.
- Have students spend a short time discussing the Find It on the Page questions. Then ask all the number threes to stand if they know the answer to the question. If any of them do not know, go back to discussion time.
- Continue the activity until all members of all groups have had the opportunity to answer.

Assist Students Having Difficulty If students struggle to keep track of the stories in the article, help them organize their thoughts.

- Have students create a three-row, two-column graphic organizer in their notebooks. Have them label each row with either *Indiana man,* *Pennsylvania man,* or *New Jersey woman.*
- Go through the article and show students the most important points in each person's story.
- Have students write those points in the right column and appropriate row.

WRITING JOURNAL

Extend

Write About It Students write a TV public service announcement about the lottery.

- Read and discuss the Writing Prompt (Journal, p. 2). Review the Writing Rubric. Encourage students to add more points to the rubric to guide their work.
- Model how to use the organizer.
- Students should use the Check It and Fix It section and the Writing Checklist to revise and evaluate their work.

Model how to use the organizer to gather ideas. Use this Think Aloud:

> **THINK ALOUD** *I know what my opinion is, but I need ideas to explain it. The organizer will help me plan what I want to say. I think people should not play the lottery. A man in the article says that he was happier before he won so much money. I put that in the first lower oval because it is a good reason why not to play.*

Vocabulary Workshop Students extend their thinking about Word Bank words.

- Students work in pairs or small groups on the Define It organizer (Journal, p. 4).
- Have students add words to the Your Choice box and their personal word bank.
- Use the Show You Know exercise to assess students' understanding.

Teaching Tip To follow up on the All in the Family and prefix activities, have students think of words that begin with *im-* or *in-*. Write their suggestions on the board. Work with students to discover whether the prefixes of their words mean "not." For example, *important* does not mean "not portant," whereas *impossible* does mean "not possible."

High Flyers

PROGRAM RESOURCES

ANTHOLOGY pp. 8–11

TEACHING GUIDE AND RESOURCES
- Main Idea Map **p. 146**
- Answer Key **p. 113**

REAL WORLD WRITING JOURNAL pp. 6–9

ANTHOLOGY

Preteach

Activate Prior Knowledge Take a poll for each question in the Real-Life Connection. Students will revisit the poll after reading.

Build Background *There are more kinds of aerial acts than the trapeze. There are hanging hoops and long ropes. Performers climb, wrap themselves in the rope, and pose in amazing positions.*

Introduce Vocabulary

- Use each of the vocabulary words in a sentence. Have students tell you whether the word is a noun or a verb.
- Have students use the words to complete an Article Dictionary. Using information from the Word Bank and article, have students write definitions and example sentences.
- *Build Academic Vocabulary* Ask volunteers to tell you where they would be most likely to find the academic vocabulary words *associate, context,* and *differentiate:* in an English assignment, a biology test, or a math test. Have students explain their answers.

Teach

Focus on the Big Question Ask the Article BQ, *Could I be a trapeze artist?* Students will answer this question after reading.

- *Connect to the Unit Big Question* Discuss what students believe they can do. Ask why they might think they cannot do something.

Preread the Article Help students prepare to read by activating their prior knowledge.

- *What do you know about the trapeze?*
- *Look at the pictures in the article. Do the pictures help you remember anything?*

Remind students that if they think about what they already know about a topic while they are reading about it, reading will become easier and more enjoyable.

Conduct a Guided Reading Read the article to students as they follow along. Pause after each section to monitor students' comprehension.

- After each section, revisit the Real-Life Connection statements. Ask which of the statements can now be proven true or false based on the information in the article.

Reflect on the Article After reading the article, review ideas introduced before or during reading.

- Have students look at their answers from the Real-Life Connection. Have answers changed? Discuss why.
- Ask students whether their prior knowledge helped them understand the article.

Practice and Apply

Discuss the Questions Gauge students' comprehension and help them develop critical reading skills (Answer Key, p. 113).

Connect to the Big Question Have a class discussion to help students answer the BQ.

- Write the word *perception* on the board.

> **THINK ALOUD** *Before I read the article, my perception was that the only place a person could learn the trapeze was in a special circus school. My perception told me that the answer to the BQ was "No." Now, I know that there are trapeze schools in many places and even I could go to one.*

Tell students that active readers are open to changing their perceptions as they read and gather new information. Have volunteers answer the BQ. Discuss whether they changed their perceptions after reading the article.

Assess

Use the Main Idea Map to prepare students to write a short summary of the article. Explain to students that they should begin by stating the main idea of the article and then state important supporting ideas. Remind them that a good summary includes important ideas without going into unnecessary detail.

Reach All Learners

Build Fluency Choose a section from the article for a choral reading.

- Read the section aloud as students read the section silently.
- Reread the section aloud and have students read it aloud with you.
- Then have students read the section aloud without you. Stop and correct any pronunciation or fluency errors.

Use Small Groups Engage students with a write-around activity.

- In groups of four, have each student begin with a piece of paper with the third Use Clues question written across the top.
- Have students write a response for one minute and then pass their papers to the right. The one-minute writing begins again, and students add to the paper in front of them responding to the idea that is already there.
- Continue until all students have written on each paper. Discuss with the class.

Assist Students Having Difficulty If students struggle with writing the summary or keeping track of main ideas in the article, go over the Main Idea Map using an overhead transparency.

- Allow time after reading the article to fill out the organizer with the class.
- Ask, *What ideas were presented? What was the most important idea?*
- Ask, *What are some details that support that idea?*

WRITING JOURNAL

Extend

Write About It Students will plan and write a radio report for teens about "flying" as a career.

- Read and discuss the Writing Prompt (Journal, p. 6). Review the Writing Rubric. Encourage students to add more points to the rubric to guide their work.
- Model how to use the organizer.
- Students should use the Check It and Fix It section and the Writing Checklist to revise and evaluate their work.

Teaching Tip Help students complete the Prewrite It organizer by reminding them that they do not have to write in complete sentences. Have students create their own or a class shorthand for writing notes. Post the shorthand in the classroom.

Vocabulary Workshop Students extend their thinking about Word Bank words.

- Students work in pairs or small groups on the Define It organizer (Journal, p. 8).
- Have students add words to the Your Choice box and their personal word bank.
- Use the Show You Know exercise to assess students' understanding.

To help students think of sentences, model by thinking aloud:

> **THINK ALOUD** *When I am having trouble thinking of a sentence, I look up how the word was used in the article. That sometimes gives me an idea. If I look at the sentence that uses the word* perception, *that gives me an idea for a sentence:* "My perception about trapeze artists changed."

Going to Extremes

PROGRAM RESOURCES

ANTHOLOGY pp. 12–15

TEACHING GUIDE AND RESOURCES
- T-Chart **p. 151**
- Answer Key **p. 113**

REAL WORLD WRITING JOURNAL pp. 10–13

ANTHOLOGY

Preteach

Activate Prior Knowledge Have students fill out the Real-Life Connection chart. Students will revisit their charts after reading.

Build Background *Webster's Online Dictionary says that extreme sports "feature a combination of speed, height, danger and spectacular stunts." However, some activities and sports are not called "extreme" even if they fit the definition.*

Introduce Vocabulary

- Find the boldface words in the article. Read the sentences and use context to determine each word meaning.
- Compare meanings to those listed in the Word Bank. Discuss similarities and differences. How does context change or clarify meaning?
- *Build Academic Vocabulary* Discuss the academic vocabulary words *comprehend, confirm, evaluate,* and *focus.* Ask volunteers to give examples of how they would use each word in a science class.

Teach

Focus on the Big Question Ask the Article BQ, *Are some challenges just too dangerous to be worthwhile?* Students will answer this question after reading.

- *Connect to the Unit Big Question* Ask students to write down an answer to the Article BQ. Tell them that they will revisit this answer after they have read the article.

Preread the Article Before students read, make sure they understand the meaning of the phrase "going to extremes." Point out the alliteration in the subheads and the pun in the first subhead. Have each student write one prediction.

Conduct a Guided Reading Read the article to students as they follow along. Pause after each section to monitor students' comprehension. Have students use the T-Chart to take notes on what they are reading. Pause after reading each section to give students time to complete their organizers. Model how to complete the organizer:

> **THINK ALOUD** *Now that I have read the introductory paragraphs, I realize that this article is about extreme sports. Therefore, I will write "extreme sports" above the chart on the organizer. I also know that the Article Big Question is whether these sports are a noble adventure or a needless risk. I will write "noble adventure" on the left of the T-Chart and "needless risk" on the right. As I read, I will add details from the article to my T-Chart.*

Reflect on the Article After reading the article, review ideas introduced before or during reading.

- Have students look at their Real-Life Connection charts. Discuss whether their predictions were fulfilled.
- Revisit the T-Chart. Did the article answer the Article BQ?

Practice and Apply

Discuss the Questions Gauge students' comprehension and help them develop critical reading skills (Answer Key, p. 113).

Connect to the Big Question Have students look at what they wrote to answer the Article BQ before they read. Has their perception of reality changed? If so, how? Have volunteers use information from the article to answer the question.

Assess

Place students in two groups: one that is *for* extreme sports and one that is *against* extreme sports. Have each group come up with a reason or two to support its position. Students should use reasons from the article. Informally assess students' understanding of the article by circulating throughout the room and listening.

Reach All Learners

Build Fluency Choose a section from the article for an echo read.

- Discuss text cues that are important for fluent reading: punctuation, line breaks, headings.
- Read the section sentence by sentence, as students repeat after you. Have students echo your pauses for commas and periods. Make sure students do not pause at line breaks.

Use Small Groups Use an art activity to engage students.

- In groups, have students choose an extreme sport about which to make a poster.
- Students select information from the article and their own experience to describe the sport. Have them suggest ways that people can be safe while participating. Display the posters in the classroom.

Assist Students Having Difficulty If students struggle to understand longer sentences, teach them how to turn lengthy sentences into shorter, more understandable chunks.

- Point out a compound sentence in the selection. Read it aloud as two sentences. Ask students if they understand the two sentences. Then read the compound sentence. Ask students if they understand the whole sentence.
- Have students find a different compound sentence and repeat the process.

WRITING JOURNAL

Extend

Write About It Students will use an Opinion and Reasons graphic organizer to plan and write a paragraph explaining their opinion.

- Read and discuss the Writing Prompt (Journal, p. 10). Review the Writing Rubric. Encourage students to add more points to the rubric to guide their work.
- Model how to use the organizer.
- Students should use the Check It and Fix It section and the Writing Checklist to revise and evaluate their work.

As students plan their paragraph, model how to organize ideas by thinking aloud:

> **THINK ALOUD** *Readers are more likely to agree with my opinion if I support it with reasons. I will give a good reason first and then end with my strongest reason. That way, I will build to a strong conclusion, and my readers will remember my best reason.*

Vocabulary Workshop Students extend their thinking about Word Bank words.

- Students work in pairs or small groups on the Define It organizer (Journal, p. 12).
- Have students add words to the Your Choice box and their personal word bank.
- Use the Show You Know exercise to assess students' understanding.

Teaching Tip Have students create a "Class Word Bank Wall" by defining each Word Bank word on its own notecard and posting the notecards on a classroom wall. Maintain the Class Word Bank Wall throughout the year. Organize games and contests connected to the Word Bank to improve students' vocabulary.

UNIT 1

Women's Wage Gap

PROGRAM RESOURCES

ANTHOLOGY pp. 16–19

TEACHING GUIDE AND RESOURCES
- T-Chart **p. 151**
- Answer Key **p. 114**

REAL WORLD WRITING JOURNAL pp. 14–17

ANTHOLOGY

Preteach

Activate Prior Knowledge Discuss reactions to the Real-Life Connection scenario. Students will revisit their reactions after they read.

Build Background *The minimum amount per hour that an employer can pay a worker is set by the federal government. Under the Fair Minimum Wage Act of 2007, the minimum wage is being gradually increased from the $5.85 an hour that went into effect shortly after the law was enacted to $7.25 an hour by spring 2009.*

Introduce Vocabulary

- Ask volunteers to read aloud the sentences from the article in which boldface vocabulary words appear. Discuss what each Word Bank word means in context.
- *Build Academic Vocabulary* The academic vocabulary words are *intent* and *objective*. Have students discuss similarities and differences in how these words would be used in a science class and a history class.

Teach

Focus on the Big Question Ask the Article BQ, *Are women treated fairly at work?* Students will answer this question after reading.

- *Connect to the Unit Big Question* Write the Unit and Article BQs on the board. Discuss with students what they think would be most people's answer to that question. Do they think that "reality" is accurate?

Preread the Article Before students read, have them read the first sentence of each paragraph. Then have them write a prediction of what the article will be about and one question they have.

Conduct a Guided Reading Read the article to students as they follow along. Pause after each section to monitor students' comprehension.

- Have students ask questions to clarify understanding.
- Ask a volunteer to explain the main idea of the section.

Reflect on the Article After reading the article, review ideas introduced before or during reading.

- Have students revisit the Real-Life Connection scenario. Have opinions changed? Why or why not?
- Discuss questions students posed before and during reading. Have volunteers answer them. Add other questions and discuss where students could find the answers.

Practice and Apply

Discuss the Questions Gauge students' comprehension and help them develop critical reading skills (Answer Key, p. 114).

Connect to the Big Question Refocus students' attention on the Article BQ. Have students fill out the T-Chart graphic organizer.

- Write the Article BQ at the top of the page and the words *yes* and *no* at the top of each column.
- Have students find facts that support each answer. Use a Think Aloud to model how:

> **THINK ALOUD** *When I read the BQ, I realize that it is asking about women at work in today's world, not in the past. I will look to see if women are paid the same as men now.*

- Volunteers can use their information to answer the BQ.

Assess

Work with the class to create a large list of jobs. Then ask students whether these are jobs associated with women or with men. In groups, have students discuss which jobs pay more and whether they should pay more. Circulate to assess students' understanding of the article.

Reach All Learners

Build Fluency Choose a section from the article for a group reading.

- Direct one student to read the first sentence aloud. Help the student use the correct emphasis and tone to signal the end of the sentence.
- Have the next student read the next sentence. Repeat the process with the entire group.
- Repeat the activity, but during the second reading tell students to read the section more quickly and move more smoothly from one reader to the next.

Use Small Groups Engage students with a write-around activity.

- Distribute sentence frames with the vocabulary words, such as the following: *Journalists need to be objective about what they write because* _____.
- Have students add to each and pass their papers to the right.
- Continue until all students have written on each paper. Discuss similarities and differences with groups.

Assist Students Having Difficulty If students struggle to keep track of the numbers and time frames in the "Mind the Gap" section of the article, draw a graph on the board.

- The x axis is the years 1963 through the present.
- The y axis is the wage gap.
- As you read through the section, mark the appropriate points on the graph.
- After you have finished the article, draw a line to indicate how the wage gap has decreased over the years.

WRITING JOURNAL

Extend

Write About It Students will use an Opinion and Reasons Organizer to plan and write a letter of advice to women workers.

- Read and discuss the Writing Prompt (Journal, p. 14). Review the Writing Rubric. Encourage students to add more points to the rubric to guide their work.
- Model how to use the organizer.
- Students should use the Check It and Fix It section and the Writing Checklist to revise and evaluate their work.

Teaching Tip If students have difficulty wording their thoughts, have them work with partners. Students should explain to their partners what their advice would be and why, and partners should take notes on what students say. Partners should then read the notes to the students, helping them word ideas when necessary.

Vocabulary Workshop Students extend their thinking about Word Bank words.

- Students work in pairs or small groups on the Define It organizer (Journal, p. 16).
- Have students add words to the Your Choice box and their personal word bank.
- Use the Show You Know exercise to assess students' understanding.

If students are having difficulty completing the Define It exercise, model how to do so by thinking aloud:

> **THINK ALOUD** *The next word on the list is* intent. *What is my connection to the word? I really do not know. The example sentence might help me. Can I use that sentence to help me think of something? Yes! It reminds me of when I helped my friend paint her house. My* intent *was to be nice to my friend, not learn new things about house painting.*

Happy Together

PROGRAM RESOURCES

ANTHOLOGY pp. 20–23

TEACHING GUIDE AND RESOURCES
- Web Map **p. 156**
- Answer Key **p. 114**

REAL WORLD WRITING JOURNAL pp. 18–21

ANTHOLOGY

Preteach

Activate Prior Knowledge Discuss responses to the quotations in the Real-Life Connection. Students will revisit their responses after reading.

Build Background *The World Database of Happiness lists Denmark as the happiest country and Tanzania as the least happy. The United States is seventeenth on the list.*

Introduce Vocabulary

- Write the definitions of the vocabulary words on the board.
- Ask students which definition on the board matches each Word Bank word.
- *Build Academic Vocabulary* Use the Web Map. Have students write the name of one of their classes in the center circle and the academic vocabulary words *discern, evaluate,* and *results* in the outer circles. Ask volunteers to explain how the words relate to the class of their choice.

Model how to use the graphic organizer:

> **THINK ALOUD** *The first word I am looking at is* discern. *How would that relate to science? Well, if I am doing a science experiment, I might be able to* discern *some important information by doing an experiment.*

Teach

Focus on the Big Question Ask the Article BQ, *What makes people happy?* Students will answer this question after reading.

- *Connect to the Unit Big Question* Write the Unit and Article BQs on the board. Discuss what happiness is. How can people be happy? What makes people happy?

Preread the Article Before students read, remind them to use the Article BQ to set a purpose for reading.

- Discuss what students already know about the topic of the article.
- Discuss questions students might have.
- Direct students to read to answer the question "What makes people happy?"

Conduct a Guided Reading Read the article to students as they follow along. Pause after each section to monitor students' comprehension.

- Direct students to write questions they have about what they read. Encourage students to clarify the meaning of sentences or passages they do not understand.
- Call for volunteers to make connections between the article and their own experiences.

Reflect on the Article After reading the article, review ideas introduced before or during reading.

- Revisit responses to the Real-Life Connection. Would students change their responses? Why or why not?
- Call for volunteers to ask further questions about the article or the topic. Discuss where students might look to find answers to their questions.

Practice and Apply

Discuss the Questions Gauge students' comprehension and help them develop critical reading skills (Answer Key, p. 114).

Connect to the Big Question Have students answer the BQ.

- Discuss with students whether they have changed their opinion about what makes people happy.
- Call for volunteers to answer the BQ. Ask students to support their answers with reasons based on the article.

Assess

Have students work in small groups to come up with plans for increasing happiness in their community. Students should base their plan on information provided in the article. Each group should write down its plan, including specific suggestions for how to accomplish it. Informally assess students' understanding of the article by circulating through the room and listening as they make their plans. Post "happiness plans" on a classroom bulletin board.

Reach All Learners

Build Fluency Choose a section from the article for a group reading.

- Discuss the flow of the phrases. Tell students that part of reading fluently is not to read word by word, but to read phrases with expression.
- Call for a volunteer to read the first sentence. Remind students to approach the text as a series of meaningful phrases.
- Ask the next student to read the next sentence. Repeat the process with the entire group.

Use Small Groups Use a debate to engage students.

- Place students in groups. Have each group discuss its answers to the Use Clues question "Do you agree that people do not need much money to be happy?"
- Members of each group should choose a side and use details from the article to support their opinion. Make sure every group has members who agree with the Use Clues statement as well as members who do not.
- Direct group members to debate their answers. Discuss which side was the most persuasive.

Assist Students Having Difficulty If students struggle to keep track of the main idea in the article, provide them with four sticky notes.

- Tell students to place the sticky notes next to the text that is the most important.
- Go over the passages where students have placed the notes.
- Discuss each idea. Is it the most important idea of the article? Why or why not?

WRITING JOURNAL

Extend

Write About It Students will use a summary and comparison graphic organizer to plan and write a summary describing the class's top answers in a poll.

- Read and discuss the Writing Prompt (Journal, p. 18). Review the Writing Rubric. Encourage students to add more points to the rubric to guide their work.
- Model how to use the organizer.
- Students should use the Check It and Fix It section and the Writing Checklist to revise and evaluate their work.

As students check their work, model by thinking aloud:

> **THINK ALOUD** *After I have written something, I read it out loud to hear how it sounds. That way, I can tell if I have any incomplete or run-on sentences. I make sure I read it out loud slowly and carefully so that I can tell if I have left out any words. I also check to make sure I used the right verb endings, such as -s or -ed.*

Vocabulary Workshop Students extend their thinking about Word Bank words.

- Students work in pairs or small groups on the Define It organizer (Journal, p. 20).
- Have students add words to the Your Choice box and their personal word bank.
- Use the Show You Know exercise to assess students' understanding.

Teaching Tip To have students connect with the idea of multiple-meaning words, introduce them to the idea of puns:

- There was once a cross-eyed teacher who could not control his pupils.
- To write with a broken pencil is pointless.
- Math teachers have lots of problems.

UNIT 1

Winners and Losers

PROGRAM RESOURCES

ANTHOLOGY pp. 24–27

TEACHING GUIDE AND RESOURCES
- Two-Column Journal **p. 153**
- Answer Key **p. 114**

REAL WORLD WRITING JOURNAL pp. 22–25

ANTHOLOGY

Preteach

Activate Prior Knowledge Have students complete the Real-Life Connection web. Students will revisit the webs after they read.

Build Background *Though many people in the United States believe that competition is good, some groups disagree. In many Native American cultures, for example, cooperation among members of the community is considered to be good, and competition is thought to be bad. The accomplishments of the group are more important than the accomplishments of an individual.*

Introduce Vocabulary

- Ask students which Word Bank words they have already studied (*context, differentiate, evidence, subjective*) and what each means.
- Discuss the meaning of the word *crucial*. Have students make connections between the words.
- *Build Academic Vocabulary* Ask students the difference between *subjective* and *objective*. Why might an evaluation of a piece of art be more subjective than a score on a true-false quiz?

Teach

Focus on the Big Question Ask the Article BQ, *Are people naturally competitive?* Students will answer this question after reading.

- *Connect to the Unit Big Question* Confirm that students know what *competitive* means.

Preread the Article Preview the article with students. Read aloud the introduction, the title, and the subheads. Direct students to study the photographs and read the captions. Then have students write a prediction about how the article will answer the BQ about competition.

Conduct a Guided Reading Read the article to students as they follow along. Pause after each section to monitor students' comprehension.

- Call on a volunteer to summarize the section.
- Have a volunteer ask a question based on the section. Write the question on the board.

Model how to do this by using a think aloud:

> **THINK ALOUD** *As I read the first page, I am really surprised that the author has not focused on sports, because that was the first thing I thought of when I heard the word* competitive. *My first question is, "Will there be anything about sports in this article?"*

Reflect on the Article After reading the article, review ideas introduced before or during reading.

- Revisit the Real-Life Connection webs. Discuss additions based on the article.
- Revisit students' predictions about the article. Were they correct? Why or why not?

Practice and Apply

Discuss the Questions Gauge students' comprehension and help them develop critical reading skills (Answer Key, p. 114).

Connect to the Big Question Have students use the Two-Column Journal to answer the Article BQ.

- Direct students to reread the article to find four statements related to the BQ. Write these statements in the "Ideas from the Article" column.
- Have students write their own responses in the "My Thoughts" column.
- Call for volunteers to answer the BQ. Ask students to support their opinions with ideas from their organizers.

Assess

Informally assess students' understanding of the article by asking these questions:

- *What is one good thing children can learn by being involved in sports?*
- *What is one bad effect competition can have on children?*
- *What was the most persuasive fact in the article?*
- *Did your opinion about competition change after reading? Why or why not?*
- *What else would you like to know about competition?*

Reach All Learners

Build Fluency Choose a section from the article for a group reading.

- Organize students into groups. Have one student in each group read one line from the text aloud. Then have the next student read the second line.
- Direct students to move as seamlessly as possible from one to another in their reading.
- Encourage students to give each other feedback as they read to improve the flow of reading.

Use Small Groups Use the RCRC method to help students check comprehension.

- Group students. Give each group member a short section of the article to read.
- Explain the process of RCRC to students:
  Read the text.
  Cover it up.
  Retell what they have just read.
  Check to see if they were correct.
- Have each group practice RCRC until all group members have had a chance to test their comprehension.

Assist Students Having Difficulty If students struggle with writing notes, remind them that notes do not have to be complete sentences.

- Work with students to make a list of abbreviations to use when taking notes.
- Give examples of notes for different activities in the lesson.

WRITING JOURNAL

Extend

Write About It Students will use a two-column graphic organizer to plan a guide for parents about competition.

- Read and discuss the Writing Prompt (Journal, p. 22). Review the Writing Rubric. Encourage students to add more points to the rubric to guide their work.
- Model how to use the organizer.
- Students should use the Check It and Fix It section and the Writing Checklist to revise and evaluate their work.

Teaching Tip If students are having difficulty deciding what their opinion is, have them fill out the positives and negatives columns on the graphic organizer first. Then have students review the information in the two columns. Which column is more convincing? If students have a clear preference, that preference will help them formulate their opinion of competition.

Vocabulary Workshop Students extend their thinking about Word Bank words.

- Students work in pairs or small groups on the Define It organizer (Journal, p. 24).
- Have students add words to the Your Choice box and their personal word bank.
- Use the Show You Know exercise to assess students' understanding.

As students read about the suffix -*ate*, model by thinking aloud:

> **THINK ALOUD** *This says that the suffix -ate means "to make or to do," but if I try to apply that definition literally the sentence does not make sense to me. You do not literally "make the twins not the same" by their clothes. You make a decision about the difference between the twins by their clothes. Now I see how the meaning of the suffix applies.*

Follow up by holding a brainstorming session. Ask students to list words that end in -*ate*. Together, think of a class in which students might use each word on the list. For example, students might use *pollinate* in a science class and *calculate* in a math class.

Shark Story

PROGRAM RESOURCES

ANTHOLOGY pp. 28–31

TEACHING GUIDE AND RESOURCES
- Cause and Effect Map **p. 140**
- Answer Key **pp. 114–115**

REAL WORLD WRITING JOURNAL pp. 26–29

ANTHOLOGY

Preteach

Activate Prior Knowledge Take a poll about students' reactions to sharks: *Like/Do Not Like/Do Not Know.* Students will revisit the poll after reading.

Build Background *There are around four hundred different species of sharks. The fastest shark is the shortfin mako, which can swim up to 20 miles per hour. The largest shark is also the largest fish in the ocean. It is the whale shark. It eats only plankton and can be as long as 60 feet.*

Introduce Vocabulary

- Divide the class into groups and assign each group one of the words.
- Have each group work on a presentation about the word it has been assigned.
- Ask groups to teach their words to the class.
- *Build Academic Vocabulary* To review the academic vocabulary words *approach* and *observe,* ask the following question: *What* approach *would you use to* observe *how a bird builds a nest?*

Teach

Focus on the Big Question Ask the Article BQ, *How dangerous are sharks?* Students will answer this question after reading.

- *Connect to the Unit Big Question* Write the Unit and Article BQs on the board. Remind students what the word *perception* means. Have students discuss their perceptions of sharks.

Preread the Article Before students read, use the following Think Aloud to model how to preview and activate prior knowledge to help predict what the article will be about:

THINK ALOUD *The title of this article is "Shark Story," and the first subhead is "Fear of a Fish." I wonder if the article is about when a shark attacked someone. Then I think about the Big Question and the articles we have been reading. All of them ask us to think about subjects in a new way. I think I will learn something new about sharks.*

Have students preview other elements of the article and write a prediction.

Conduct a Guided Reading Read the article to students as they follow along. Pause after each section to monitor students' comprehension.

- Have students create sticky notes with check marks, minus marks, plus marks, and question marks on them.
- Explain that a check mark is for information that students already know. A minus is for information that is different from what they thought. A question mark is for information they do not understand, and a plus mark is for new information.
- As students read, they should attach the appropriate sticky note next to passages.

Reflect on the Article After reading the article, review ideas introduced before or during reading.

- Retake the poll. Have poll results changed?
- Review predictions. Were they accurate?

Practice and Apply

Discuss the Questions Gauge students' comprehension and help them develop critical reading skills (Answer Key, pp. 114–115).

Connect to the Big Question Discuss what students thought about sharks before reading the article and after.

Assess

Have students work in groups to create a fact sheet that contains information about ways that people are dangerous to sharks. Tell each group to choose at least three important facts from the article. Post students' fact sheets on a classroom bulletin board.

Reach All Learners

Build Fluency Choose a section from the article for a paired reading.

- Pair students and have them read silently.
- Direct one student to read aloud while the other follows along making notes.
- The listener provides suggestions and feedback. Students then reverse roles.

Use Small Groups Engage students with a peer learning exercise.

- In small groups, have students review their sticky notes from Conduct a Guided Reading. Clarify the meaning of passages that students did not understand.

Assist Students Having Difficulty If students struggle to understand the ideas in the article, provide them with the Cause and Effect Map.

- Have students write "More people swim in the ocean" or "the movie *Jaws*" in the Cause section of the organizer.
- Help students look through the article and record the effects of either cause.

WRITING JOURNAL

Extend

Write About It Students will use a web graphic organizer to plan and write an informational brochure about sharks.

- Read and discuss the Writing Prompt (Journal, p. 26). Review the Writing Rubric. Encourage students to add more points to the rubric to guide their work.
- Model how to use the organizer.
- Students should use the Check It and Fix It section and the Writing Checklist to revise and evaluate their work.

To help students organize, model by thinking aloud:

> **THINK ALOUD** *I have a pretty good idea what facts to include about this subject, but I can make sure I have enough interesting facts if I use this organizer. The article says that a person is more likely to be hit by lightning than be attacked by a shark. I will put that on the web because it is a convincing fact.*

Vocabulary Workshop Students extend their thinking about Word Bank words.

- Students work in pairs or small groups on the Define It organizer (Journal, p. 28).
- Have students add words to the Your Choice box and their personal word bank.
- Use the Show You Know exercise to assess students' understanding.

Teaching Tip If students are having difficulty with the Show You Know story, help them by brainstorming different story ideas as a class.

The ABCs of Antioxidants

PROGRAM RESOURCES

ANTHOLOGY pp. 32–35
TEACHING GUIDE AND RESOURCES
- T-Chart **p. 151**
- Answer Key **p. 115**
REAL WORLD WRITING JOURNAL pp. 30–33

ANTHOLOGY

Preteach

Activate Prior Knowledge Have students fill in the Real-Life Connection chart. Students will revisit their charts after they read.

Build Background *Many foods that have deep, rich colors are full of antioxidants: red cherries and tomatoes; orange carrots, papaya, and mangos; and blue or purple blueberries, blackberries, and grapes.*

Introduce Vocabulary

- Have volunteers read aloud the sentences from the article in which boldface vocabulary words appear. As a class, discuss what each word means in context.
- Read the definitions from the Word Bank. Discuss similarities and differences in meaning.
- *Build Academic Vocabulary* Ask students questions about the academic vocabulary *consequence, refer,* and *discern.* For example, if they wanted to find out the meaning of a word, would they *refer* to a dictionary or *discern* a dictionary? What is the *consequence* if vinegar is added to baking soda?

Teach

Focus on the Big Question Ask the Article BQ, *Can we eat our way to good health?* Students will answer this question after reading.

- *Connect to the Unit Big Question* Discuss what makes a person healthy. How much do students know about health?

Preread the Article Before students read, use the following Think Aloud to model how to prepare to read:

| THINK ALOUD | *I know I have some reading to do. I need to be able to concentrate when I read, so I find a quiet place. Then I look at how many pages the assignment is. It is three pages. Next, I look at the title and other text features to preview the article. I ask myself, What do I already know about this topic? What do I predict this article will be about? What do I want to find out about the topic of the article?* |

Have students write a prediction about the article and a question they would like to have answered.

Conduct a Guided Reading Read the article to students as they follow along. Pause after each section to monitor students' comprehension.

- Ask questions to check meaning. Have students volunteer questions they have.

Reflect on the Article After reading the article, review ideas introduced before or during reading.

- Have students revisit what they wrote in the Real-Life Connection chart. Have answers changed? Why or why not?
- Discuss questions students posed during reading. What else do students wonder?

Practice and Apply

Discuss the Questions Gauge students' comprehension and help them develop critical reading skills (Answer Key, p. 115).

Connect to the Big Question Use the T-Chart to have students answer the Article BQ.

- Have students write the Article BQ on their organizers and the words *yes* and *no* at the top of each column.
- Go through the points in the article and ask students if they support a *yes* or *no* answer.

Assess

Have students write a few sentences that describe the difference between what free radicals do and what antioxidants do. Students should use information from the article.

Reach All Learners

Build Fluency Choose a section from the article for a class reading.

- Have students read the selection in pairs and coach each other on fluency. Tell students that if disagreements arise, they should ask for your help.
- Then have each student read one or two sentences from the section aloud to the entire class.

Use Small Groups

- In groups of three or four, have students create a menu for a day's meals using healthful foods full of antioxidants.
- Have the groups present their menus to the class. Post the menus on a bulletin board.

Assist Students Having Difficulty If students struggle to understand the behavior of free radicals, illustrate by drawing an example of a free radical on the board and showing how it "takes" an electron from another molecule.

WRITING JOURNAL

Extend

Write About It Students will use a question and answer graphic organizer to plan and write a FAQ for a Web page on healthful eating.

- Read and discuss the Writing Prompt (Journal, p. 30). Review the Writing Rubric. Encourage students to add more points to the rubric to guide their work.
- Model how to use the organizer.
- Students should use the Check It and Fix It section and the Writing Checklist to revise and evaluate their work.

Teaching Tip If students are having difficulty thinking of questions, remind them of the questions they wrote for themselves before reading and of the questions they asked during reading. Remind students that no question is too obvious or simple for a FAQ.

Vocabulary Workshop Students extend their thinking about Word Bank words.

- Students work in pairs or small groups on the Define It organizer (Journal, p. 32).
- Have students add words to the Your Choice box and their personal word bank.
- Use the Show You Know exercise to assess students' understanding.

Help students with the Root Words Exercise by thinking aloud:

> **THINK ALOUD** *If I am having trouble understanding what the other -fer words mean, I will think about what the prefix means. Trans- means "across," so transfer means "to carry or to bring across." Con- means "with or together," so confer means "to bring together" or "to talk together."*

UNIT 1
WRAP UP

Is there a difference between reality and truth?

Introduce the Unit Project

Interview Students will participate in interviews and present their partner's answer to the Big Question: *Is there a difference between reality and truth?*

- Read through the steps of the assignment with students.
- Point out the rubric so that students will know their goals for the assignment. Add other rubric points with students to guide their work.
- Allow time for students to practice and present their work. Encourage listeners to offer their feedback and advice on the presentation.

Model Model how to strengthen a presentation by thinking aloud:

> **THINK ALOUD** *I already interviewed my partner and I have her answer to the Big Question, but as I look through my notes, I realize that I do not understand all of her answers. If I am going to have a great presentation, I need to understand all of her thoughts. I can ask clarifying questions to strengthen my presentation.*

Teaching Tip Let students know that when they practice their presentation, they should also make sure that their notes are legible and easy to read by glancing down at them. Students should practice more than once so that they are comfortable with what they will say.

Conclude the Unit

Review Unit Objectives Return to the unit objectives and ask students to evaluate how well they mastered each one on a scale of 1 to 5, with 1 being low and 5 being high. Discuss how lower scores could be improved.

Reflect on the Learning Examine the bulletin board with students. Ask them to reflect on what they have learned. They can write or discuss with the class or in small groups. Prompt students' thinking with questions such as:

- *What was the most interesting article you read? What did you like about it?*

- *How did your ideas about reality and truth change as you read through the articles?*
- *Which topic would you like to know more about? What do you still wonder about it?*
- *How did the writing assignments and the interview help you form your ideas about reality and truth?*
- *What other subjects do you think challenge people's ideas about reality? What effect would that have on how they live their lives or operate in the world?*

UNIT 1

Word Bank Quiz

WORD LIST A			
approach	discern	involves	subjective
associate	evidence	observe	uncertainty
consequence	focus	refer	verify

Ten of the unit Word Bank words are defined in parentheses in the article below. As you read the article, use Word List A, above, to figure out which word best fits each definition. Write the word on the line provided. (You will not use every word on the list.) Then go on to the next page of the quiz.

Digging Up the Past

I am an archeologist. I study the **(1. sign or proof that something is true)**

_____ of ancient cultures. This **(2. includes or requires)**

_____ digging up old bones. I have to be very careful about my

(3. organized way to do something) _____ to any new find.

Let me give you an example.

Say I have a **(4. based on feelings and opinions)** _____ belief

that women cannot be warriors. One day I find some bones. I **(5. make sure)**

_____ that they are human. I see a spear and armor. I immediately

(6. connect in my mind) _____ this with male warriors. I have

no **(7. being unsure)** _____ about my opinion. However, I am

still a scientist. I do my job, no matter what the **(8. result of the action)**

_____. When I **(9. put all my attention)** _____

closely on the bones, I **(10. become aware of)** _____ that they are

smaller than many other bones that had been found at the site.

UNIT 1 Word Bank Quiz

WORD LIST B			
comprehend	context	evaluate	perception
concrete	crucial	improbable	reality
confirm	differentiate	objective	results

Ten more Word Bank words are defined in parentheses in the rest of the
article, below. As you read the article, use Word List B, above, to figure out
which word best fits each definition. Write the word on the line provided.
(You will not use every word on the list.)

What had I found? Could it be a child? Could it be a woman? I know that scientists

have to be **(11. based on facts rather than feelings)** _____. It seems

(12. unlikely) _____ based on what we thought we knew about this

particular culture, but this might not be a man. I have to **(13. notice the difference)**

_____ between what I think I know and **(14. real and**

specific) _____ proof. It is **(15. extremely important)**

_____ that I find out what age and gender these bones are.

I run tests on the bones and wait for the **(16. outcomes)** _____.

With that information, I can **(17. form an opinion about how good or bad)**

_____ what I have found. The tests indicate that the bones were

those of a female. This is hard for me to **(18. understand)** _____.

It changes my **(19. understanding based on thoughts and senses)**

_____ of this culture. Perhaps I also need to rethink my ideas about

(20. things in the actual world) _____.

Can progress be made without conflict?

Unit Overview

The articles in this unit explore what progress is and how progress is made. Students will read about issues such as sibling rivalry, identity theft, problems with teen drivers, and the possibility of a flu epidemic. As they read, students will decide for themselves whether conflict and progress are related.

Launch the Unit

Connect to the Big Question Prompt students to think about the unit opener. Read the introduction to students and examine the illustration together. Ask questions such as these:

- *Why might the shopping mall be progress? Why might it not?*
- *What is the conflict in the illustration?*
- *What do you think the boys in the illustration think about the new mall?*
- *How is the conflict in the illustration connected to progress?*
- *What connections can you make to this situation?*

Use the prompt on the page as the basis for journal writing or for small group or whole class discussion.

Anchor Students' Thinking On a classroom bulletin board, post a Three-Column Chart on which you have written the Unit Big Question. Label the first column *Progress Achieved;* the second column *Was Conflict Involved?;* and the third column *Did Conflict Help or Hurt?* Throughout the unit, encourage students to add ideas to the chart and art to the bulletin board.

- Have students look through the articles and other sources for words that can be used to talk about progress. Post these words and meanings.
- Post exemplary writing from students' journal assignments. Discuss what these writings reveal about the relationship between progress and conflict.
- Challenge students to find other examples of progress. Have them bring in newspaper or magazine articles, photographs from print or online resources, or their own drawings. Link students' art to ideas in the articles and to the Unit Big Question.

Unit Objectives

Share these objectives with students. As you read the articles in this unit, you will:

- Identify connections between conflict and progress.
- Determine an answer to the Big Question: *Can progress be made without conflict?* Explain your answers using details from the articles and from your own experiences.
- Use content and academic vocabulary to talk and write about progress and conflict.
- Make a poster that answers the Big Question.

Sibling Strife

PROGRAM RESOURCES

ANTHOLOGY pp. 40–43

TEACHING GUIDE AND RESOURCES
- K-W-L Chart **p. 145**
- Main Idea Map **p. 146**
- Answer Key **p. 116**

REAL WORLD WRITING JOURNAL pp. 36–39

ANTHOLOGY

Preteach

Activate Prior Knowledge Have students copy and complete the chart in the Real-Life Connection. Students will revisit answers after they read.

Build Background *Sibling rivalry often starts right after the birth of a second child and usually continues throughout childhood and adolescence. Many factors contribute to sibling rivalry, including competition between brothers and sisters to define themselves as individuals and to get parental attention.*

Introduce Vocabulary

- Read aloud the words, definitions, and example sentences in the Word Bank.
- Choose one of the words and use it in a sentence on the board. Ask for volunteers to come to the board and add to the idea by writing another sentence with a different vocabulary word. Continue until all the words have been used.
- *Build Academic Vocabulary* Ask students to give examples of how they would use the academic vocabulary word *discuss* in different classes.

Teach

Focus on the Big Question Ask the Article BQ, *Why can it be hard for siblings to get along?* Students will answer this question after reading.

- *Connect to the Unit Big Question* Write the Article BQ on the board and read it aloud. Then ask a student to read the Unit BQ aloud. Have students discuss how the BQs are linked.

Preread the Article Have students review the title and introduction. Ask them to write down on a K-W-L Chart what they know and want to know about sibling rivalry.

Conduct a Guided Reading Read the article to students as they follow along. Pause after each section to monitor students' comprehension.

- Model how to monitor comprehension:

> **THINK ALOUD** *I should reread the first few sentences of the section, since they often state the main idea. I see that this first subhead is about why siblings are rivals for their parents' love. Which details in the section give more information about this topic? The author explains that only children get all of their parents' attention, while siblings feel that they must compete for it. They resent the other child or children taking attention from them.*

- Ask a volunteer to summarize the section.

Reflect on the Article After reading the article, review ideas introduced before or during reading.

- Review the responses to the Real-Life Connection chart. How do students' answers compare with the information in the article?
- Have students discuss their K-W-L Charts. Students should then fill in the *Want to Learn* column.

Practice and Apply

Discuss the Questions Gauge students' comprehension and help them develop critical reading skills (Answer Key, p. 116).

Connect to the Big Question Have students quickwrite about a personal experience they have had with sibling rivalry.

- Have students write a short summary of the experience. Then ask them to write about what they learned in the article that could explain the reasons behind the situation.

Assess

Have students create a learning log for you to assess informally. Students should answer these questions:

- *What did you do in class today? What did you learn?*
- *What did you find interesting?*
- *What questions do you still have?*

Reach All Learners

Build Fluency Choose sections from the article for an echo reading.

- Read the section aloud to students, modeling reading with accuracy.
- Have volunteers read the same section aloud, focusing on accuracy.
- Tell students to repeat the process with a partner. The first partner reads a section aloud, focusing on accuracy, and the second partner echo reads.

Use Small Groups Engage students with a write-around activity.

- Organize students into groups of four or five. Ask a group leader to give each group a piece of paper that has each Word Bank word for this lesson written across the top.
- Direct a member of each group to write a sentence that begins a story about sibling rivalry. The sentence must contain one Word Bank word.
- The group member who wrote the sentence then passes the paper to the right. The next group member should continue the story with another sentence and vocabulary word. Group members should continue until all vocabulary has been used at least once.

Assist Students Having Difficulty If students have trouble expressing what they learned in the article, have them complete a Main Idea Map for each section.

- Read the first section aloud, having students take turns reading the next sections.
- Complete the Main Idea Map as a class, using an overhead transparency.
- Have students complete their own charts for each section.

WRITING JOURNAL

Extend

Write About It Students will write an article about sibling rivalry.

- Read and discuss the Writing Prompt (Journal, p. 36). Review the Writing Rubric. Encourage students to add more points to the rubric to guide their work.
- Model how to use the organizer.
- Students should use the Check It and Fix It section and the Writing Checklist to revise and evaluate their work.

As you draft, model by thinking aloud:

> **THINK ALOUD** *As I write, I want to remember the requirements of the assignment about sibling rivalry: define, explain causes, give solutions, and discuss possible benefits. My article needs to include each of these in a way that will be interesting to my readers, who are teens.*

Vocabulary Workshop Students extend their thinking about Word Bank words.

- Students work in pairs or small groups on the Define It organizer (Journal, p. 38).
- Have students add words to the Your Choice box and their personal word bank.
- Use the Show You Know exercise to assess students' understanding.

Teaching Tip Write the Word Bank words across the top of the board. Have students share their sentences from the Show You Know exercise. Write examples under each word, and discuss the different ways students showed their understanding of the words.

Holding Parents Responsible

PROGRAM RESOURCES

ANTHOLOGY pp. 44–47

TEACHING GUIDE AND RESOURCES
- Two-Column Journal **p. 153**
- Cause and Effect Map **p. 140**
- Answer Key **p. 116**

REAL WORLD WRITING JOURNAL pp. 40–43

ANTHOLOGY

Preteach

Activate Prior Knowledge Have students complete the Real-Life Connection exercise on their own. Discuss responses as a class. Students will revisit answers after they read.

Build Background *States have different kinds of parental accountability laws. Many states press criminal charges against parents who contribute to the delinquency of a minor. If found guilty, parents may face a variety of consequences, including fines, required participation at court proceedings, payment of court and legal fees, payment to victims, participation in community service with their child, or jail time.*

Introduce Vocabulary

- Read aloud the sentences from the article in which boldface vocabulary words appear. Discuss what each word means in context.
- Give students the opportunity to practice the words in a new context. Work with students to create new sentences for each term.
- *Build Academic Vocabulary* Use the academic vocabulary for this lesson in this sentence: I am *inclined* to *defend* my point of view from those who *oppose* it. Challenge students to think of synonymous words or phrases for each academic vocabulary word.

Teach

Focus on the Big Question Ask the Article BQ, *Should parents be held responsible for teens' mistakes?* Students will answer this question after reading.

- *Connect to the Unit Big Question* Write both the Unit and Article BQs on the board. Have students brainstorm in pairs about the connection between the two. Then discuss their ideas as a class.

Preread the Article Ask students to read the title of the article and the first few sentences in each paragraph. Use the sentences to make an informal outline of the article. Direct students to use the outline to make a prediction about the article.

Conduct a Guided Reading Read the article to students as they follow along. Pause after each section to monitor students' comprehension.

- After each section, stop and summarize.
- Ask students, *What is the author trying to say and why? How does the author make the points clear? What is still unclear?*

Model how to find the article's main idea:

> **THINK ALOUD** *The last sentence of the three-paragraph introduction is about holding parents responsible. That idea links to the title, so I think that may be the main idea of the whole article.*

Reflect on the Article After reading the article, review ideas introduced before or during reading.

- Have students revisit their responses to the scenario in the Real-Life Connection. Have students changed their minds since reading the article?
- Ask students to discuss their predictions.

Practice and Apply

Discuss the Questions Gauge students' comprehension and help them develop critical reading skills (Answer Key, p. 116).

Connect to the Big Question Use the Two-Column Journal to help students answer the BQ.

- Have students list the reasons for and against holding parents legally responsible for teens' crimes.
- Instruct students to use the My Thoughts section to respond to each of these reasons.

Assess

Have students create a Cause and Effect Map for you to assess informally.

- Have students write *Holding Parents Responsible* in the cause circle.
- In the Effect boxes, have students list the good and bad effects of holding parents responsible.

Reach All Learners

Build Fluency Choose a section from the article for a paired reading.

- Pair students and have them read silently.
- Direct one student to read aloud while the other follows along making notes about miscues, mispronounced words, or other problems that hamper fluency.
- The listener provides suggestions and feedback. Students then reverse roles.

Use Small Groups Engage students in a small group discussion.

- Ask students to brainstorm consequences for parents of teens who commit crimes.
- Have students discuss whether they think each consequence might help prevent further crimes by teens. Ask groups to present their ideas to the class as a whole.

Assist Students Having Difficulty If students struggle with comprehension, have them use sticky notes to help them develop questioning skills.

- Provide students with a stack of small sticky notes.
- Instruct students to place notes next to confusing areas in the text. Have students write specific questions on the sticky notes.
- Allow time to discuss and answer the questions as a class.

WRITING JOURNAL

Extend

Write About It Students will write a letter to their senator about their views on parental responsibility laws.

- Read and discuss the Writing Prompt (Journal, p. 40). Review the Writing Rubric. Encourage students to add more points to the rubric to guide their work.
- Model how to use the organizer.
- Students should use the Check It and Fix It section and the Writing Checklist to revise and evaluate their work.

Teaching Tip Allow students to talk in pairs after their prewriting exercises. Students should review each other's lists and provide feedback about things that might add to the letter or make the ideas more convincing.

Vocabulary Workshop Students extend their thinking about Word Bank words.

- Students work in pairs or small groups on the Define It organizer (Journal, p. 42).
- Have students add words to the Your Choice box and their personal word bank.
- Use the Show You Know exercise to assess students' understanding.

Use a Think Aloud to model how to do the word root exercise:

> **THINK ALOUD** *In the first sentence, I see the root* pos *in the word* pose. *I know that* pos *usually means "to put or place." I should also look at the context of the sentence to get a better idea of exactly what* pose *means. Since the sentence is talking about an artist wanting me to do something for a portrait, or picture, I think* pose *means "to put or place myself for a picture."*

UNIT 2

Identity Theft

PROGRAM RESOURCES

ANTHOLOGY pp. 48–51

TEACHING GUIDE AND RESOURCES
- Guess It and Check It Chart **p. 143**
- Answer Key **pp. 116–117**

REAL WORLD WRITING JOURNAL pp. 44–47

ANTHOLOGY

Preteach

Activate Prior Knowledge Take a poll for each question in the Real-Life Connection. Students will revisit answers after they read.

Build Background *While a 2007 survey found that the number of victims of identity theft decreased from the previous year, there were still 8.9 million victims in the United States. In fact, most people know someone whose identity has been stolen. The best way to fight identity theft is summed up by the Federal Trade Commission as* Deter, Detect, *and* Defend.

Introduce Vocabulary

- Read aloud the definitions and examples in the Word Bank.
- Have students work in pairs to use each word in a sentence. Ask for volunteers to share their sentences with the class.
- *Build Academic Vocabulary* The academic vocabulary words for this lesson are *motive, produce,* and *radical.* Point out that the word *radical* means one thing in social studies and another thing in math. Discuss the differences in the definitions.

Teach

Focus on the Big Question Ask the Article BQ, *Is someone out to steal your identity?* Students will answer this question after reading.

- *Connect to the Unit Big Question* Write both the Unit and Article BQs on the board. Have volunteers read each aloud. Ask students how technological progress has increased identity theft.

Preread the Article Before students read, model how to preview and predict:

> **THINK ALOUD** *I see that the title of the article is "Identity Theft." In the illustration on the first page, I see a girl using a computer. This makes me think that there are probably many ways for thieves to get a person's personal information by using the Internet and e-mail. I will review the first few sentences of each section to make a prediction about how the picture is related to the article.*

Model how to preview the other text features: subheads, pullout quotation, and bulleted list. Ask students to write a prediction about the article.

Conduct a Guided Reading Read the article to students as they follow along. Pause after each section to monitor students' comprehension.

- Ask students to identify the main idea of each section.
- Ask a volunteer to summarize the section.

Reflect on the Article After reading the article, review ideas introduced before or during reading.

- Retake the poll from the Real-Life Connection. Have answers changed? Ask students why or why not.
- Discuss with students how accurate their predictions were. Discuss any changes they would make.

Practice and Apply

Discuss the Questions Gauge students' comprehension and help them develop critical reading skills (Answer Key, pp. 116–117).

Connect to the Big Question Ask students to list ways to protect themselves from identity theft.

- Have students reread the article for help.
- Remind students that the article states some recommendations, but others must be inferred.

Assess

Have students write questions about the article's content for you to assess informally.

- Have students write two questions on slips of paper.
- Ask students to trade their questions with a classmate.
- Direct students to answer each other's questions.

Reach All Learners

Build Fluency Choose a section from the article and work on difficult or unfamiliar words. For example, the section "Phish and Spam" contains the words *reputation, data, site, register, attachment,* and *virus.*

- Have students read a section and write down difficult or unfamiliar words.
- Make a list on the board and coach students on ways to figure out how to pronounce the words and infer what the words mean.
- Have students reread the section.

Use Small Groups Engage students in a word game.

- Divide the class into groups of three or four. One student should take the role of artist, while the others will be guessers.
- Provide artists with different lists of key words from the article.
- Have the artists come to the board and draw pictures that lead their groups to guess the word. Set a timer to make the game more challenging. The team with the most correct guesses wins.

Assist Students Having Difficulty If students struggle with vocabulary in the article, provide them with a Guess It and Check It Chart.

- Have students write difficult words on the organizer as they read. They may refer to their lists from the Build Fluency exercise.
- Instruct students to use the organizer to write down clues from the context, a guess at the meaning, and the dictionary definition.

WRITING JOURNAL

Extend

Write About It Students will write a list of guidelines about safe Internet use.

- Read and discuss the Writing Prompt (Journal, p. 44). Review the Writing Rubric. Encourage students to add more points to the rubric to guide their work.
- Model how to use the organizer.
- Students should use the Check It and Fix It section and the Writing Checklist to revise and evaluate their work.

Teaching Tip Allow students to work with a partner to make a poster using the guidelines they wrote. Ask students to make their final products eye-catching. Provide an art center in the room for the creation of the final poster; include items such as markers, scissors, and construction paper. To make the writing assignment more meaningful, get permission to post some of students' guidelines in a school computer lab or library. Have students work in pairs to ensure that their guidelines are error-free.

Vocabulary Workshop Students extend their thinking about Word Bank words.

- Students work in pairs or small groups on the Define It organizer (Journal, p. 46).
- Have students add words to the Your Choice box and their personal word bank.
- Use the Show You Know exercise to assess students' understanding.

Model how to approach the Show You Know exercise with this Think Aloud:

> **THINK ALOUD** *For my clues, I don't want to just repeat the definitions from the Word Bank. I won't learn as much if I do. I want to come up with clues that are similar to the definitions and likely to help my partner and me learn the words. For example, for the word* discuss *I might say, "When we talk over ideas in small groups, we do this."*

UNIT 2

Tracking Teen Drivers

PROGRAM RESOURCES

ANTHOLOGY pp. 52–55

TEACHING GUIDE AND RESOURCES
- T-Chart **p. 151**
- Answer Key **p. 117**

REAL WORLD WRITING JOURNAL pp. 48–51

ANTHOLOGY

Preteach

Activate Prior Knowledge Have students complete the Real-Life Connection charts on their own. Then take a poll of student answers. Students will revisit answers after they read.

Build Background *Car accidents caused by teens are the number one cause of death for teens in the United States. Though inexperience is likely a factor, studies also show that teens are distracted by things such as friends in the car, music, cell phone calls, and text messages.*

Introduce Vocabulary

- Have students brainstorm different contexts or situations in which each word might be useful. Write their ideas on the board.
- Then ask students to create sentences for the words using the different contexts.
- *Build Academic Vocabulary* The academic vocabulary words for this lesson are *oppose* and *unify*. Ask students how they might use *oppose* in gym class and *unify* in social studies.

Teach

Focus on the Big Question Ask the Article BQ, *Are tracking systems lifesavers or invasions of privacy?* Students will answer this question after reading.

- *Connect to the Unit Big Question* Have students write down both the Unit and Article BQs. Ask students to work with a partner to explain how the article BQ is related to progress and conflict.

Preread the Article Before students read the article, ask them to read the title, introduction, and caption for the first photo. Challenge students to explain what "tracking" refers to. Work with students to determine what the opening paragraph tells them about the article. Then have students write a prediction.

Conduct a Guided Reading Read the article to students as they follow along. Pause after each section to monitor students' comprehension.

- Ask five *W*'s and an *H* questions.

Model asking and answering the questions:

> **THINK ALOUD** *Who is the article about and what is the subject? It is about teen drivers and the use of tracking systems. Where and when are they used? They are used in the cars of teen drivers, and they keep track of the cars' location all the time. Why are the devices used? Parents use them to keep track of their children's location and driving habits. How do the devices work? They use a satellite to keep track of the car. They also allow for cameras in the car and tracking of information like speed.*

- Ask students to use their own words to retell what they read in a section.

Reflect on the Article After reading the article, review ideas introduced before or during reading.

- Retake the poll from the Real-Life Connection. Have answers changed? Ask students why.
- Ask students how the article differs from their predictions and expectations.

Practice and Apply

Discuss the Questions Gauge students' comprehension and help them develop critical reading skills (Answer Key, p. 117).

Connect to the Big Question Use a T-Chart to have students answer the BQ.

- Have students label the columns *For Tracking Systems* and *Against Tracking Systems*.
- Direct students to refer to the article to find supporting ideas for both opinions. Have students list these ideas in their chart.
- Call for volunteers to answer the BQ.

Assess

Have students write a personal journal entry about how they would feel if they had tracking devices in their cars. Instruct students to address how they feel about the pros and cons of the devices, as described in the article.

Reach All Learners

Build Fluency Choose sections from the article and have students work on appropriate expression.

- Ask students to read short sections aloud. Provide suggestions and feedback.
- Model different kinds of expression to show how tone and intonation affect understanding.
- Then ask students to reread the section.

Use Small Groups Engage students in a role-playing activity.

- Have small groups imagine a conversation between a concerned parent and his or her teenager about the use of a tracking device.
- Assign each group one of the two roles: either the role of the parent or the teenager. Have each group write either the parent's explanation speech or the child's response speech.
- Call on volunteers to perform the conversations for the class.

Assist Students Having Difficulty If students struggle to keep track of main ideas in the article, provide them with a skeleton outline for taking notes.

- The outline should include the article title and subheads with space for notes.
- Allow time after reading the article to go over the outline, using an overhead transparency. Ask students the following questions:
- *What questions do you still have?*
- *What was the point of today's lesson?*

WRITING JOURNAL

Extend

Write About It Students will write a letter to a newspaper editor about the pros and cons of using teen tracking devices.

- Read and discuss the Writing Prompt (Journal, p. 48). Review the Writing Rubric. Encourage students to add more points to the rubric to guide their work.
- Model how to use the organizer.
- Students should use the Check It and Fix It section and the Writing Checklist to revise and evaluate their work.

As you draft, model by thinking aloud:

> **THINK ALOUD** *I want my letter to be convincing so that readers will agree with my argument. To be convincing, I need to include plenty of evidence to support my argument. I also need to organize my evidence in a clear way. It is helpful if I think about people who might disagree with me. What arguments might they make? This way, I can address some of those points in my letter.*

Vocabulary Workshop Students extend their thinking about Word Bank words.

- Students work in pairs or small groups on the Define It organizer (Journal, p. 50).
- Have students add words to the Your Choice box and their personal word bank.
- Use the Show You Know exercise to assess students' understanding.

Teaching Tip After the Word Ending exercise, put students in pairs or small groups and have them compete to see who can come up with the most words that end with the suffixes *-ity* or *-ty*.

The Greed Game

PROGRAM RESOURCES

ANTHOLOGY pp. 56–59

TEACHING GUIDE AND RESOURCES
- Cause and Effect Map **p. 140**
- Web Map **p. 156**
- Answer Key **p. 117**

REAL WORLD WRITING JOURNAL pp. 52–55

ANTHOLOGY

Preteach

Activate Prior Knowledge Copy the chart from the Real-Life Connection onto the board. Complete the chart as a class. Students will revisit answers after they read.

Build Background *One of the most common ways companies advertise to teens is through celebrity spokespeople. Athletic shoe and clothing companies have paid millions to athletes like Tiger Woods and LeBron James. Gwyneth Paltrow and Fergie have endorsed cosmetics. Beyoncé and Britney Spears have done commercials for soft drinks. Companies cash in on teens' dreams of being like their favorite stars.*

Introduce Vocabulary

- Ask students to brainstorm synonyms for each word that will fit in the example sentence.
- Have students try their synonyms in the article sentences where boldface vocabulary words appear. What, if any, meaning do they lose with these substitutions?
- *Build Academic Vocabulary* The academic vocabulary words for this lesson are *conclude, debate,* and *former.* Ask students to use each word in a sentence with an academic context and then in a sentence with a non-academic context. Write examples on the board.

Teach

Focus on the Big Question Ask the Article BQ, *Do today's teens want too much?* Students will answer this question after reading.

- *Connect to the Unit Big Question* Write the Unit BQ on the board and read it aloud. Ask students to discuss conflicts that might occur when teens make decisions about buying. Can progress come from this conflict?

Preread the Article Ask students to preview the title and subheads and use these text features to make a prediction.

Conduct a Guided Reading Read the article to students as they follow along. Pause after each section to monitor students' comprehension.

- Ask students to give examples of key words and phrases. Model with this Think Aloud:

> **THINK ALOUD** *In the opening section, the author talks about advertising, teen consumers, materialistic teens, and the idea that teens are never satisfied. The author seems to be saying that advertising is aimed at teens because they are a big consumer group that just keeps wanting more and more.*

- Ask students to use the words and phrases to determine the main idea of the section.

Reflect on the Article After reading the article, review ideas introduced before or during reading.

- Turn students' attention to their answers to the Real-Life Connection. Ask students if they think advertising has been effective in their lives.
- Have students recall their predictions about the article. Discuss the accuracy of their predictions.

Practice and Apply

Discuss the Questions Gauge students' comprehension and help them develop critical reading skills (Answer Key, p. 117).

Connect to the Big Question Have students make a list of five things they would buy at the mall if money were no object. Ask students to answer the following questions about each item:

- *Where did they hear about it?*
- *Is it worth the amount of money it costs?*

Assess

Have students create a Web Map for you to assess informally.

- Ask students to write *Pitfalls of Teen Spending* in the center circle.
- In the outer circles, students should write potential pitfalls for teens who spend a lot of money on clothes, electronics, or cars.

Reach All Learners

Build Fluency Choose sections from the article and have students work on using punctuation to guide expression.

- First, read a section aloud using appropriate rate and expression as dictated by punctuation.
- Ask students to discuss how you used punctuation to guide your reading.
- Then have students take turns reading sections aloud. Provide coaching and feedback on how students used punctuation to guide their reading.

Use Small Groups Have students make acrostics for key words in the article.

- Have students work in groups of three or four.
- Place key words and phrases on small slips of paper; examples include *greed game, advertising, commercials,* and *credit cards.* Have each group draw slips from a box.
- Groups should write each word or phrase vertically on a piece of paper. Then they should write describing words and phrases that start with each letter in the word. Have groups share their acrostics on the board.

Assist Students Having Difficulty If students have trouble expressing what they learned from reading the article, have them complete a Cause and Effect Map for each section.

- Distribute a Cause and Effect Map to students.
- Use an overhead transparency of the organizer to model how to complete the *Cause* section.
- Have students complete their own organizers for each section.

WRITING JOURNAL

Extend

Write About It Students will write an advice blog for a teen under peer pressure to buy.

- Read and discuss the Writing Prompt (Journal, p. 52). Review the Writing Rubric. Encourage students to add more points to the rubric to guide their work.
- Model how to use the organizer.
- Students should use the Check It and Fix It section and the Writing Checklist to revise and evaluate their work.

Teaching Tip Ask students to recall times when they have received advice. Have them consider the following questions: *Why can some people give advice in a way that seems helpful, while other people just seem to be lecturing you? What makes you want to follow a person's advice? How can you tell good advice from bad advice?* Ask students to use their answers to the questions to guide their writing.

Vocabulary Workshop Students extend their thinking about Word Bank words.

- Students work in pairs or small groups on the Define It organizer (Journal, p. 54).
- Have students add words to the Your Choice box and their personal word bank.
- Use the Show You Know exercise to assess students' understanding.

Do the first Word Play sentence together. Model by thinking aloud:

> **THINK ALOUD** *I know that debate means "a discussion of arguments in favor of and against a certain action or viewpoint." What words or phrases mean something similar to debate? Argument, discussion, and deliberation are good examples. If I substitute these words in my example sentence, how does the meaning change? For example, "Dad and Juan had an argument about driving at age sixteen" is different from, "Dad and Juan had a debate about driving at age sixteen." Argument sounds as if it involves more conflict than debate.*

Learning from Crime Victims

PROGRAM RESOURCES

ANTHOLOGY pp. 60–63

TEACHING GUIDE AND RESOURCES
- Main Idea Map **p. 146**
- Answer Key **pp. 117–118**

REAL WORLD WRITING JOURNAL pp. 56–59

ANTHOLOGY

Preteach

Activate Prior Knowledge Have students complete the Real-Life Connection. Students will revisit answers after they read.

Build Background *Drugs and alcohol can play a major role in crimes involving teens. These substances impair judgment and lead people to do things they would never dream of doing otherwise. Offender/victim meetings may show offenders how out of control they are when under the influence.*

Introduce Vocabulary

- Write the Word Bank words across the board. Do not put them in alphabetical order.
- Ask for volunteers to come to the board and draw a line between two of the words. Students should then write a sentence using both words.
- *Build Academic Vocabulary* The academic vocabulary word for this lesson is *inestimable*. Have students identify the prefix, suffix, and base word. Discuss how the word parts change the meaning and part of speech of the word.

Teach

Focus on the Big Question Ask the Article BQ, *Can teen offenders learn from their victims?* Students will answer this question after reading.

- *Connect to the Unit Big Question* Read aloud both the Unit BQ and Article BQ. Ask students to brainstorm ways in which the two questions are connected.

Preread the Article Before students read, have them read the title and introductory section. Instruct students to answer the following questions about the topic: *What do you know? What do you think you know? What do you want to know?*

Conduct a Guided Reading Read the article to students as they follow along. Pause after each section to monitor students' comprehension.

- Have students find the main idea and details of each section.
- Model with this Think Aloud:

> **THINK ALOUD** *I should reread the first sentence, since that sentence is usually the topic sentence. I see that this section is about programs that bring together offenders and victims. The author explains that the purpose of these meetings is not reconciliation but forgiveness and understanding, as well as a change in the offender's behavior. The meeting is a conversation. Both sides gain understanding from this conversation. These details lead me to believe that the main idea of this section is that meetings between offenders and victims can allow both sides a chance to vent their feelings and move on from the experience in a positive way.*

Reflect on the Article After reading the article, review ideas introduced before or during reading.

- Have students review their answers to the Real-Life Connection. Discuss how they would change their answers after reading the article.
- Ask students if the article confirmed what they knew and thought they knew about the topic. Did the article answer their questions?

Practice and Apply

Discuss the Questions Gauge students' comprehension and help them develop critical reading skills (Answer Key, pp. 117–118).

Connect to the Big Question Have students support different answers to the BQ.

- Write the Article BQ on the board. Write *Yes* on one side of the board and *No* on the other.

Assess

Have students create a Main Idea Map for you to assess informally. The chart should include the main idea and at least four supporting details. Students may add more details boxes to the chart if they wish.

Reach All Learners

Build Fluency Choose sections from the article for an echo reading.

- First, have students echo your reading as a class.
- Then, have smaller groups, such as rows, echo your reading.
- Finally, call on individual students to echo read.

Use Small Groups Engage students in small group discussions.

- Have students work in groups of three or four. Provide each group with a question that extends thoughts on the article. For example: *How could an offender/victim meeting be detrimental instead of helpful? What kind of preparation should both sides undertake before the meeting? How can you measure the success of these programs?*
- After the exercise, ask groups to share their thoughts with the class.

Assist Students Having Difficulty If students have trouble expressing what they learned in the article, have them write one-sentence summaries for each paragraph.

- Choose a paragraph and have a student read it aloud.
- Work with students to summarize the paragraph in one sentence.
- Have students write their own sentences for the remaining paragraphs.
- Review the sentences aloud and point out that they make a kind of outline for the article.

WRITING JOURNAL

Extend

Write About It Students will write a paragraph about whether or not victims and offenders should meet.

- Read and discuss the Writing Prompt (Journal, p. 56). Review the Writing Rubric. Encourage students to add more points to the rubric to guide their work.
- Model how to use the organizer.
- Students should use the Check It and Fix It section and the Writing Checklist to revise and evaluate their work.

As you draft, model by thinking aloud:

> **THINK ALOUD** *As I write, I want to remember that some people may disagree with my opinion. Threfore, I want to carefully organize my paragraph to convince readers that my opinion is right. I must first clearly state my opinion. Then I need to search through the article for information that supports my opinion. Plenty of support for my opinion will help make my argument convincing.*

Vocabulary Workshop Students extend their thinking about Word Bank words.

- Students work in pairs or small groups on the Define It organizer (Journal, p. 58).
- Have students add words to the Your Choice box and their personal word bank.
- Use the Show You Know exercise to assess students' understanding.

Teaching Tip Start a chart of prefixes and suffixes that can be added to base words to create word families. Post the chart in the front of the room and add to it as students learn more vocabulary.

Preparing for the Flu

PROGRAM RESOURCES

ANTHOLOGY pp. 64–67

TEACHING GUIDE AND RESOURCES
- Problem and Solution Map **p. 149**
- Answer Key **p. 118**

REAL WORLD WRITING JOURNAL pp. 60–63

ANTHOLOGY

Preteach

Activate Prior Knowledge Ask students to share their responses to the Real-Life Connection. Students will revisit their answers after they read.

Build Background *The flu makes some people only mildly sick and others severely ill. The flu can even cause death. The U.S. Centers for Disease Control and Prevention (CDC) reports that an average of 5 percent to 20 percent of the population gets the flu each year; 200,000 people are hospitalized, and 36,000 die. The CDC recommends that people get a flu vaccination each year, particularly older people, young children, and those with health conditions that put them at high risk for flu complications.*

Introduce Vocabulary

- Read aloud the words, definitions, and example sentences.
- Ask students to give examples of synonyms and antonyms for each word.

Model how to think about the first word:

| THINK ALOUD | *I see that* debate *means "a discussion of arguments in favor of and against a certain action or viewpoint." Therefore, a debate involves discussion. I could also say that it is a dispute or an argument. What words or phrases are the opposite of what* debate *means? A debate is not an agreement. It is not harmony or accord between people.* |

- *Build Academic Vocabulary* The academic vocabulary words for this lesson are *debate, emphasis,* and *radical.* Ask students to rate how often they use each word: often, sometimes, or never. Then ask students to write a sentence for each word.

Teach

Focus on the Big Question Ask the Article BQ, *Have we made enough progress in fighting the flu?* Students will answer this question after reading.

- *Connect to the Unit Big Question* Write the Unit and Article BQs on the board. With students, circle similar words and ideas to show how the BQs are linked.

Preread the Article Have students review text features of the article and brainstorm what the features reveal about content. Ask students to make a prediction about the article.

Conduct a Guided Reading Read the article to students as they follow along. Pause after each section to monitor students' comprehension.

- Help students identify the main idea in each section and then summarize the section.

Reflect on the Article After reading the article, review ideas introduced before or during reading.

- Have students review their responses to the Real-Life Connection.
- Discuss with students how the text features led to their predictions. Have them explain how the article differed from their predictions.

Practice and Apply

Discuss the Questions Gauge students' comprehension and help them develop critical reading skills (Answer Key, p. 118).

Connect to the Big Question Have students use a Problem and Solution Map to answer the BQ.

- Begin by writing "The U.S. is not prepared for the bird flu" in the Problem section.
- Ask students to review the article to find possible solutions.
- In the End Result section, students should write what steps they think should be taken.

Assess

Have students create a learning log for you to assess informally. Students should answer these questions:

- *What did you do in class today? What did you learn?*
- *What did you find interesting?*
- *What questions do you still have?*

Reach All Learners

Build Fluency Choose sections from the article and have students do oral repeated readings.

- Have students take turns reading small sections aloud.
- Provide feedback about aspects of fluency, including rate, expression, and identification of clues that help guide reading.
- Have students reread after coaching.

Use Small Groups Engage students with a debate.

- On the board, write some of the important controversial points in the article, such as mass producing vaccines, deciding who should get the vaccine first, and using the National Guard to quarantine affected areas.
- Divide students into groups of five or six and assign each a debate topic. Have the group divide into two subgroups for each controversial point: pro and con.
- Each subgroup should write a short speech supporting its side of the argument. Have the subgroups debate the issues for the class.

Assist Students Having Difficulty If students have trouble with comprehension, have them use their own words to retell what they read.

- Ask students to read short sections of the article.
- Have students retell content using their own words.
- Work with students to fill in any blanks in their retellings.

WRITING JOURNAL

Extend

Write About It Students will write suggestions for a town emergency plan for an outbreak of the bird flu.

- Read and discuss the Writing Prompt (Journal, p. 60). Review the Writing Rubric. Encourage students to add more points to the rubric to guide their work.
- Model how to use the organizer.
- Students should use the Check It and Fix It section and the Writing Checklist to revise and evaluate their work.

Use a Think Aloud to model how to draft:

> **THINK ALOUD** *As I write, I must make sure that each of my suggestions is practical and realistic. If there is any information that I can include to improve my suggestions, I should include those as well.*

Vocabulary Workshop Students extend their thinking about Word Bank words.

- Students work in pairs or small groups on the Define It organizer (Journal, p. 62).
- Have students add words to the Your Choice box and their personal word bank.
- Use the Show You Know exercise to assess students' understanding.

Teaching Tip To reinforce students' understanding of context clues, have them write sentences with three key words they choose from the article. Students should not use Word Bank words. Direct students to underline the words and include plenty of context in their sentences to make the word meaning clear. Have students exchange sentences with a partner and follow the same instructions from the Context Clues exercise.

UNIT 2

The Development Debate

ANTHOLOGY pp. 68–71

TEACHING GUIDE AND RESOURCES
- Web Map **p. 156**
- Making Personal Connections Organizer **p. 147**
- Answer Key **p. 118**

REAL WORLD WRITING JOURNAL pp. 64–67

ANTHOLOGY

Preteach

Activate Prior Knowledge Brainstorm possible answers to the Real-Life Connection with students. Students will revisit answers after they read.

Build Background *Many U.S. cities are expanding at a rapid pace and, in many cases, much faster than their population is growing. One study reports that the average American spends more than 100 hours commuting to work each year. That's even more than the two weeks' vacation time the average worker gets. As cities expand, parks and farmland disappear, while pollution and congestion increase.*

Introduce Vocabulary

- Read aloud the words, definitions, and example sentences.
- Write the following sentence frames on the board, and ask students to fill in the blanks about each word: "This word reminds me of _____. It would also be useful for talking about _____." Ask volunteers to share their ideas.
- *Build Academic Vocabulary* The academic vocabulary words for this lesson are *motive, resolve,* and *unify.* Have students write two sentences for each word, showing how the word would be useful in two different classes.

Teach

Focus on the Big Question Ask the Article BQ, *How much land development is too much?* Students will answer this question after reading.

- *Connect to the Unit Big Question* Have students write both the Unit and Article BQs on a piece of paper. Give them a few minutes to brainstorm on their own about how the two are connected. Then have students share their ideas in pairs.

Preread the Article Before students read, ask them to review the title and the first few sentences of each section. Have students write key phrases from each topic sentence on a piece of paper and then tell what they think the main idea of the article is.

Conduct a Guided Reading Read the article to students as they follow along. Pause after each section to monitor students' comprehension.

- Ask students what they can infer about the effects of development from reading each section.
- Model how to infer with a Think Aloud:

> **THINK ALOUD** *In the section titled "Suburban Sprawl," the author discusses the massive amount of farmland that has been lost to development. From this information, I can infer that the United States may face a problem in producing enough food for its growing population if development continues.*

Reflect on the Article After reading the article, review ideas introduced before or during reading.

- Ask students whether they would change their answers to the Real-Life Connection now.
- Discuss whether students' predictions came true.

Practice and Apply

Discuss the Questions Gauge students' comprehension and help them develop critical reading skills (Answer Key, p. 118).

Connect to the Big Question Have students write about the negative effects of development.

- Use the following prompt: "Development has gone too far when…"
- Students should refer to the article to find examples to finish the prompt.

Assess

Have students create a Web Map for you to assess informally.

- Have students write *Benefits of Restricting Development* in the center of their organizer.
- Ask students to write a benefit in each of the outer circles. Some answers may be inferred from the text.

Reach All Learners

Build Fluency Choose sections from the article for an echo reading.

- Read the section aloud to students, modeling reading with accuracy.
- Have volunteers read the same section aloud, focusing on accuracy.
- Tell students to repeat the process with a partner. The first student reads a section aloud, focusing on accuracy, and the partner echo reads.

Use Small Groups Engage students in a word game.

- Write key words from the article on slips of paper and put them in a box.
- Divide students into groups of four or five and explain that the object of the game is to get teammates to guess the meaning of a word. Teams should designate one person to give hints and three or four people to guess.
- The student giving hints has a limited amount of time to draw words, give hints, and get the team to guess the words. The team with the most correct guesses wins.

Assist Students Having Difficulty To help students connect with the topic, have them complete a Making Personal Connections Organizer.

- As they read, students should list on their organizer events and details from the article that bring to mind a personal connection.
- Students should then explain the connection in the bottom left box.
- In the bottom right box, students should think about other connections they can make with the article.

WRITING JOURNAL

Extend

Write About It Students will write speeches about development to deliver at a city council hearing.

- Read and discuss the Writing Prompt (Journal, p. 64). Review the Writing Rubric. Encourage students to add more points to the rubric to guide their work.
- Model how to use the organizer.
- Students should use the Check It and Fix It section and the Writing Checklist to revise and evaluate their work.

Teaching Tip Remind students that they are preparing a speech. Take a few minutes to discuss what makes a speech good or bad. Emphasize the importance of word choice, and provide examples of lively verbs and describing words that will add excitement to their ideas. Allow time for students to pair up and provide feedback about word choice in their speeches.

Vocabulary Workshop Students extend their thinking about Word Bank words.

- Students can work in pairs or small groups on the Define It organizer (Journal, p. 66).
- Have students add words to the Your Choice box and their personal word bank.
- Use the Show You Know exercise to assess students' understanding.

Model how to do the All in the Family exercise with this Think Aloud:

> **THINK ALOUD** *Another form of the word* unit *is* unity. Unity *is a noun that means "the state of being together as one." An example sentence for* unity *would be "Our baseball team felt a sense of unity after working so much throughout the year."*

 # Can progress be made without conflict?

Introduce the Unit Project

Poster Students will create a poster to answer the Big Question: *Can progress be made without conflict?*

- Read through the steps of the assignment with students.
- Point out the rubric so that students will know their goals for the assignment. Add other rubric points with students to guide their work.
- Provide time for students to create their posters. Provide materials that all students can use. Allow time for students to practice and present their work.

Model Model how to organize thoughts:

> **THINK ALOUD** *I have chosen my articles and have written notes about what I want on my poster. I need to figure out which examples should be written and which examples should be pictures or illustrations. I want to use the example of the healing power of meetings between victims and offenders. I do not know how to illustrate that, so I will write that phrase on my poster. I underline the phrases I want to write but circle the things I want to try to find pictures of, such as a picture of a sit-in to illustrate the conflict that helped the Civil Rights Movement bring social progress.*

Teaching Tip Encourage students to think of conflicts beyond what they read. They can make connections to other classes where they are learning about conflict and progress.

Conclude the Unit

Review Unit Objectives Return to the unit objectives and ask students to evaluate how well they mastered each one on a scale of 1 to 5, with 1 being low and 5 being high. Discuss how lower scores could be improved.

Reflect on the Learning Examine the Three-Column Chart with students. Ask them to reflect on what they have learned. They can write or discuss with the class or in small groups. Prompt students' thinking with questions such as the following:

- *What was the most interesting article you read? What did you like about it?*
- *How did your ideas about conflict and progress change as you read through the articles?*
- *Which topic would you like to know more about? What do you still wonder about it?*
- *How did the writing assignments and the interview help you form your ideas about progress?*
- *What other subjects do you think might help to answer the Big Questions? Where might you find that information?*

Word Bank Quiz

WORD LIST A			
change	discuss	oppose	resolve
debate	former	radical	reveal
defend	inclined	reconciliation	unify

Ten of the unit Word Bank words are defined in parentheses in the article below. As you read the article, use Word List A, above, to figure out which word best fits each definition. Write the word on the line provided. (You will not use every word on the list.) Then go on to the next page of the quiz.

Doctors Without Borders

In 1971, a group of people decided a **(1. something different)**

_____ was needed to help people in countries at war or struck by disaster. The group decided to bring emergency medical care to other countries, no matter how **(2. extreme)** _____ or dangerous the countries' situations were. The group also hoped to **(3. show something that has been hidden)**

_____ the countries' plights to the rest of the world. This was the beginning of Doctors Without Borders. Since 1971, it has managed to help **(4. bring together)** _____ people across the globe. Its main purpose is to

(5. end an argument by settling it) _____ the problem of how to get medical care to people who lack it. The group goes to places other aid organizations are not **(6. likely)** _____ to go. Doctors Without Borders does not **(7. discuss arguments in favor of and against)** _____ which side is right when bringing aid. The group wants only to **(8. argue in support of)**

_____ and help people. One of the only things the doctors

(9. are against) _____ is the spread of disease. They bring people together to **(10. talk about)** _____ ways to fight its spread.

UNIT 2 Word Bank Quiz

WORD LIST B			
adversity	conclude	motive	produce
compromise	confrontation	negotiate	progress
concession	inestimable	oppose	struggle

Ten more Word Bank words are defined in parentheses in the rest of the article, below. As you read the article, use Word List B, above, to figure out which word best fits each definition. Write the word on the line provided. (You will not use every word on the list.)

Doctors Without Borders serves people facing many different kinds of **(11. troubles caused by bad luck)** _____. People who are in the middle of **(12. meeting of people who are in an argument)** _____ or natural disaster benefit from the group's services. In addition, the group helps people who **(13. keep on trying though it is hard)** _____ against the spread of contagious diseases, such as cholera and measles. Doctors Without Borders does not **(14. settle an argument between sides by both giving up something)** _____ in its efforts to provide good medical care.

Many of the medical tools that Doctors Without Borders use come from **(15. something that has gotten better)** _____ in the field of technology. The doctors **(16. make)** _____ medical kits to take on their missions. Because Doctors Without Borders has to work to **(17. try to reach an agreement)** _____ with different governments in order to do its work, many of its representatives are good at conflict management.

It is easy to **(18. make a judgment based on information)** _____ that Doctors Without Borders has a positive effect on the communities it reaches out to. In truth, its impact is **(19. too great to be measured)** _____. Perhaps that is because its main **(20. reason for doing something)** _____ for going into other countries is to help people.

What kind of knowledge changes our lives?

Unit Overview

The articles in this unit explore the topics of knowledge and information. As students read about different subjects, they will increase their knowledge of those subjects. Then they will decide for themselves whether that knowledge can change someone's life.

Launch the Unit

Connect to the Big Question Prompt students' thinking about the unit opener. Read the introduction with students and examine the illustration. Ask questions such as these:

- *Why does knowledge sometimes lead to increased responsibility?*
- *Describe what is happening in the two frames of the illustration.*
- *What knowledge has the new driver gained?*
- *What kind of knowledge is depicted in this situation? Is it knowledge from books or from personal experience? What are some other kinds of knowledge?*
- *What connections do you have to this situation?*

Use the prompt on the page as the basis for journal writing or for small group or whole class discussion. Students can share their ideas with partners or in small groups.

Anchor Students' Thinking Post a Big Question chart on a classroom bulletin board. Write the Big Question on a piece of flip-chart paper or poster board. Throughout the unit, have students suggest ways that the knowledge they have gained can or has changed their lives. Use these ideas:

- After reading each article, identify the kind of knowledge it explores. Then discuss how the knowledge might change someone's life.
- Post exemplary writing from students' writing journal assignments. Discuss what they reveal about ways that knowledge changes people.
- Encourage students to add to their knowledge of article topics. Sources might include Web sites; encyclopedia, newspaper, or magazine articles; or interviews. Link new knowledge to the Unit Big Question.

Unit Objectives

Share these objectives with students. As you read the articles in this unit, you will:

- Become aware of new information and ways it may affect us.
- Determine an answer to the Big Question: *What kind of knowledge changes our lives?* Explain your answers using details from the articles and from your own experiences.
- Use content and academic vocabulary to talk and write about different kinds of knowledge.
- Form an opinion for a TV commercial and support that opinion with facts.

Sixth Sense Survival

PROGRAM RESOURCES

ANTHOLOGY pp. 76–79

TEACHING GUIDE AND RESOURCES
- Two-Column Journal p. 153
- Answer Key p. 120

REAL WORLD WRITING JOURNAL pp. 70–73

ANTHOLOGY

Preteach

Activate Prior Knowledge Discuss the Real-Life Connection scenario. Have students fill in the chart. Students will revisit answers after they read.

Build Background *The five senses are sight, hearing, taste, touch, and smell. Some people say there are also the sense of balance, the sense of one's body in space, the sense of heat, and the sense of pain.*

Introduce Vocabulary

- Read aloud the definitions and sentences in the Word Bank. Discuss what each word means in context.
- Place students in pairs. Have each pair find a boldface word in the selection and take turns reading the sentence aloud to each other.
- *Build Academic Vocabulary* All the Word Bank words are academic vocabulary. Have students give an example of how they would use each word in a class.

Teach

Focus on the Big Question Ask the Article BQ, *What do we know about the sixth sense?* Students will answer this question after reading.

- *Connect to the Unit Big Question* Ask students whether they believe in a sixth sense.

Preread the Article Before students read, model how to preview and predict:

> **THINK ALOUD** *I see the title is "The Sixth Sense." I remember a movie with that title, but I do not think that is what this article will be about. Reading the subheads reminds me what the sixth sense is.*

Ask students what they think the title and each subhead mean. Then direct students to write a prediction about the article.

Conduct a Guided Reading Read the article to students as they follow along. Pause after each section to monitor students' comprehension.

- After each section, ask a volunteer to state the section's main idea.
- Ask another a volunteer to provide a supporting detail.

Reflect on the Article After reading the article, review ideas introduced before or during reading.

- Revisit the Real-Life Connection. Have answers changed? Why or why not?
- Ask students whether their predictions were accurate. Why or why not?

Practice and Apply

Discuss the Questions Gauge students' comprehension and help them develop critical reading skills (Answer Key, p. 120).

Connect to the Big Question Have students use the Two-Column Journal to answer the BQ.

- Have students write the Article BQ on their organizers.
- Ask students to fill in the organizer.
- Call for students to use the "My Thoughts" column to answer the Article BQ.

Assess

Have students identify situations in which their sixth sense might come in handy. Together, brainstorm when it would be helpful to have a sixth sense. Follow up by asking students to write a few sentences describing a "sixth-sense situation" and ways that the sixth sense might help them.

Reach All Learners

Build Fluency Choose a section from the article for a choral reading.

- Read the selection aloud slowly and clearly. Use as much expression as possible.
- Have students follow along silently.
- Reread the selection aloud while students echo your reading, copying your expression.

Use Small Groups Use a "numbered heads together" activity to increase peer teaching. Have each group work to answer the Use Clues questions.

- Organize students into groups of three. Count off one through three.
- After a brief time for discussion, ask all the "number threes" to stand if they know the answer to the third question. If any of them do not know, go back to discussion time.
- Continue the activity until all members of all groups have had the opportunity to answer either the first, second, or third question.

Assist Students Having Difficulty Students may have difficulty understanding Rensink's experiment. Explain that the gray field was shown so quickly that people did not even realize they had seen it. However, because they knew that Rensink would periodically show a gray field before showing a change in a picture, people expected to see the gray field and changes. Their expectations may have led them to push the button a few seconds before the gray field actually appeared. It is not clear whether some people simply guessed correctly or truly had intuition that the changed picture would appear.

WRITING JOURNAL

Extend

Write About It Students will use a graphic organizer to plan and write a handout for a science fair presentation.

- Read and discuss the Writing Prompt (Journal, p. 70). Review the Writing Rubric. Encourage students to add more points to the rubric to guide their work.
- Model how to use the organizer.
- Students should use the Check It and Fix It section and the Writing Checklist to revise and evaluate their work.

Use a Think Aloud to model how to organize ideas:

> **THINK ALOUD** *After I look through the article for scientific proof to back up my opinion, I am going to number each fact. I will label the strongest or most interesting fact "1." I will save the number 1 fact for last. That way, I will end with my most convincing idea rather than my least convincing idea. That is an advantage, because people tend to remember first and last ideas in a paper or a speech.*

Vocabulary Workshop Students extend their thinking about Word Bank words.

- Students work in pairs or small groups on the Define It organizer (Journal, p. 72).
- Have students add words to the Your Choice box and their personal word bank.
- Use the Show You Know exercise to assess students' understanding.

Teaching Tip Ask students to suggest verbs to which you can add *-tion* to form nouns. Write students' suggestions on the board. Ask for volunteers to use each noun in a sentence.

UNIT 3

Looking over Your Shoulder

PROGRAM RESOURCES

ANTHOLOGY pp. 80–83

TEACHING GUIDE AND RESOURCES
- Opinion and Reasons Organizer **p. 148**
- Answer Key **p. 120**

REAL WORLD WRITING JOURNAL pp. 74–77

ANTHOLOGY

Preteach

Activate Prior Knowledge Take a poll of students' answers to the Real-Life Connection questions. Students will revisit answers after they read.

Build Background *The Global Positioning System includes twenty-four satellites that orbit the earth every twelve hours. The Department of Defense started working on the system in the early 1970s. It was not fully operational until the 1990s.*

Introduce Vocabulary

- Ask volunteers to read aloud the definitions. Discuss what each word means in context.
- *Build Academic Vocabulary* Ask these questions: *When you* revise *an English paper, what are you doing? If your class schedule was* modified *to give you time for another class, what happened? If a dance teacher says someone has good* technique *but not enough passion, what does she mean?*

Teach

Focus on the Big Question Ask the Article BQ, *When does gathering information threaten the right to privacy?* Students will answer this question after reading.

- *Connect to the Unit Big Question* Confirm that students understand what GPS is and what *privacy* means.

Preread the Article Before students read, model how to make predictions after previewing:

| THINK ALOUD | *I made predictions before I read by using the* |

subheads. Two are "Location Information" and "GPS Saves Lives." I predict that the article will explain how satellites beam information to Earth.

Conduct a Guided Reading Read the article to students as they follow along. Pause after each section to monitor students' comprehension. Stop and confirm that students know the more difficult words used in the article, including *surveillance, device, satellite, track,* and *monitor.* After each section, ask a volunteer to recite a detail he or she remembers from the section.

Reflect on the Article After reading the article, review ideas introduced before or during reading.

- Revisit the poll from the Real-Life Connection. Have answers changed? Why or why not?
- Ask students whether their predictions were accurate. Why or why not?

Practice and Apply

Discuss the Questions Gauge students' comprehension and help them develop critical reading skills (Answer Key, p. 120).

Connect to the Big Question Have students use the Opinion and Reasons Organizer to answer the BQ.

- Have students write the Article BQ on their organizers and decide whether GPS threatens privacy.
- Ask students to fill in their organizers using facts from the article.
- Call for volunteers to answer the BQ using information from the article and their own thoughts.

Assess

Informally assess students' understanding of the article by asking them to complete a learning log. Students should answer these questions:

- *What was today's article about?*
- *What in the article did you already know?*
- *Did you learn anything new?*
- *What else do you wonder about the topic?*

Reach All Learners

Build Fluency Choose a section from the article for a choral reading.

- Read the section aloud as students read the section silently.
- Reread the section aloud and have students choral read it with you.
- Then have students choral read the section without you. Stop and correct any pronunciation or fluency errors.

Use Small Groups Have students do a write-around to answer the second Use Clues question.

- Organize the class into groups of three or four.
- Have a member of each group write the second question on the top of a piece of paper. Afterward, the student should write a response for one minute and then pass the paper to the right. The one-minute writing begins again, as the next student responds to the first student's ideas.
- Continue until all students have written on their group's paper. Discuss responses.

Assist Students Having Difficulty If students have trouble understanding how GPS works, show them a drawing, diagram, or 3-D model. Make sure it includes satellites sending signals to the Earth. Also show a variety of photographs of GPS receivers and GPS satellites. Images of these are readily available on the Internet.

WRITING JOURNAL

Extend

Write About It Students will use an Opinion and Reasons Organizer to plan and write a paragraph or two stating their opinion.

- Read and discuss the Writing Prompt (Journal, p. 74). Review the Writing Rubric. Encourage students to add more points to the rubric to guide their work.
- Model how to use the organizer.
- Students should use the Check It and Fix It section and the Writing Checklist to revise and evaluate their work.

Teaching Tip If students are having trouble organizing their thoughts, point out the sentence frames they will be using in the drafting portion of their assignment. Tell students that an opinion is "I think," the reason is "because," and the examples from the article are "for example."

Vocabulary Workshop Students extend their thinking about Word Bank words.

- Students work in pairs or small groups on the Define It organizer (Journal, p. 76).
- Have students add words to the Your Choice box and their personal word bank.
- Use the Show You Know exercise to assess students' understanding.

Model how to fill out the Your Choice box:

> **THINK ALOUD** *There were quite a few words in this article that I would like to put in a personal word bank. Disadvantage is one of them. I hear that word all the time. People say that someone is disadvantaged, which often means that someone does not have much money or education, but people also say that someone is at a disadvantage, which often means the person does not have adequate information.*

UNIT 3

Dressing by the Book

PROGRAM RESOURCES

ANTHOLOGY pp. 84–87

TEACHING GUIDE AND RESOURCES
- Main Idea Map p. 146
- Answer Key p. 120

REAL WORLD WRITING JOURNAL pp. 78–81

ANTHOLOGY

Preteach

Activate Prior Knowledge Are students for or against dress codes? Take a poll. Make sure students fill out the Real-Life Connection word web. Students will revisit answers after they read.

Build Background *No state has passed a law that makes all students wear school uniforms, but more than half the states and the District of Columbia have laws that allow dress codes.*

Introduce Vocabulary

- Have students tell you which words are nouns and which are verbs. Then ask students to complete the following sentences:
  - "If you *influence* a *process,* you…";
  - "If you *question* a *statement,* you…";
  - "If you *reflect* on a *statement,* you…"
- *Build Academic Vocabulary* Tell students that the academic vocabulary word *process* is often used in science. Have students create sentences to link the other word academic vocabulary word—*statement*—to different subject areas.

Teach

Focus on the Big Question Ask the Article BQ, *Do schools need dress codes, or should kids dress any way they want?* Students will answer this question after reading.

- *Connect to the Unit Big Question* Ask students whether anything would make them change their answers to the poll. Model how to use new information to alter an opinion:

THINK ALOUD *I believe that dress codes are good because dressing like professionals helps students take their studies seriously. However, I might change my opinion if I learn that dress codes do not have this effect.*

Preread the Article Before students read, discuss the importance of setting a purpose for reading. Discuss different purposes, such as the following: to answer a question, to learn how to do something, to evaluate information. Remind students that a main purpose for reading the article is to answer the BQ. Then ask students to identify another purpose they would like to fulfill by reading.

Conduct a Guided Reading Read the article to students as they follow along. Pause after each section to monitor students' comprehension. Have students use the Main Idea Map to make notes on what they are reading. Pause after each section and help students fill in their organizer.

Reflect on the Article After reading the article, review ideas introduced before or during reading.

- Retake the poll from the Real-Life Connection. Have answers changed? Why or why not?
- Have students describe whether they fulfilled their purposes for reading.

Practice and Apply

Discuss the Questions Gauge students' comprehension and help them develop critical reading skills (Answer Key, p. 120).

Connect to the Big Question Discuss the Article BQ, using the results of the two polls (taken before and after reading). Have volunteers use what they know to answer the BQ.

Assess

Have each student write a school dress code.

- To help students get started, have a class discussion about their school dress code or another dress code they know about.
- Tell students their dress codes must include at least four rules.
- Each rule must include a reason why it is part of the code.

Reach All Learners

Build Fluency Choose a section from the article. Read it aloud as students follow along silently.

- Point out to students when and why you paused for commas and periods. Point out how to read smoothly through line breaks. Discuss the difference between lines and sentences.
- Reread the section sentence by sentence as students read aloud with you. Have students echo your pauses for commas and periods. Make sure students do not pause at line breaks.

Use Small Groups Use small groups to help students complete the first two Find It on the Page questions.

- Place students in small groups. Have students use sticky notes to mark sentences in the article that answer their questions.

Assist Students Having Difficulty If students struggle to come up with a purpose for reading, help them consider various purposes they might have. Ask students how reading the article might help them answer the post-reading questions, write their journal assignments, and learn Word Bank words. Help students use their responses to formulate purposes.

WRITING JOURNAL

Extend

Write About It Students will use a graphic organizer to record benefits and drawbacks of school dress codes. The organizer will, in turn, help students plan and write an article for the school newspaper.

- Read and discuss the Writing Prompt (Journal, p. 78). Review the Writing Rubric. Encourage students to add more points to the rubric to guide their work.
- Model how to use the organizer.
- Students should use the Check It and Fix It section and the Writing Checklist to revise and evaluate their work.

Use a Think Aloud to model how to complete the organizer:

> **THINK ALOUD** *I am going to organize my thoughts before I start writing. I will reread the article and my notes from class. In the Benefits column, I will put all the positive things I see about dress codes. In the Drawbacks column, I will put all the negative things. When I start writing, I will use ideas from the organizer.*

Vocabulary Workshop Students extend their thinking about Word Bank words.

- Students work in pairs or small groups on the Define It organizer (Journal, p. 80).
- Have students add words to the Your Choice box and their personal word bank.
- Use the Show You Know exercise to assess students' understanding.

Teaching Tip To help students understand that the same word can have different meanings, ask students to look up the noun *view* in their dictionaries. Discuss the different meanings, such as "opinion" and "scenery visible from a window or other place." Have students illustrate these different meanings of *view* in sentences.

Textbook Technology

PROGRAM RESOURCES

ANTHOLOGY pp. 88–91

TEACHING GUIDE AND RESOURCES
- T-Chart **p. 151**
- Answer Key **p. 121**

REAL WORLD WRITING JOURNAL pp. 82–85

ANTHOLOGY

Preteach

Activate Prior Knowledge Have students make predictions by filling in the Real-Life Connection chart. Students will revisit predictions after they read.

Build Background *There are many sites where students can find the texts of classic works online. One of the best is the Internet Public Library, or IPL.*

Introduce Vocabulary

- Write the definitions of the Word Bank words on the board. Pronounce the words aloud.
- Have students tell you which definition on the board matches the word you just said.
- *Build Academic Vocabulary* Ask students which school subject might include a play that has been *adapted* from a story; which subject might explain how animals *adapt* to seasonal changes; and what the *subject* of this lesson's article is.

Teach

Focus on the Big Question Ask the Article BQ, *Would electronic textbooks foster learning more than printed textbooks do?* Students will answer this question after reading.

- *Connect to the Unit Big Question* Ask students what they already know about e-texts.

Preread the Article Before students read, remind them that asking questions is an important part of reading. Model by thinking aloud:

| **THINK ALOUD** | *I know a little bit about e-texts, but I want to* |

know if there are e-texts that are more than just words on a screen. I will read to find out.

Have students write down one question they have about e-textbooks.

Conduct a Guided Reading Read the article to students as they follow along. Pause after each section to monitor students' comprehension. Tell students that understanding how a text is organized can help them understand what they are reading.

- Point out the "Pro/Con" text structure of the article. Distribute the T-Chart. Have students label the first column *Pros* and the second column *Cons*.
- Direct students to take notes as they read. They should write advantages of e-textbooks in the first column and disadvantages in the second column.

Reflect on the Article After reading the article, review ideas introduced before or during reading.

- Revisit the Real-Life Connection chart. Were predictions correct?
- Have students write answers to the questions they posed before reading.

Practice and Apply

Discuss the Questions Gauge students' comprehension and help them develop critical reading skills (Answer Key, p. 121).

Connect to the Big Question Discuss students' answers to the Article BQ.

- Revisit the T-Chart. Use the information to answer the BQ.
- Call for volunteers to answer the BQ. Ask students to support their opinions with reasons based on the article.

Assess

Remind students of the example at the beginning of the article—a multimedia presentation of the Normandy invasion. Have students write another example of how an electronic textbook might facilitate learning. Then have students review the article to find and write down either a drawback of e-texts or an advantage of printed textbooks.

Reach All Learners

Build Fluency Choose a section from the article for a group reading.

- Direct one student to read the first sentence aloud. Help the student use the correct emphasis and tone to signal the end of the sentence.
- Have the next student read the next sentence. Repeat the process with the entire group.
- Repeat the activity, but during the second reading tell students to read the section more quickly and move more smoothly from one sentence to the next.

Use Small Groups Place students in two to four groups to debate whether e-texts should be used in the classroom.

- Assign each group either a pro or con position to present and defend.
- Tell each group to list reasons that support its position.
- During the debate, make sure that each member of each group participates.

Assist Students Having Difficulty If students struggle to take notes, point out that notes do not have to be complete sentences.

- Work with students to review and add to the list of abbreviations to be used when taking notes.
- Model how to take notes.

WRITING JOURNAL

Extend

Write About It Students will use a reason-and-example graphic organizer to plan and write a letter of advice to their principal.

- Read and discuss the Writing Prompt (Journal, p. 82). Review the Writing Rubric. Encourage students to add more points to the rubric to guide their work.
- Model how to use the organizer.
- Students should use the Check It and Fix It section and the Writing Checklist to revise and evaluate their work.

Teaching Tip The writing assignment provides a good opportunity for students to think about why they should consider their audience and practice how to do so. Help students plan their arguments by asking them to think not only of reasons *they* think are good, but also reasons the *principal* will think are good. Ask students to think about what is important to the principal.

Vocabulary Workshop Students extend their thinking about Word Bank words.

- Students work in pairs or small groups on the Define It organizer (Journal, p. 84).
- Have students add words to the Your Choice box and their personal word bank.
- Use the Show You Know exercise to assess students' understanding.

Use a Think Aloud to help students complete the Define It organizer:

> **THINK ALOUD** History *is connected to* enlighten *because when people know history they are enlightened about the past.* Subject *is connected to* understanding *because a complete knowledge of a subject will lead to an understanding of it.*

UNIT 3

The Witness Dilemma

PROGRAM RESOURCES

ANTHOLOGY pp. 92–95

TEACHING GUIDE AND RESOURCES
- Problem and Solution Map **p. 149**
- Answer Key **p. 121**

REAL WORLD WRITING JOURNAL pp. 86–89

ANTHOLOGY

Preteach

Activate Prior Knowledge Hold a class discussion about the subject of witnessing crimes. Have students fill in the Real-Life Connection chart. Students will revisit answers after they read.

Build Background *Crime Stoppers is an organization created in 1976. It gives people a place to call when they have information about a crime. The people who call Crime Stoppers can remain anonymous and do not have to appear in court as witnesses.*

Introduce Vocabulary

- Read the example sentences from the Word Bank.
- Ask a volunteer to tell you what each word means.
- *Build Academic Vocabulary* Point out the academic vocabulary in the Word Bank: *evolve, represent, revise.* Ask volunteers to tell you in which of the following sources they would be most likely to find each word: an English assignment, an algebra book, a biology test. Have students explain their answers.

Teach

Focus on the Big Question Ask the Article BQ, *Should witnesses to a crime be forced to appear in court?* Students will answer this question after reading.

- *Connect to the Unit Big Question* Take a yes/no poll on the Article BQ. What other information do students need to formulate an informed answer to the BQ?

Preread the Article Before students read the entire article, have them read the first sentence of each paragraph. Then have students write down a prediction about the article and one question they have about the topic.

Conduct a Guided Reading Read the article to students as they follow along. Pause after each section to monitor students' comprehension. Model how to monitor comprehension:

> **THINK ALOUD** *When I finished reading the first section of this article, I could not remember what I had just read. I was distracted by thoughts about the work I have to do after this class. I will take a minute to clear my head. Then I will reread the section.*

Reflect on the Article After reading the article, review ideas introduced before or during reading.

- Revisit the Real-Life Connection charts. Would students change their answers? If predictions were wrong, discuss why. Was anything misleading? Did students remember to preview all major text elements? Remind students that it is OK if their predictions were wrong. The process of predicting is still beneficial.
- Have students answer the questions they posed prior to reading.

Practice and Apply

Discuss the Questions Gauge students' comprehension and help them develop critical reading skills (Answer Key, p. 121).

Connect to the Big Question

- Retake the Article BQ poll.
- Have students complete the following sentence frame: *I _____ (did/did not) change my answer because _____.*

Assess

Ask students to answer these questions:

- *What is a witness?*
- *How would it feel to be a witness to a crime?*
- *What is one word in this article that you did not (or still do not) understand?*
- *What did you learn from the article that you did not know before?*
- *What else do you wonder about the topic?*

Reach All Learners

Build Fluency Choose a section from the article. Read it aloud as students follow along silently. Emphasize the flow of the phrases. Tell students that part of reading fluently is to read phrases with expression and to avoid reading word for word.

- Direct a student to read the first sentence. Help the student approach reading the text as a series of phrases rather than separate words.
- Have the next student read the next sentence. Repeat the process with the entire group.

Use Small Groups Place students in small groups. Give each group a copy of the Problem and Solution Map.

- Present all the groups with this problem: Witnesses are too afraid to go to the police.
- Have group members work together to figure out a possible solution to the problem.
- Ask each group to present its solution to the class.

Assist Students Having Difficulty If students struggle to understand longer sentences, teach them how to turn lengthy sentences into shorter, more understandable chunks.

- Point out a compound sentence in the selection. Read the sentence aloud as two sentences. Ask students if they can understand the two sentences. Then read the compound sentence again. Ask students if they understand the whole sentence.
- Have students find a different compound sentence and repeat the process.

WRITING JOURNAL

Extend

Write About It Students will use an Opinion and Reasons graphic organizer to plan and write a memo with a suggestion for a debate topic.

- Read and discuss the Writing Prompt (Journal, p. 86). Review the Writing Rubric. Encourage students to add more points to the rubric to guide their work.
- Model how to use the organizer.
- Students should use the Check It and Fix It section and the Writing Checklist to revise and evaluate their work.

Use a Think Aloud to model how to check writing:

> **THINK ALOUD** *After I have written something, I read it out loud to "hear" how it sounds. That way, I can tell if I have any incomplete or run-on sentences. I make sure I read very slowly and carefully so that I can also tell if I have left out any words.*

Vocabulary Workshop Students extend their thinking about Word Bank words.

- Students work in pairs or small groups on the Define It organizer (Journal, p. 88).
- Have students add words to the Your Choice box and their personal word bank.
- Use the Show You Know exercise to assess students' understanding.

Teaching Tip If students have difficulty figuring out synonyms and antonyms for the Define It exercise, remind them to look at the definitions for clues. For example, a synonym for *evolve* might be *change,* and an antonym might be *decrease.*

UNIT 3

Instant Friends

PROGRAM RESOURCES

ANTHOLOGY pp. 96–99

TEACHING GUIDE AND RESOURCES
- Three-Column Chart **p. 152**
- Two-Column Journal **p. 153**
- Answer Key **p. 121**

REAL WORLD WRITING JOURNAL pp. 90–93

ANTHOLOGY

Preteach

Activate Prior Knowledge Have students complete the chart in the Real-Life Connection. Students will revisit answers after they read.

Build Background *An early social networking site started in 1997. It was called SixDegrees.com. However, not enough people were online then and the site closed in 2000.*

Introduce Vocabulary

- Ask students which Word Bank words they have already studied (*enlighten, history, insight,* and *modified*) and what each means.
- Read aloud the meaning of the word *concise.* Call for volunteers to make connections between the Word Bank words they know and the new word.
- *Build Academic Vocabulary* Ask these questions: If you have *insight* into a story's theme, what class are you in? If your gym teacher *modified* the exercise routine, what happened? If your history teacher asked you to write a *concise* report, what did he or she mean?

Teach

Focus on the Big Question Ask the Article BQ, *Is the Internet keeping people from truly knowing one another?* Students will answer this question after reading.

- *Connect to the Unit Big Question* Ask how many students use social networking sites. Discuss the kinds of information available on these sites.

Preread the Article Distribute copies of the Three-Column Chart. Have students label the first column *Text Element,* the second column *Information,* and the third column *Meaning.* Have students complete their chart on their own or with partners.

Conduct a Guided Reading Read the article to students as they follow along. Pause after each section to monitor students' comprehension.

- Call on a volunteer to summarize the section.
- Have a volunteer ask a question based on information in the section. Write the question on the board. Model for students:

> **THINK ALOUD** *On the first page, the author says that electronic communication has created a modified idea of friendship. That makes me wonder how it has done that. I consider the people I meet online to be my friends. What is a modified friendship like?*

Reflect on the Article After reading the article, review ideas introduced before or during reading.

- Have students reexamine their charts from the Real-Life Connection. Did answers change?
- Revisit the Three-Column Charts. Were answers correct? What else would students add?

Practice and Apply

Discuss the Questions Gauge students' comprehension and help them develop critical reading skills (Answer Key, p. 121).

Connect to the Big Question Have students use the Two-Column Journal to answer the Article BQ.

- Have students find four statements related to the BQ and write them in the *Ideas from the Article* column.
- Have students write their own responses in the *My Thoughts* column.
- Have volunteers answer the BQ using their organizers.

Assess

Students should write a summary of the article for you to assess informally. Students can use these questions to pinpoint important ideas to include:

- *What is one good thing and one bad thing about social networking sites?*
- *Do you think online friendships are different from face-to-face friendships? Why or why not?*
- *Did this article change how you felt about meeting people online? Why or why not?*
- *What else do you wonder about social networking sites?*

Reach All Learners

Build Fluency Choose a section from the article and do a group reading to practice fluency.

- Put students into groups of three or four. Have one student in each group read aloud one sentence from the text. Then have the next student read the second sentence.
- Direct students to move as seamlessly as possible from one to another.
- If any student has difficulty with a word or sentence, have the group repeat the sentence aloud until everyone is comfortable saying it.

Use Small Groups Use the RCRC method to build students' comprehension.

- Place students in groups of three or four. Give each student in each group a short section of the article to read.
- Explain the process of RCRC to students:

    Read the text.

    Cover it up.

    Retell what you have just read.

    Check to see if you were correct.
- Have each group practice RCRC until all group members have had a chance to test their comprehension.

Assist Students Having Difficulty If students struggle to summarize, tell them to organize their summaries the same way the text is organized.

- Identify the pro/con text structure.
- Then use the text structure to take students through the summarizing process.

WRITING JOURNAL

Extend

Write About It Students will use a web graphic organizer to plan and write an article about the best way to communicate with friends.

- Read and discuss the Writing Prompt (Journal, p. 90). Review the Writing Rubric. Encourage students to add more points to the rubric to guide their work.
- Model how to use the organizer.
- Students should use the Check It and Fix It section and the Writing Checklist to revise and evaluate their work.

Teaching Tip If students have difficulty using transitions when they write, review the list of transitions in the Grammar Handbook section titled Paragraph Coherence and Transitions (Journal, p. 222). Ask students to choose transitions they might use. Write the words on the board so that students can see them as they write.

Vocabulary Workshop Students extend their thinking about Word Bank words.

- Students work in pairs or small groups on the organizer (Journal, p. 92).
- Have students add words to the Your Choice box and their personal word bank.
- Use Show You Know to assess students' understanding.

Use a Think Aloud to model how to write a dialogue:

> **THINK ALOUD** *I know that a dialogue is a talk between two people, but I am having a hard time thinking of something to write. If I start with a question, that might help. My first line will be "Do you know the history of Mexico?" Then I can use another Word Bank word in my answer.*

UNIT 3

The Newest Newcomers

PROGRAM RESOURCES

ANTHOLOGY pp. 100–103

TEACHING GUIDE AND RESOURCES
- Cause and Effect Map **p. 140**
- Answer Key **p. 122**

REAL WORLD WRITING JOURNAL pp. 94–97

ANTHOLOGY

Preteach

Activate Prior Knowledge Have students answer the Real-Life Connection true-false questions. Students will revisit their answers after they read.

Build Background *In the late nineteenth and early twentieth centuries, many immigrants came through Ellis Island in New York. There was a lot of prejudice against immigrants during that period.*

Introduce Vocabulary

- Divide the class into pairs. Have each pair work together to create a scenario that contains the words *ignorance, understanding,* and *empathy.* Call for volunteers to present their scenarios to the class.
- *Build Academic Vocabulary* Have students write sentences that relate the academic vocabulary words—*argument* and *adapt*—to one of their classes.

Teach

Focus on the Big Question Ask the Article BQ, *What does the United States offer immigrants today?* Students will answer this question after reading.

- *Connect to the Unit Big Question* Immigration may be a sensitive topic for your class. Have students respond to the BQ privately, in writing.

Preread the Article Before students read, have them write down one fact they know about immigration or the name of a source that has taught them about immigration, such as a movie, book, or article.

Model how to activate prior knowledge:

> **THINK ALOUD** *I think I know a lot about immigration. Throughout our history, immigrants have come to the United States to live. I can imagine pictures of immigrants that I have seen in textbooks and documentaries. I also know that my grandparents were immigrants.*

Conduct a Guided Reading Read the article to students as they follow along. Pause after each section to monitor students' comprehension.

- Have students create sticky notes with √, –, +, and ? marks.
- A checkmark denotes information that students already know. A minus sign denotes information that is different from what students thought. A question mark denotes information that students do not understand. A plus sign denotes new information.
- Students use sticky notes to respond as they read.

Reflect on the Article After reading the article, review ideas introduced before or during reading.

- As a class, review students' sticky notes. Answer any questions. Share similarities and differences in responses.
- Have students review the Real-Life Connection questions. Discuss whether answers changed.

Practice and Apply

Discuss the Questions Gauge students' comprehension and help them develop critical reading skills (Answer Key, p. 122).

Connect to the Big Question Discuss whether anything in the article changed how students think. Have volunteers use the information to answer the BQ.

Assess

Ask pairs of students to choose one of the five freedoms and write a dialogue between two foreigners who are considering immigrating to the United States to obtain that freedom. Informally assess students' understanding of the article by listening to students' dialogues.

Reach All Learners

Build Fluency Choose a section from the article for a paired reading.

- Pair students and have them read silently.
- Direct one student to read aloud while the other follows along making notes about the student's strengths and weaknesses as an oral reader.
- The listener provides feedback and suggestions. Students then reverse roles.

Use Small Groups Engage students with a peer learning exercise.

- Have students get into small groups and skim the article. Students should add question-mark sticky notes to anything they do not understand, including words.
- Have group members review their sticky notes and help each other answer their questions.

Assist Students Having Difficulty If students struggle to understand the ideas in the article, provide them with copies of the Cause and Effect map.

- Have students write *Immigration* in the effect section of the map.
- Help students review the article to find at least two causes of the effect. Then have students include one example from the article for each cause.

WRITING JOURNAL

Extend

Write About It Students will use a graphic organizer to plan and write a speech describing which freedoms immigrants consider the most important.

- Read and discuss the Writing Prompt (Journal, p. 94). Review the Writing Rubric. Encourage students to add more points to the rubric to guide their work.
- Model how to use the organizer.
- Students should use the Check It and Fix It section and the Writing Checklist to revise and evaluate their work.

Use a Think Aloud to model how to draft:

> **THINK ALOUD** *Since this is a speech, I want to make it interesting to listen to but easy to understand. I will use simple sentences. I also will be careful about my word choice. I want to use the most effective words so that I convince people about my argument. I will think about why I chose that freedom above all the others. Did one example move me more than any other? Did I connect that freedom to something in my own experience? Thinking about this will help me write an effective speech.*

Vocabulary Workshop Students extend their thinking about Word Bank words.

- Students work in pairs or small groups on the organizer (Journal, p. 96).
- Have students add words to the Your Choice box and their personal word bank.
- Use Show You Know to assess students' understanding.

Teaching Tip To help students understand the meaning of the prefix *in-*, challenge them to brainstorm a list of words that begin with the prefix. Examples might include *inactive, incapable,* and *inbred.* Ask students what the *in-* prefix on each word means.

UNIT 3

Hip-Hop: Keeping It Real

PROGRAM RESOURCES

ANTHOLOGY pp. 104–107

TEACHING GUIDE AND RESOURCES
- Main Idea Map **p. 146**
- Answer Key **p. 122**

REAL WORLD WRITING JOURNAL pp. 98–101

ANTHOLOGY

Preteach

Activate Prior Knowledge Have students fill in the Real-Life Connection web. Students will revisit their webs after they read.

Build Background *In 1988, MTV introduced the show "Yo! MTV Raps." This was ten years after the first rap hit. "Yo! MTV Raps" made rap more popular in rural and suburban areas.*

Introduce Vocabulary

- Read aloud the Word Bank words and their definitions. Have students give synonyms for the words. To help students remember the definition of *imitate*, have pairs of students do a mirror exercise in which one student imitates the other.
- *Build Academic Vocabulary* Have students use the academic vocabulary words for this lesson (*awareness, influence, reflect, imitate*) in two sentences. Use a Think Aloud to model how:

> **THINK ALOUD** *How could I use the words* influence *and* awareness *in one sentence? Well, the words make me think of history class. My sentence is "The* awareness *that there was free land in the West* influenced *many people to migrate."*

Teach

Focus on the Big Question Ask the Article BQ, *When is hip-hop the real deal?* Students will answer this question after reading.

- *Connect to the Unit Big Question* Discuss responses to the BQ. What else might students need to know to answer it?

Preread the Article Before students read, have them write a prediction about the article and explain which elements of the article prompted the prediction.

Conduct a Guided Reading Read the article to students as they follow along. Pause after each section to monitor students' comprehension.

- After each section, stop and ask students if they have any questions.
- If there are no questions, ask your own.
- Remind students to monitor their own comprehension when they read. Two ways to do so are to ask questions and reread in order to understand.

Reflect on the Article After reading the article, review ideas introduced before or during reading.

- Have students revisit what they wrote in the Real-Life Connection web. Which words would they add or delete? Why?
- Ask students whether their predictions were accurate. Why or why not?

Practice and Apply

Discuss the Questions Gauge students' comprehension and help them develop critical reading skills (Answer Key, p. 122).

Connect to the Big Question Have students write an answer to the Article BQ.

- *Is the answer different from the answer they wrote before reading?*
- *If not, then how did information in the article support the first answer?*
- *If so, then what new information in the article caused the change?*

Assess

Direct students to write a poem, list, or rap about whether hip-hop has become too commercial. They can work in groups and use the information from the article to support their opinion. Informally assess students' understanding by having each group perform and discussing the conclusion at which each group arrived.

Reach All Learners

Build Fluency Choose a section from the article and have students do a class reading to practice fluency.

- Have students read the selection in pairs and coach each other on fluency. Tell students that if disagreements arise, they should ask for your help.
- Then have each student read aloud one or two lines from the section to the entire class.

Use Small Groups Use a write-around activity to engage students.

- Organize students into groups of three or four. Have a member of each group write Use Clues question six across the top of a piece of paper.
- Have the same group members write responses for one minute and then pass their papers to the right. Have the next student respond or add to the first student's words.
- Continue until all group members have written on each paper. Discuss similarities and differences in responses.

Assist Students Having Difficulty If students struggle to write a poem, list, or rap for the assessment, have them write a summary of the article. Use a transparency to go over the Main Idea Map.

- Allow time after reading the article to fill out the organizer with the class.
- What was the most important idea in the article?
- What is the best detail to support that idea?

WRITING JOURNAL

Extend

Write About It Students will use a graphic organizer to plan and write a presentation that defines what they think hip-hop really is.

- Read and discuss the Writing Prompt (Journal, p. 98). Review the Writing Rubric. Encourage students to add more points to the rubric to guide their work.
- Model how to use the organizer.
- Students should use the Check It and Fix It section and the Writing Checklist to revise and evaluate their work.

Teaching Tip If students feel they are more knowledgeable about hip-hop than the article is, allow them to use their own information rather than facts from the article, but tell them they must explain how they got that information. For example, "Rap is not what keeps hip-hop real, dance is. I know this because my cousin was a hip-hop dancer back in the nineties. He told me."

Vocabulary Workshop Students extend their thinking about Word Bank words.

- Students work in pairs or small groups on the Define It organizer (Journal, p. 100).
- Have students add words to the Your Choice box and their personal word bank.
- Use the Show You Know exercise to assess students' understanding.

Use a Think Aloud to help students with the Define It exercise:

> **THINK ALOUD** *If I am not sure whether I really understand what a word means, I try to say what it means in my own words. For example, I think the word* imitate *means "acts like." Then I look at the definition and I see that it means "try to be like." That is pretty close, so I will circle 4.*

What kind of knowledge changes our lives?

Introduce the Unit Project

Commercial Students will create a commercial to present an answer to the Big Question: *What kind of knowledge changes our lives?*

- Read through the steps of the assignment with students.
- Point out the rubric so that students will know their goals for the assignment. Add other rubric points with students to guide their work.
- Allow time for students to practice and present their work. Encourage listeners to offer their feedback and advice on the presentation.

Model Use a Think Aloud to model how to strengthen an argument:

> **THINK ALOUD** *As I draft my commercial, I realize that I need to use persuasive language to convince people. Every time I want to write* very, *I use a more interesting word such as* extremely *or* amazingly. *I use shorter, simpler sentences to strengthen the impact of what I am saying. I make sure that I do not use language that shows uncertainty or lack of enthusiasm. I want to avoid words like* kind of, sort of, *or* almost.

Teaching Tip Students will be using a persuasive argument in a commercial. Let them know that it is important to lead the listener from one point to another. Transitions for showing the consequence of something include *therefore, for this reason,* and *otherwise.*

Conclude the Unit

Review Unit Objectives Return to the unit objectives and ask students to evaluate how well they mastered each one on a scale of 1 to 5, with 1 being low and 5 being high. Discuss how lower scores could be improved.

Reflect on the Learning Examine the unit chart with students. Ask them to reflect on what they have learned. They can write or discuss with the class or in small groups. Prompt students' thinking with questions such as:

- *What was the most interesting article you read? What did you like about it?*

- *How did your ideas about knowledge change as you read through the articles?*
- *Which topic would you like to know more about? What do you still wonder about it?*
- *How did the writing assignments and the commercial help you form your ideas about conflict?*
- *What other kinds of knowledge do you think could be included in this unit? What knowledge has changed your life the most?*

UNIT 3

Word Bank Quiz

WORD LIST A			
awareness	evolve	influence	reaction
empathy	growth	insight	reflect
enlighten	ignorance	question	represent

Ten of the unit Word Bank words are defined in parentheses in the article below. As you read the article, use Word List A, above, to figure out which word best fits each definition. Write the word on the line provided. (You will not use every word on the list.) Then go on to the next page of the quiz.

Homework Helpline

My story is one of (**1. undergoing development**) _____.

I volunteered for a grade school's homework helpline because I thought it would

look good on my record. I was in complete (**2. a situation of little or no knowledge**)

_____ about how volunteering might help me. I also had no

(**3. knowledge that something exists**) _____ that some children

have a hard time learning arithmetic. Therefore, at first, my (**4. feeling in response**)

_____ to working for the helpline was kind of negative. Soon,

however, I began to feel (**5. understanding and sharing other people's feelings**)

_____ for kids who needed help. I began to (**6. think calmly and

carefully**) _____ about how I could help. I began to (**7. challenge

the truth about**) _____ my plans to go into business one day

and started thinking about becoming a teacher. As you can see, tutoring had a big

(**8. effect**) _____ on me. I gained new (**9. clear understanding**)

_____ into who I am and what I want to do in the future. Now,

I try to (**10. give information to help**) _____ others about the

benefits of volunteering.

UNIT 3 Word Bank Quiz

WORD LIST B			
adapt	distinguish	modified	subject
argument	history	process	technique
concise	imitate	revise	understanding

Ten more Word Bank words are defined in parentheses in the article below. As you read the article, use Word List B, above, to figure out which word best fits each definition. Write the word on the line provided. (You will not use every word on the list.)

Freelance Journalism

Journalism is a rewarding but difficult career. You have to pick a **(11. topic of discussion)** _____ that a magazine or newspaper editor thinks is interesting. You have to show a good **(12. knowledge of what something means)** _____ of it. You have to be able to state your **(13. reason given to support or oppose a point of view)** _____ clearly in very few words. In other words, the ability to be **(14. using as few words as possible to get your meaning across)** _____ is essential. There is a **(15. way of doing something)** _____ to writing journalism, but you also need have an original style. You do not want your writing to **(16. try to be like another person)** _____ anyone else's. Then there is the publication **(17. series of steps to complete a task)** _____. Every article is **(18. has small changes made)** _____ by the editors. You have to be able to **(19. change in order to fit a new situation)** _____ to make changes the editor wants you to make. Finally, you have to be able to **(20. make corrections or improve)** _____ your work quickly.

 Does all communication serve a positive purpose?

Unit Overview

The articles in this unit explore what communication is and whether all communication is positive. As students read about different forms of communication—for example, text messaging, protests, movies, and rap music—they will decide for themselves what purposes communication serves.

Launch the Unit

Connect to the Big Question Prompt students to think about the unit opener. Read the introduction with students and examine the illustration. Ask questions such as these:

- *How can communication be difficult?*
- *What difficulty in communicating is the girl in the illustration having?*
- *What do you think might solve her communication problem?*
- *Why do you think some methods of communication are positive? Why do you think some are negative?*
- *When have you had positive communication experiences? Negative experiences?*

Use the prompt on the page as the basis for journal writing or for small group or whole class discussion. Students can share their ideas with partners or in small groups.

Anchor Students' Thinking Create a bulletin board for the unit. Post the Unit Big Question at the top. Encourage students to add to the bulletin board as they work through the unit.

- Have students list forms of communication discussed in each article and put a check mark next to those that are positive.
- Ask students to look through the articles and other sources for words that can be used to talk about communication. Post the words and their meanings.
- Post exemplary writing from students' writing assignments. Discuss what the writings reveal about positive and negative communication.
- Encourage students to post clippings that illustrate forms of communication. Link illustrations to the Unit Big Question.

Unit Objectives

Share these objectives with students. As you read the articles in this unit, you will:

- Identify ways in which people communicate and determine purposes that communication serves.
- Determine an answer to the Unit Big Question: *Does all communication serve a positive purpose?* Explain your answers using details from the articles and from your own experiences.
- Use content and academic vocabulary to talk and write about communication.
- Form an opinion for a debate and support that opinion with facts.

UNIT 4

Ooooh, Scary!

PROGRAM RESOURCES

ANTHOLOGY pp. 112–115

TEACHING GUIDE AND RESOURCES
- Guess It and Check It Chart **p. 143**
- Making Personal Connections Organizer **p. 147**
- Answer Key **p. 123**

REAL WORLD WRITING JOURNAL pp. 104–107

ANTHOLOGY

Preteach

Activate Prior Knowledge Take a poll of students' answers to the Real-Life Connection. Students will revisit answers after they read.

Build Background *The Motion Picture Association of America, Inc., has rated many popular horror films "R" or "NC-17." Movie theaters will not admit a person younger than seventeen to see an R-rated movie unless he or she is accompanied by an adult. Movie theaters cannot admit a person younger than seventeen to see an NC-17 movie, regardless of who accompanies the person. The primary reason for an R or NC-17 rating is the graphic depiction of violence.*

Introduce Vocabulary

- Read aloud the words, definitions, and example sentences.
- Ask students to respond to the following prompt about each of the words: "This word reminds me of . . ."
- *Build Academic Vocabulary* The academic vocabulary words for this lesson are *convey, isolation,* and *pattern.* Ask students to write a sentence for each word that shows how the word might be used in one of their classes.

Teach

Focus on the Big Question Ask the Article BQ, *Are today's horror movies too horrible?* Students will answer this question after reading.

- *Connect to the Unit Big Question* Have a student read the Article BQ aloud. Then write the Unit BQ on the board. Ask students to write for two minutes about how the two are related. Share responses as a class.

Preread the Article Before students read, model how to preview and predict:

THINK ALOUD *This title, "Ooooh, Scary!" makes me think that the article will be frightening. The opening sentence asks a question:* Do I love scary movies, or do they give me nightmares? *I predict that the article is going to explore what makes movies scary.*

- Have students silently read the rest of the first paragraph. Work with them to identify clues about the content of the article. Ask students to make a prediction about the article.

Conduct a Guided Reading Read the article to students as they follow along. Pause after each section to monitor students' comprehension.

- Ask a volunteer to identify key words and phrases in the section.
- Ask five *W*'s and an *H* questions.

Reflect on the Article After reading the article, review ideas introduced before or during reading.

- Revisit the Real-Life Connection statements. Has the article made students want to change any answers? Why?
- Ask students whether their predictions were correct and how they made them.

Practice and Apply

Discuss the Questions Gauge students' comprehension and help them develop critical reading skills (Answer Key, p. 123).

Connect to the Big Question Ask students to list things that make a movie scary.

- Mention examples from the article, such as realistic makeup and violent acts.
- Ask students to answer the following question about each item on the list: *How might this item be taken too far?*

Assess

Have students complete a Making Personal Connections Organizer for you to assess informally.

- In the top box, have students write the Article BQ.
- Then ask students to fill in the other boxes with their personal experiences and additional connections. If students struggle to make additional connections, direct them to review the article to find statements to which they can react.

Reach All Learners

Build Fluency Choose a section from the article for a paired reading.

- Pair students and have them read silently.
- Then direct one student to read aloud while the other follows along, making notes.
- The listener provides feedback and suggestions. Students then reverse roles.

Use Small Groups Engage students in writing an acrostic.

- Put students in groups of three or four and provide each group with a large piece of paper.
- Down the left side of the page, students should write *Horror Movies* vertically.
- Challenge groups to come up with describing words or phrases for horror movies that start with each of the letters.

Assist Students Having Difficulty If students have trouble with vocabulary in the article, have them complete a Guess It and Check It Chart. Students will need access to dictionaries for this exercise.

- As students read, they should list unfamiliar words.
- At the end of each section, students should use the chart to write the words, context clues, guesses at the meanings, and the dictionary meanings.

WRITING JOURNAL

Extend

Write About It Students will write a feature article about horror movies for a teen magazine.

- Read and discuss the Writing Prompt (Journal, p. 104). Review the Writing Rubric. Encourage students to add more points to the rubric to guide their work.
- Model how to use the organizer.
- Students should use the Check It and Fix It section and the Writing Checklist to revise and evaluate their work.

Use a Think Aloud to model how to draft:

> **THINK ALOUD** *I need to know how horror movies of the past and present are alike and different. Then I need to explain why I think one kind of horror movie is better than the other. For example, both old and new horror movies use makeup to make characters frightening. However, the makeup in old movies sometimes looks fake in comparison to the advanced makeup used today. Still, I definitely prefer the older, perhaps less realistic makeup because there is a certain innocence and simplicity to it.*

Vocabulary Workshop Students extend their thinking about Word Bank words.

- Students work in pairs or small groups on the organizer (Journal, p. 106).
- Have students add words to the Your Choice box and their personal word bank.
- Use the Show You Know exercise to assess students' understanding.

Teaching Tip To go over the Define It exercise, make three large boxes on the board and label them *Thinking, Talking,* and *Feeling*. Ask students to share examples of their sentences. Write them on the board in the appropriate boxes. This will provide a visual aid to show how words can be used in different ways.

UNIT 4

Up a Tree

PROGRAM RESOURCES

ANTHOLOGY pp. 116–119

TEACHING GUIDE AND RESOURCES
- Problem and Solution Map **p. 149**
- Answer Key **p. 123**

REAL WORLD WRITING JOURNAL pp. 108–111

ANTHOLOGY

Preteach

Activate Prior Knowledge Discuss responses to the Real-Life Connection scenario. Students will revisit answers after they read.

Build Background *What makes a forest endangered? Scientists and activists have a variety of answers for this question. Many would agree that forests most in need of protection are forests that remain mostly intact and untouched, forests with rare trees, forests with diverse species of plants and animals, and forests in areas with little remaining forestation.*

Introduce Vocabulary

- Write the words and definitions on the board.
- Call for volunteers to come to the board and draw lines between words that may be connected. Volunteers should then write a sentence that contains both words. Repeat the process until all words have been used at least twice.
- *Build Academic Vocabulary* The academic vocabulary words for this lesson are *define, discourse,* and *frequently.* Ask students to use each word in two sentences, one with an academic context and one with a non-academic context.

Teach

Focus on the Big Question Ask the Article BQ, *Do some kinds of protest do more harm than good?* Students will answer this question after reading.

- *Connect to the Unit Big Question* Write both the Unit and Article BQs on the board. Ask students to identify words or ideas in each that are related. Use students' ideas to discuss how the BQs are connected.

Preread the Article Ask students to read the article title, look at the photograph, and read the caption and the first subhead. Model how to preview and predict:

> **THINK ALOUD** *I see that the title of the article is "Up a Tree." This title could refer to forests, animals, or a predicament.* Up a tree *is slang for "in a tough situation." The photograph shows a woman in a tree. The caption says that the woman is Julia Hill and that she protected redwoods, which are a kind of tree. I think that this article will describe how Hill protected trees.*

Have students add information from subheads and make predictions.

Conduct a Guided Reading Read the article to students as they follow along. Pause after each section to monitor students' comprehension.

- Ask five *W*'s and an *H* questions.
- Ask a volunteer to summarize the section.

Reflect on the Article After reading the article, review ideas introduced before or during reading.

- Remind students of the Real-Life Connection scenario. Did their answers change?
- Was previewing helpful in predicting the content of the article? How so? If not, why not?

Practice and Apply

Discuss the Questions Gauge students' comprehension and help them develop critical reading skills (Answer Key, p. 123).

Connect to the Big Question Have students consider the effects of Hill's protest.

- Ask students to make a list of the people and resources affected by Hill's protest.
- Next to each item, have students write positive and negative effects of the protest.
- Call for volunteers to read their answers. Discuss how the answers relate to the BQ.

Assess

Have students create a Problem and Solution Map for you to assess informally.

- In the top box, students should summarize the problem between Pacific Lumber and the Earth First! organization.
- In the other boxes, students should summarize Hill's solution, the responses to it, and the end results of her protest.

Reach All Learners

Build Fluency Choose a section of the article for an echo reading.

- Read aloud the section sentence by sentence. Have students echo your reading as a class.
- Have smaller groups, such as rows, read aloud sentences for other groups to echo.
- Provide assistance as needed.

Use Small Groups Engage students in a debate.

- On the board, write the debate question: *Did Julia Hill's protest do more harm than good?*
- Divide the class into groups of six. Have each group subdivide into groups of three. One subgroup should take the position that the protests were harmful, and the other subgroup should argue that the protests were helpful.
- Each subgroup should write a short speech supporting its position. Have both sides of each group present their speeches to the class. Listeners should provide feedback to the groups.

Assist Students Having Difficulty If students have trouble with comprehension, have them write questions as they read.

- As you read a section aloud, stop at the end of each paragraph and ask students if they have questions. Write their questions on the board.
- At the end of the section, stop and answer the questions together as a class.
- Have students keep track of their own questions for the remaining sections. Leave time at the end of each section to answer and discuss students' questions.

WRITING JOURNAL

Extend

Write About It Students will write an opinion paragraph about the actions of Julia Hill.

- Read and discuss the Writing Prompt (Journal, p. 108). Review the Writing Rubric. Encourage students to add more points to the rubric to guide their work.
- Model how to use the organizer.
- Students should use the Check It and Fix It section and the Writing Checklist to revise and evaluate their work.

Teaching Tip Help students identify run-on sentences in their writing. On an overhead transparency, write a few run-ons from students' past writing assignments. Do not say who wrote the run-ons. Ask students to turn to the section on run-on sentences in the Grammar Handbook (Journal, p. 217). Discuss the examples and the ways to fix run-ons. Then call for volunteers to explain why the sentences on the transparency are run-ons. Use a variety of methods to revise each sentence.

Vocabulary Workshop Students extend their thinking about Word Bank words.

- Students work in pairs or small groups on the organizer (Journal, p. 110).
- Have students add words to the Your Choice box and their personal word bank.
- Use the Show You Know exercise to assess students' understanding.

> **THINK ALOUD** *If* link *is a good synonym for* connection, *it should fit well into the example sentence in the Word Bank:* Jaime saw a clear link between his new workout and winning the race. Link *works well as a synonym in this sentence. It shows that the new workout and the win are connected events.*

As Big As All Outdoors

PROGRAM RESOURCES

ANTHOLOGY pp. 120–123

TEACHING GUIDE AND RESOURCES
- Cause and Effect Map **p. 140**
- Answer Key **p. 123**

REAL WORLD WRITING JOURNAL pp. 112–115

ANTHOLOGY

Preteach

Activate Prior Knowledge Have students complete the Real-Life Connection chart. Students will revisit answers after they read.

Build Background *Many people and organizations have an interest in catching your eye. Advertising is used by businesses, politicians, charity groups, and public safety organizations. Outdoor advertising works; it is effective in part because it has a captive audience. Most people sit in cars, trains, or other forms of transportation for a certain amount of time each day in order to commute to work or school, so advertisers are practically guaranteed to have people's attention.*

Introduce Vocabulary

- After reading aloud the words, definitions, and example sentences, work with students to brainstorm situations in which students might use each word.
- *Build Academic Vocabulary* The academic vocabulary words for this lesson are *explanation, interact,* and *respond.* Ask students to answer these questions: *In which classes might you be asked to write an* explanation *of something? In what situations might you* interact *in a PE class? What are some methods you can use to* respond *to questions?*

Teach

Focus on the Big Question Ask the Article BQ, *Should we put more limits on outdoor ads?* Students will revisit this question after reading.

- *Connect to the Unit Big Question* Write both the Unit and Article BQs on the board. Then put students in pairs and have them discuss how the questions are related.

Preread the Article Ask students to read the article title and subheads. Have students consider the ideas presented in the subheads in order to predict the author's purpose in the article. Give students examples of possible purposes, such as these: to entertain, to explore a problem and its solutions, to describe.

Conduct a Guided Reading Read the article to students as they follow along. Pause after each section to monitor students' comprehension.

- At the end of each section, ask students to question the author: what is he or she saying? What is the author's purpose in saying it? Model how to think about the opening section:

> **THINK ALOUD** *I think the author is trying to say that in the United States it is difficult to escape billboards, though some states have banned them. I think the author is saying this to make us question whether or not billboards are a good idea.*

Reflect on the Article After reading the article, review ideas introduced before or during reading.

- Revisit the Real-Life Connection chart. Did answers change? Have students explain why.
- Review the author's purpose. Students should see that the primary purpose is to explore a problem and its solutions.

Practice and Apply

Discuss the Questions Gauge students' comprehension and help them develop critical reading skills (Answer Key, p. 123).

Connect to the Big Question Have students complete a Cause and Effect Map to answer the BQ.

- In the circle, have students write *Outdoor Advertising.* In the Effects boxes, ask students to write possible negative effects of outdoor advertising. Some are listed in the article.
- Call for volunteers to answer the BQ.

Assess

Have students create a main idea outline for you to assess informally.

- Provide students with a skeleton outline.
- The outline should include the title, subheads, and space for important details from each section. At the end of each section, leave a space for students to write the main idea.
- Students should list several details that support each main idea they list.

Reach All Learners

Build Fluency Choose a section from the article to practice using punctuation as a reading guide.

- Read a section aloud as students follow along.
- Ask students to comment on how you used punctuation to guide your rate, intonation, and expression.
- Put students in pairs and have them read the section. They should focus on pausing for commas and periods.

Use Small Groups Engage students in a write-around activity to answer a Use Clues question.

- Divide the class into groups of three or four. Have a member of each group begin by writing Use Clues question 5 ("How might you test whether outdoor ads are dangerous?") across the top of a piece of paper.
- Next, have the same group members write a response for one minute and then pass their papers to the right. The one-minute writing begins again, and students add to the paper in front of them, responding to the idea that is already there.
- Continue until all students have written on each paper. Discuss responses as a class.

Assist Students Having Difficulty If students struggle to relate to the issue explored in the article, help them make a personal connection to it.

- Ask students to list and describe outdoor ads in their neighborhood.
- Have students discuss how the ads affect them and their community.
- Have students reconsider their answer to the Article BQ.

WRITING JOURNAL

Extend

Write About It Students will write a speech about limiting outdoor advertising.

- Read and discuss the Writing Prompt (Journal, p. 112). Review the Writing Rubric. Encourage students to add more points to the rubric to guide their work.
- Model how to use the organizer.
- Students should use the Check It and Fix It section and the Writing Checklist to revise and evaluate their work.

Use a Think Aloud to model how to prewrite:

> **THINK ALOUD** *My opinion is that outdoor advertising should be limited. How do I support that? I see in the article that billboards are one type of advertising. They are good because they reach many people and provide something interesting to look at on a long road trip. They are bad because they take away from the natural landscape and can be distracting to drivers. I can use this to support my argument, because there are many other ways to reach people that do not mar the landscape or make driving more dangerous.*

Vocabulary Workshop Students extend their thinking about Word Bank words.

- Students work in pairs or small groups on the organizer (Journal, p. 114).
- Have students add words to the Your Choice box and their personal word bank.
- Use the Show You Know exercise to assess students' understanding.

Teaching Tip For the Show You Know activity, ask students to make their dialogues interesting by writing about a school event or other topic relevant to them. Then have students perform their dialogues for the class.

Put Me In, Coach!

PROGRAM RESOURCES

ANTHOLOGY pp. 124–127

TEACHING GUIDE AND RESOURCES
- Two-Column Journal **p. 153**
- Answer Key **p. 124**

REAL WORLD WRITING JOURNAL pp. 116–119

ANTHOLOGY

Preteach

Activate Prior Knowledge Have students share responses to the Real-Life Connection exercise. Students will revisit answers after they read.

Build Background *There are around 10,000 life coaches working in the United States. Many people say that coaches have helped them improve themselves, change, and reach goals. It is important to note, however, that life coaches do not need any license or certification.*

Introduce Vocabulary

- Read aloud the words, definitions, and example sentences.
- Work with students to break down the words into prefixes, suffixes, and root words. Help students figure out how the combinations create the meanings of the words.
- *Build Academic Vocabulary* The academic vocabulary word for this lesson is *isolation*. Ask students how the word might be used in science and social studies.

Teach

Focus on the Big Question Ask the Article BQ, *Do teens need life coaches to help them set goals?* Students will answer this question after reading.

- *Connect to the Unit Big Question* Remind students of the Unit BQ. Then ask a volunteer to read the Article BQ aloud. Have the class brainstorm about how the two BQs are linked.

Preread the Article Ask students to read the article title and the bar graph titled "Who Influences Teens the Most on Important Issues?" (Anthology, p. 126). Point out that the horizontal axis identifies groups of influential people; the vertical axis provides the percentage of respondents who identified each group. Help students figure out what each bar means; then ask them to make a prediction about the article.

Conduct a Guided Reading Read the article to students as they follow along. Pause after each section to monitor students' comprehension.

- Ask students to recast each subhead that is not a question into question form. Direct students to read to answer the question.

Model how to form a question:

> **THINK ALOUD** *The first subhead is "Life Coaches Defined." I can turn the subhead into a question or two by using the five W's and an H. For example, I could say "How are life coaches defined?" or "What is the definition of a life coach?" Then I'll read to answer the question.*

- Work with students to answer the question provided in the second subhead. Then ask students to turn the last subhead into a question and read to answer it.

Reflect on the Article After reading the article, review ideas introduced before or during reading.

- Revisit the Real-Life Connection chart. Discuss whether students would call the person whom they identified as a life coach.
- Review students' answers to subhead questions.

Practice and Apply

Discuss the Questions Gauge students' comprehension and help them develop critical reading skills (Answer Key, p. 124).

Connect to the Big Question Ask students the following question:

- *Aside from the media, what things might influence young people to believe they can become professional athletes?*

As an example, point out that at some schools star athletes are important figures whom students and faculty admire. After discussion, have students answer the BQ.

Assess

Have students write a personal journal entry for you to assess informally.

- Ask students to recall a personal challenge they have faced. Have students summarize it on a piece of paper.
- Then have students write about what they think would have happened if a life coach had tried to help them overcome the challenge. What would the coach have done? Would it have worked? Remind students to use information from the article to generate ideas.

Reach All Learners

Build Fluency Read a section of the article, focusing on challenging words.

- Read the section aloud.
- Work with students to identify difficult pronunciations. Practice the words together.
- Pair students and ask them to read the section to each other.

Use Small Groups Engage students in a discussion.

- Put students in groups of three or four and provide each group with this discussion starter: "A life coach may be a bad idea for teens because . . ."
- Direct the groups to assign each member a role, such as time-keeper, recorder, moderator, and reporter.
- When finished, the reporter from each group should share group ideas with the class.

Assist Students Having Difficulty If students have trouble recalling information from the article, have them retell information in their own words.

- Have students read short sections, stopping periodically to paraphrase what they read.
- Work with students to identify information that they missed or misunderstood.
- Show students how their notes create a kind of outline for the article.

WRITING JOURNAL

Extend

Write About It Students will write a memo to their principal about hiring two school life coaches.

- Read and discuss the Writing Prompt (Journal, p. 116). Review the Writing Rubric. Encourage students to add more points to the rubric to guide their work.
- Model how to use the organizer.
- Students should use the Check It and Fix It section and the Writing Checklist to revise and evaluate their work.

Use a Think Aloud to model how to prewrite:

> **THINK ALOUD** *It is important to remember that I am writing for the purpose of persuading the principal that my opinion is correct. In order to persuade someone about my opinion, I have to support it with plenty of good reasons. I must also present my opinion and reasons in a clear way. This means that my memo must be neat and free of errors. That way, anyone reading it knows that I feel strongly enough about my opinion to check my work thoroughly.*

Vocabulary Workshop Students extend their thinking about Word Bank words.

- Students work in pairs or small groups on the organizer (Journal, p. 118).
- Have students add words to the Your Choice box and their personal word bank.
- Use the Show You Know exercise to assess students' understanding.

Teaching Tip Reverse the process of the Show You Know exercise. Choose five key words from the article and write them on the board with their definitions. Have students write sentences with the words, providing enough context that a reader could define the words. Have volunteers write their sentences on the board, and work together as a class to identify the context clues.

UNIT 4

Longing to Be Like Mike

PROGRAM RESOURCES

ANTHOLOGY pp. 128–131

TEACHING GUIDE AND RESOURCES
- K-W-L Chart **p. 145**
- Web Map **p. 156**
- Answer Key **p. 124**

REAL WORLD WRITING JOURNAL pp. 120–123

ANTHOLOGY

Preteach

Activate Prior Knowledge Take a poll of student responses to the Real-Life Connection. Students will revisit answers after they read.

Build Background *Most pro athletes spend their careers in development or minor leagues, where they make little money. For example, a basketball player in the NBA development league makes between $12,000 and $24,000 per season; a minor league baseball player will earn no more than $1,100 per month for the first season, with salary negotiation after that. Only a few pros will get a chance to play in the big leagues, and only a few of those will succeed there.*

Introduce Vocabulary

- Ask students to find the boldface words in the article and read them in context.
- Have students identify context clues to word meanings. Compare students' definitions to those in the Word Bank.
- *Build Academic Vocabulary* All the Word Bank words for this lesson are academic vocabulary. Direct students to think of at least one school subject for which each word would be useful.

Teach

Focus on the Big Question Ask the Article BQ, *Do the media communicate the wrong message about sports careers?* Students will answer this question after reading.

- *Connect to the Unit Big Question* Write both the Unit and Article BQs on the board. Discuss the message most often communicated about sports careers.

Preread the Article Have students read the article title and opening paragraph. Distribute copies of the K-W-L Chart and ask students to write down what they know and want to know about the topic.

Conduct a Guided Reading Read the article to students as they follow along. Pause after each section to monitor students' comprehension.

- Help students identify the main idea of the section and the details that support it.

Model how to think about the main idea:

> **THINK ALOUD** *The main idea of the first section is that the media have helped create a society where most people's heroes are famous. One detail that supports this is the author's explanation that people used to admire local celebrities, but now local celebrities are overshadowed by famous people promoted by the media.*

- Have students jot down the main idea of each section.

Reflect on the Article After reading the article, review ideas introduced before or during reading.

- Revisit the Real-Life Connection statements. Have responses changed? Ask students why.
- Have students read aloud the main ideas they wrote for each section.
- Discuss students' responses to the K-W-L Chart. What do students still want to learn?

Practice and Apply

Discuss the Questions Gauge students' comprehension and help them develop critical reading skills (Answer Key, p. 124).

Connect to the Big Question Ask students the following question:

- *Aside from the media, what are some other reasons that young people might believe they can become professional athletes?*

Assess

Have students create a learning log for you to assess informally. Students should answer these questions:

- *What did you do in class today? What did you learn?*
- *Did today's lesson confirm or change any feelings you already had about the topic you studied? What, and why?*
- *What questions do you still have?*

Reach All Learners

Build Fluency Choose a section from the article and have students do coached repeated readings.

- Pair students and have them read the section to each other. As one student reads, the other takes notes about rate, pronunciation, and expression.
- Have pairs repeat the reading until they are comfortable reading aloud and can read with some fluency.

Use Small Groups Engage students in a creative exercise about the media.

- Divide the class into groups of three or four and provide each group with a piece of poster board or large piece of paper.
- Ask students to create a poster that glamorizes a profession not often portrayed by the media, like a business person or a teacher.
- Direct students to think about how the media portray athletes and then apply media methods to the "ordinary" profession.
- Hang posters on a bulletin board.

Assist Students Having Difficulty If students have trouble following the arguments in the article, have them complete an informal outline.

- Provide students with a skeleton outline that consists of subheads followed by blank spaces for note taking.
- Help students outline the arguments.

WRITING JOURNAL

Extend

Write About It Students will write a blog about the media portrayal of sports careers.

- Read and discuss the Writing Prompt (Journal, p. 120). Review the Writing Rubric. Encourage students to add more points to the rubric to guide their work.
- Model how to use the organizer.
- Students should use the Check It and Fix It section and the Writing Checklist to revise and evaluate their work.

Teaching Tip Have rows or small groups of students create "threads" with their blogs. Have students pass their papers systematically and respond to the prior blog. Create an overhead transparency of some threads and discuss them as a class. Focus on how the threads change direction as people respond, and discuss the quality of the arguments and ideas presented.

Vocabulary Workshop Students extend their thinking about Word Bank words.

- Students work in pairs or small groups on the organizer (Journal, p. 122).
- Have students add words to the Your Choice box and their personal word bank.
- Use the Show You Know exercise to assess students' understanding.

Use a Think Aloud to model how to think about the Word Sort exercise:

> **THINK ALOUD** *In addition to the Word Bank words,* professional *and* intellectual *are two important words in the article.* Professional *is an adjective that describes someone who does a certain job for a living.* Intellectual *is also an adjective. It describes something that has to do with using the mind. I could use both of those words in a sentence:* If you enjoy intellectual work, you could become a professional teacher or lawyer.

UNIT 4

Time to Serve

PROGRAM RESOURCES

ANTHOLOGY pp. 132–135

TEACHING GUIDE AND RESOURCES
• Cause and Effect Map **p. 140**
• Answer Key **pp. 124–125**
REAL WORLD WRITING JOURNAL pp. 124–127

ANTHOLOGY

Preteach

Activate Prior Knowledge Discuss students' responses to the Real-Life Connection activity. Students will revisit the charts after they read.

Build Background *In 1993, Americorps was established. It is a national program to help Americans contribute to needs in education, public health, and the environment. In 2002, Freedom Corps was established. It involves senior citizens in communities and organizes volunteers to respond to emergencies.*

Introduce Vocabulary

• Point out that the Word Bank words comprise two nouns and two verbs. Ask students to write two sentences, each using one of the nouns and one of the verbs.
• Have volunteers write their sentences on the board. Discuss the sentences as a class.
• *Build Academic Vocabulary* All the Word Bank words except *language* are academic vocabulary. Ask students to identify at least two classes in which each word might be useful.

Teach

Focus on the Big Question Ask the Article BQ, *What message would a national draft send to young people?* Students will answer this question after reading.

• *Connect to the Unit Big Question* Write both the Unit and Article BQs on the board. Discuss how national service might send a positive message. How might the message be negative?

Preread the Article Ask students to read the title and first paragraph of the article. What opinions do they think the author is going to present? What support might the author cite?

Conduct a Guided Reading Read the article to students as they follow along. Pause after each section to monitor students' comprehension.

• Have students identify the text structures of each section. The first and second sections are organized chronologically; the last section is organized around opinions and reasons.

Model how to identify text structures:

> **THINK ALOUD** *The subhead* Draft History *makes me think the events described in this section may be organized chronologically, or in the order in which they actually happened. Histories are usually organized that way. I am going to skim to see if I am right. I see the dates* 1860s *and* 1900s, *so it looks as if this section is in chronological order.*

• Have students repeat this process with a partner for each section.

Reflect on the Article After reading the article, review ideas introduced before or during reading.

• Discuss additions students would make to their Real-Life Connection charts based on the article.
• Discuss the text structures students identified while reading the article.

Practice and Apply

Discuss the Questions Gauge students' comprehension and help them develop critical reading skills (Answer Key, pp. 124–125).

Connect to the Big Question Ask the following questions to spark discussion:

• *Would you participate in national service?*
• *What message do you think a national service draft would send and why?*
Have volunteers use information from the article and the class opinion to answer the BQ.

Assess

Have students imagine that a national service draft has just been instituted and that they will be required to perform some type of service after they turn eighteen. Direct them to answer the following questions using information from the article and their personal experience:

- *Why do you think the country is instituting the draft?*
- *What might be the result of this draft?*

Reach All Learners

Build Fluency Choose a section from the article and have students work on emphasizing words.

- Work with students to identify words needing special emphasis, such as those in italics, those in quotations, and those following a dash.
- Model how to emphasize words. Have students echo your reading.
- Then call for volunteers to read the section aloud. Provide feedback and suggestions.

Use Small Groups Engage students in a question and answer game.

- Put students in groups of three or four and ask groups to write five fact questions and one discussion question about the article.
- Pair groups and have them ask each other questions.

Assist Students Having Difficulty If students have trouble with comprehension, have them list difficult words and concepts as they read.

- Instruct students to write "I need to know more about . . ." across the top of a piece of paper.
- If students do not understand a word or concept while they are reading, they should write it on the paper, leaving a line or two between each item.
- When students are finished, discuss words and concepts that students did not know.

WRITING JOURNAL

Extend

Write About It Students will write a letter to a congressperson about a national service draft.

- Read and discuss the Writing Prompt (Journal, p. 124). Review the Writing Rubric. Encourage students to add more points to the rubric to guide their work.
- Model how to use the organizer.
- Students should use the Check It and Fix It section and the Writing Checklist to revise and evaluate their work.

Teaching Tip To help students evaluate and revise their work, draw their attention to the Editing Checklist (Journal, p. 232). Discuss each item listed. Remind students that they can review rules related to each item by using their Grammar Handbook (Journal, pp. 189–231). Then discuss the proofreaders' marks at the bottom of the Checklist. On the board, write a few sentences with errors in them. Then call for volunteers to use the marks to correct the errors.

Vocabulary Workshop Students extend their thinking about Word Bank words.

- Students work in pairs or small groups on the organizer (Journal, p. 126).
- Have students add words to the Your Choice box and their personal word bank.
- Use the Show You Know exercise to assess students' understanding.

To help students with the It's Academic exercise, model how to think about ways to use the word *interact*:

> **THINK ALOUD** *I know that* interact *means to talk with or have another kind of exchange with another. When would I interact in my classes? One example would be during a class discussion in my English class. With whom do I interact? One example would be talking with other students in a small group. A good sentence with these examples would be:* I interact with other students when we talk about books in English class. *What other ways can I use* interact *when I talk about my classes?*

UNIT 4

Hip-Hop into Hall of Fame

PROGRAM RESOURCES

ANTHOLOGY pp. 136–139

TEACHING GUIDE AND RESOURCES
- Draw-Define-Use Organizer **p. 142**
- T-Chart **p. 151**
- Answer Key **p. 125**

REAL WORLD WRITING JOURNAL pp. 128–131

ANTHOLOGY

Preteach

Activate Prior Knowledge Have students complete the Real-Life Connection chart. Students will revisit answers after they read.

Build Background *The term* hip-hop *also refers to the whole culture that inspired rap music. The urban roots of hip-hop include deejaying (or "turntabling"), rapping, graffiti painting, and dancing. Though the roots of hip-hop may be urban and associated with African American culture, it became the best-selling genre of music in the late 1990s, and it generates sales in many other industries, like fashion and electronics.*

Introduce Vocabulary

- Write a sentence using one of the Word Bank words. This sentence will be a story-starter.
- Call on students to continue the story with other sentences using more Word Bank words. Continue until all words have been used.
- *Build Academic Vocabulary* All the Word Bank words except *verbal* are academic vocabulary. Have students complete a Draw-Define-Use Organizer for each.

Model how to complete the organizer:

> **THINK ALOUD** *I will use the word misinterpret for my organizer. I know that it means "misunderstand," so I write that. I think that I will draw two stick figures with speech bubbles. One will say, "Why don't you want to go?" and the other will say, "Who says I don't?" as an illustration. My sentence is* Sometimes, my mom and dad accidentally misinterpret what I mean.

Teach

Focus on the Big Question Ask the Article BQ, *Do rap musicians belong in the Rock and Roll Hall of Fame?* Students will answer this question after reading.

- *Connect to the Unit Big Question* Have a student read the Article BQ aloud. Then write the Unit BQ on the board. Ask students to think about the ways in which rap music is a form of communication.

Preread the Article Direct students to jot down what they know and want to know about the topic.

Conduct a Guided Reading Read the article to students as they follow along. Pause after each section to monitor students' comprehension.

- Have students state the main idea in their own words.
- Ask a volunteer to summarize the section.

Reflect on the Article After reading the article, review ideas introduced before or during reading.

- Ask students if the article confirmed or refuted what they already knew about hip-hop. What did they learn?
- Do any questions remain unanswered? What are they?

Practice and Apply

Discuss the Questions Gauge students' comprehension and help them develop critical reading skills (Answer Key, p. 125).

Connect to the Big Question Have students complete a T-Chart to answer the BQ.

- Provide students with a T-Chart and ask them to write the BQ and the headings *Yes* and *No*.
- Have students use ideas from the article to fill in reasons for both sides of the argument.
- When students are finished, discuss the BQ.

Assess

Have students write about the challenge of defining music.

- Remind students of the article BQ. Ask them to write it on a piece of paper.
- Beneath the BQ, students should write, "This question is difficult to answer because…"
- Have students answer this question by listing reasons. Direct them to refer to the article for ideas.

Reach All Learners

Build Fluency Choose a section from the article for a paired reading.

- Pair students and have them read silently.
- Direct one student to read aloud while the other follows along making notes.
- The listener provides suggestions and feedback. Students then reverse roles.

Use Small Groups Engage students in a discussion.

- Put students in groups of three or four and provide groups with the following discussion questions: *Why is it hard to categorize rap music under an existing genre of music? Why do you think rap remains so popular?*
- Groups should share their ideas with the class.

Assist Students Having Difficulty If students struggle to keep track of main ideas in the article, provide them with a skeleton outline for taking notes.

- The outline should include the article title and subheads, with space for notes.
- Allow time after reading the article to go over the outline using an overhead transparency.
- Ask, *What questions do you still have? What did you learn from today's lesson?*

WRITING JOURNAL

Extend

Write About It Students will write a letter to the editor of a teen music magazine about allowing hip-hop stars into the Rock and Roll Hall of Fame.

- Read and discuss the Writing Prompt (Journal p. 128). Review the Writing Rubric. Encourage students to add more points to the rubric to guide their work.
- Model how to use the organizer.
- Students should use the Check It and Fix It section and the Writing Checklist to revise and evaluate their work.

Use a Think Aloud to model how to prewrite:

> **THINK ALOUD** *I think the Hall should be free to honor any outstanding musician in any genre of popular music. One of the first supporting facts is that rock and roll itself grew out of other forms of music, such as R&B and country. Since rock and roll has some of its roots in other forms, why can't hip-hop have some of its roots in rock and roll? There is my first sentence!*

Vocabulary Workshop Students extend their thinking about Word Bank words.

- Students work in pairs or small groups on the organizer (Journal, p. 130).
- Have students add words to the Your Choice box and their personal word bank.
- Use the Show You Know exercise to assess students' understanding.

Teaching Tip To go over the Define It exercise, use an overhead transparency of the organizer. Fill it in as a class, and then have volunteers share sentences they wrote about the different subjects.

UNIT 4

Texting on Trial

PROGRAM RESOURCES

ANTHOLOGY pp. 140–143

TEACHING GUIDE AND RESOURCES
- Draw-Define-Use Organizer **p. 142**
- Making Personal Connections Organizer **p. 147**
- Answer Key **p. 125**

REAL WORLD WRITING JOURNAL pp. 132–135

ANTHOLOGY

Preteach

Activate Prior Knowledge Take a poll of students' answers to the Real-Life Connection. Students will revisit answers after they read.

Build Background *Some say texting takes the personal responsibility out of communication. People might be more likely to be unkind or untruthful in a text message. Also, without the benefit of nonverbal cues, like facial expressions and other gestures, the brief nature of texts might lead to misunderstanding.*

Introduce Vocabulary
- Ask students to complete a Draw-Define-Use Organizer for each word.
- Have volunteers share their sentences.
- *Build Academic Vocabulary* The academic vocabulary words for this lesson are *continuum* and *frequently*. Ask students to rate each word in two ways: knowledge and use. They should rate each as *a lot, some,* or *little*. Direct students to write a sentence for each word.

Teach

Focus on the Big Question Ask the Article BQ, *Is text messaging a good tool for young people?* Students will answer this question after reading.

- *Connect to the Unit Big Question* Put students in groups. Direct them to read both BQs and brainstorm connections between the questions.

Preread the Article Ask students to read the article title and look at the photograph and chart in the article. Read the opening and discuss the author's purpose.

Conduct a Guided Reading Read the article to students as they follow along. Pause after each section to monitor students' comprehension.

- Have a student state the opinion discussed in each section, then identify the support, or proof, for each side.

Model how to identify opinions and support:

> **THINK ALOUD** *In Argument 1, the opinion under discussion is that texting is a distraction in class. The prosecution says that students are texting when they should be listening and that some even cheat with texts. The defense says that texting is no different from passing a note or talking. If students are bored, that is not texting's fault.*

Reflect on the Article After reading the article, review ideas introduced before or during reading.

- Revisit the Real-Life Connection chart. Did answers change? Have students explain.
- Reflect on the opinions noted by students. Which did they think were the most persuasive? Why?

Practice and Apply

Discuss the Questions Gauge students' comprehension and help them develop critical reading skills (Answer Key, p. 125).

Connect to the Big Question Have students complete a Making Personal Connections Organizer to help them answer the Article BQ.

- Have students write "Text Messaging" in the top box.
- Direct students to use the other boxes to write about their own experiences with texting as well as ideas they have gotten from other connections with texting.
- Follow up by asking whether texting has been a good tool in students' lives.

Assess

Have students write a judgment on the case presented in the article.

- Ask students to imagine that they are a judge presiding over the case presented in the article.
- Have students write their judgment using the following prompt: "In the case of Texting vs. No Texting, I am ruling in favor of _____. I am ruling this way because…"
- Instruct students to use ideas from the article in explaining their ruling.

Reach All Learners

Build Fluency Choose a section from the article for a reader's theater exercise.

- Discuss how attorneys present their cases to a judge or jury in a convincing way. Brainstorm with the class about ways attorneys use expression to be convincing.
- Call on students to take the roles of prosecution and defense. Have students read their portion of the argument aloud.
- Discuss with the class and provide feedback. Have students repeat the reading.

Use Small Groups Engage students in a critique of the article arguments.

- Put students in groups of three or four and assign each group an argument from the article.
- Ask students to have a group member read the argument aloud.
- Groups should then answer the following questions: *Which argument is stronger, and why? How could each side have made a stronger argument? What is the best solution to the problem presented in the argument?*

Assist Students Having Difficulty If students have trouble keeping track of the arguments in the article, have them keep a list of supporting details.

- Ask students to write the following headings on a piece of paper: *For Texting* and *Against Texting.*
- As they read, students should list the support for each side.
- Instruct students to refer to this list when answering questions about the article or considering their thoughts on the BQ.

WRITING JOURNAL

Extend

Write About It Students will write an opinion paragraph about whether they would prosecute or defend texting.

- Read and discuss the Writing Prompt (Journal p. 136). Review the Writing Rubric. Encourage students to add more points to the rubric to guide their work.
- Model how to use the organizer.
- Students should use the Check It and Fix It section and the Writing Checklist to revise and evaluate their work.

Teaching Tip To help students identify ways to be convincing, show a video of an attorney presenting a case in a film or television show. Ask students to take notes about words, expression, and other ways the attorney is convincing. Ask students to incorporate some of these techniques in their writing. Students could also read their opinion paragraphs aloud and use nonverbal cues that help them present their ideas convincingly.

Vocabulary Workshop Students extend their thinking about Word Bank words.

- Students work in pairs or small groups on the organizer (Journal, p. 134).
- Have students add words to the Your Choice box and their personal word bank.
- Use the Show You Know exercise to assess students' understanding.

Help students complete the Word Play exercise by modeling:

> **THINK ALOUD** *The words often, always, a lot, and most of the time are words and phrases that mean about the same thing as frequently. If they mean the same thing, they all should fit into the same sentence without changing the sentence's meaning. Here is a sample sentence for frequently: "I go swimming frequently when the weather is hot." All the words and phrases can be substituted for frequently, and the sentence still makes sense. Some of the words are a better fit than others, but they all work.*

UNIT 4 WRAP UP

 ## Does all communication serve a positive purpose?

Introduce the Unit Project

Debate Students will participate in a debate by choosing and presenting a response to the Unit Big Question: *Does all communication serve a positive purpose?*

- Read through the steps of the assignment with students.
- Point out the rubric so that students will know their goals for the assignment. Add other rubric points with students to guide their work.
- Allow time for students to practice and present their work. Encourage listeners to offer their feedback and advice on the presentation.

Model Use a Think Aloud to model how to select and prepare the strongest selling points:

> **THINK ALOUD** *I have selected my arguments. My side must argue that not all communication serves a positive purpose. The most important support for this should go last so that I end strongly. I think my best support is that texting is distracting and not always tied to what people are doing in the moment. I will write a 3 next to that so I know that it is last.*

Teaching Tip Explain that one part of a debate is the rebuttal. Have students prepare a response for the other side of the debate.

Conclude the Unit

Review Unit Objectives Return to the unit objectives and ask students to evaluate how well they mastered each one on a scale of 1 to 5, with 1 being low and 5 being high. Discuss how lower scores could be improved.

Reflect on the Learning Examine the bulletin board with students. Ask them to reflect on what they have learned. They can write or discuss with the class or in small groups. Prompt students' thinking with questions such as these:

- *What was the most interesting article you read? What did you like about it?*

- *How did your ideas about communication change as you read through the articles?*
- *Which topic would you like to know more about? What do you still wonder about it?*
- *How did the writing assignments and the debate help you form your ideas about whether or not all communication is positive?*
- *What other article topics do you think could be included in this unit? How would those topics help people learn more about the purposes, both positive and negative, that communication might serve?*

Name _____

Word Bank Quiz

WORD LIST A			
confusion	define	meaning	self-expression
continuum	frequently	misinterpret	tone
convey	language	possible	verbal

Ten of the unit Word Bank words are defined in parentheses in the article below. As you read the article, use Word List A, above, to figure out which word best fits each definition. Write the word on the line provided. (You will not use every word on the list.) Then go on to the next page of the quiz.

Cyberbullying

How do experts **(1. say the meaning of)** _____ *cyberbullying?*

Many experts say that the **(2. idea it expresses)** _____ is "using

the Internet to **(3. communicate in words or other ways)** _____

unkind, embarrassing, or threatening **(4. made up of words)** _____

messages." Cyberbullies may use vulgar **(5. set of words that people use to**

communicate) _____ or a threatening **(6. way of writing that**

communicates a particular feeling) _____ in their messages.

Cyberbullying covers a **(7. something that varies little by little, part by part)**

_____ of bad Internet behaviors.

It is hard to stop cyberbullies because it is **(8. able to be done)**

_____ for them to hide their identities. Cyberbullies **(9. often)**

_____ go to social networking sites and use other people's identities.

Imagine the **(10. mix-up)** _____ that causes for authorities trying to

stop cyberbullies.

UNIT 4 Word Bank Quiz

WORD LIST B			
connection	emotion	interact	pattern
define	explanation	isolation	respond
discourse	frequently	misinterpret	self-expression

Ten more Word Bank words are defined in parentheses in the rest of the article, below. As you read the article, use Word List B, above, to figure out which word best fits each definition. Write the word on the line provided. (You will not use every word on the list.)

Cyberbullying has left some victims living in fear and (**11. a feeling of being alone**) _____. The bullying may also bring out another (**12. feeling**) _____: anger. Some experts believe that there is a (**13. link**) _____ between school violence and cyberbullying. As a result, some schools include cyberbullying in their discipline policies. Students can be punished for threatening other students, in or out of school. In general, schools' (**14. statement to help you understand**) _____ for setting such policies is that it is their responsibility to keep schools safe.

Policies against cyberbullying have caused community-wide (**15. serious conversation**) _____ about how to stop bullying while preserving students' (**16. communicating one's own feelings to others**) _____ and free speech. Some people worry that schools will (**17. think it means something it does not**) _____ laws that allow them to censor students' speech, leading them to place unnecessary limits on the ways students can (**18. talk or have exchanges with others**) _____. However, most agree that something must be done before students become caught up in a (**19. routine way of doing something**) _____ of bullying. Experts suggest that students not (**20. react by speaking or doing something**) _____ to threats but instead keep a record of them and report them to authorities.

 # To what extent does experience determine what we perceive?

Unit Overview

The articles in this unit explore the topic of experience and perception. As students read about experiences and perceptions, they will decide for themselves how much experience determines what people see and understand in the world around them.

Launch the Unit

Connect to the Big Question Read the introduction with students and examine the illustration. Ask questions such as these:

- *What are some ways that experience makes parents and children perceive things differently?*
- *Describe what is happening in the illustration.*
- *Do you think the man's experience of the music is different from the girl's?*
- *Did your perception of anything change as you grew older? What was it?*

Use the prompt on the page as the basis for journal writing or for small group or whole class discussion. Students can share their ideas with partners or in small groups.

Anchor Students' Thinking Post the Unit Big Question on a bulletin board. Write the Unit Big Question at the top and the title of each selection down the left side. Throughout the unit, relate each article to the Unit Big Question. Use ideas such as the following:

- As a class, state the different perspectives of the issue described in each article. Post them on the bulletin board.
- Have students look through the articles and other sources for words that can be used to talk about experience and perspective. Post them, and periodically ask students to have "dialogue challenges" in which they use as many of the words as possible.
- Encourage students to write about how their experience has influenced their perspective at different times in their lives.

Unit Objectives

Share these objectives with students. As you read the articles in this unit, you will:
- Identify different perspectives and ways that experience affects them.
- Determine an answer to the Big Question: *To what extent does experience determine what we perceive?* Explain your answers using details from the articles and from your own experiences.
- Use content and academic vocabulary to talk and write about experience and perspective.
- Form an opinion for a write-around activity and support that opinion with facts.

Pros and Cons of Protest

PROGRAM RESOURCES

ANTHOLOGY pp. 148–151

TEACHING GUIDE AND RESOURCES
- Main Idea Map **p. 146**
- T-Chart **p. 151**
- Answer Key **p. 126**

REAL WORLD WRITING JOURNAL pp. 138–141

ANTHOLOGY

Preteach

Activate Prior Knowledge Have students copy and complete the Real-Life Connection chart. Students will revisit answers after they read.

Build Background *The Supreme Court has heard many cases over the years about whether a state law violates the First Amendment. Some of these cases are about whether high schools can limit students' freedom of speech and expression.*

Introduce Vocabulary

- Read aloud the definitions and sentences in the Word Bank. Discuss what each word means.
- Have student pairs find the boldface words in the selection and take turns reading aloud the sentences in which each word appears.
- *Build Academic Vocabulary* The academic vocabulary words for this selection are *bias* and *perspective*. Ask students how they might use the word *perspective* in an art class. How about in English class? How might students use the word *bias* in history class?

Teach

Focus on the Big Question Ask the Article BQ, *How can we keep protests from violating other people's rights?* Students will answer this question after reading.

- *Connect to the Unit Big Question* Write the Unit and Article BQs on the board. Discuss with students whether they have ever been involved in or witnessed an organized protest. Ask students how experience might influence their perceptions of people's rights.

Preread the Article The Real-Life Connection is a prediction activity. Before students read, have them use the chart to make predictions about

the article. Use the following questions to remind students about other prereading strategies:

- *Have you activated your <u>prior knowledge</u>?*
- *What is your <u>purpose</u> for reading?*
- *Do you have <u>questions</u> about the topic that you would like to answer?*

Have students share their predictions.

Conduct a Guided Reading Read the article to students as they follow along. Pause after each section to monitor students' comprehension.

- After each section, ask students to identify the main idea and supporting details.
- Call on a volunteer to summarize the section.

Reflect on the Article After reading the article, review ideas introduced before or during reading.

- Have students review their Real-Life Connection chart. Were their predictions accurate?
- Have volunteers share questions they still have about the topic.

Model how to develop new questions:

> **THINK ALOUD** *After I read this article, I wanted to know more about different student protests. I have a couple of questions: Are there a lot of student protests on college campuses? What are most about?*

Practice and Apply

Discuss the Questions Gauge students' comprehension and help them develop critical reading skills (Answer Key, p. 126).

Connect to the Big Question Have students use the T-Chart to answer the BQ.

- Students should write the Article BQ on their organizers and label the columns *Rights of Protesters* and *Rights of Others*.
- Students should take notes and use them to answer the Article BQ.

Assess

Collect students' organizers and evaluate them to do an informal comprehension assessment.

Reach All Learners

Build Fluency Choose a section from the article for a choral reading.

- Read the selection aloud slowly and clearly. Use as much expression as possible.
- Have students follow along silently.
- Reread the selection aloud while students echo your reading, copying your expression.

Use Small Groups Engage students with a small group activity to answer the Use Clues questions.

- Organize students into groups of three. Count off one through three.
- After a brief time for discussion, ask all the number threes to stand if they know the answer to the fourth question. If any of them do not know, go back to discussion time.
- Continue the activity until each member of every group has had the opportunity to answer either the fourth, fifth, or sixth question.

Assist Students Having Difficulty If students struggle to keep track of main ideas in the article, distribute a Main Idea Map to students.

- Allow time after reading the article to fill out the organizer as a class.
- Use an overhead transparency of the Main Idea Map.
- Remind students that a paragraph may start with a topic sentence that states the paragraph's main idea. Remind students to skim the first sentence or two of each paragraph.
- Help students use the topic sentences to find main ideas of sections.
- Ask students to identify the most important idea in the article. Have them find details that support the idea.

WRITING JOURNAL

Extend

Write About It Students will plan and write a paragraph explaining how college officials can protect both protestors' and non-protestors' rights.

- Read and discuss the Writing Prompt (Journal, p. 138). Review the Writing Rubric. Encourage students to add more points to the rubric to guide their work.
- Model how to use the organizer.
- Students should use the Check It and Fix It section and the Writing Checklist to revise and evaluate their work.

Use a Think Aloud to model how to prewrite:

> **THINK ALOUD** *I do not have any ideas and suggestions to write about yet. I will reread the article first. As I read, I will put a sticky note next to ideas from the article about protecting protesters as well as non-protesters. When I get an idea that is not in the article, I will write it down on the organizer in my Journal. Then I will use the sticky notes to add more ideas to my organizer.*

Vocabulary Workshop Students extend their thinking about Word Bank words.

- Students can work in pairs or small groups on the Define It organizer (Journal, p. 140).
- Have students add words to the Your Choice box and their personal word bank.
- Use the Show You Know exercise to assess students' understanding.

Teaching Tip If students are having difficulty writing the dialogues for the Show You Know exercise, place them in pairs and have each pair improvise two different dialogues. Have each pair perform its dialogues for the class. Have the class review whether words were used correctly in the dialogues.

UNIT 5

Royal Rights to Privacy

PROGRAM RESOURCES

ANTHOLOGY pp. 152–155

TEACHING GUIDE AND RESOURCES
- Opinion and Reasons Organizer **p. 148**
- Answer Key **p. 126**

REAL WORLD WRITING JOURNAL pp. 142–145

ANTHOLOGY

Preteach

Activate Prior Knowledge Discuss whether students are interested in different celebrities. Take a poll of students' answers to the questions in the Real-Life Connection. Students will revisit answers after they read.

Build Background *In 1998, California passed a law that forbids "constructive trespass." That means it is against the law there to use technologically advanced devices to watch or eavesdrop on people in situations in which they have "a reasonable expectation of privacy."*

Introduce Vocabulary

- Read aloud the sentences from the article in which boldface vocabulary words appear. Discuss what each word means in context.
- *Build Academic Vocabulary* The academic vocabulary words for this lesson are *appropriate*, *background*, and *discipline*. Ask students if it is *appropriate* to interrupt a teacher during a lecture; whether a *background* in biology would help a math teacher; whether a person needs *discipline* to study music. Have students write a sentence for each word.

Teach

Focus on the Big Question Ask the Article BQ, *Do we have the right to know about the private lives of royals?* Students will answer this question after reading.

- *Connect to the Unit Big Question* Hand out the Opinion and Reasons Organizer. Have students label the boxes *Second Opinion* and *New Reasons.* Then have students write an initial answer to the Article BQ and support it with a reason. Students will fill out the remainder of the organizer after reading.

Preread the Article Before students read, tell them that their purpose for reading this article is to find out if it will change their opinion about celebrities and privacy. Then have students write down one question they want answered by the article.

Conduct a Guided Reading Read the article to students as they follow along. Pause after each section to monitor students' comprehension.

- Ask whether any of the students' questions have been answered.
- Have a volunteer ask a new question based on the section. Write the question on the board.

Model asking a question about the section:

> **THINK ALOUD** *On the first page, the author says that freelance photographers are called paparazzi. That is a strange word! I wonder where it comes from, and why the photographers are called that.*

Reflect on the Article After reading the article, review ideas introduced before or during reading.

- Retake the poll from the Real-Life Connection. Have answers changed? Ask students why.
- Have students answer the questions they posed for themselves.

Practice and Apply

Discuss the Questions Gauge students' comprehension and help them develop critical reading skills (Answer Key, p. 126).

Connect to the Big Question Use the results of the two polls (taken before and after reading) to discuss the Article BQ.

- Ask students if reading the article has changed how they think. Have students explain why.
- Have students fill in the remaining two boxes in their organizers.
- Call on volunteers to answer the Article BQ.

Assess

Have students create a learning log for you to assess informally. Students should answer these questions:

- *What did you learn about the privacy of royals?*
- *What did you find interesting?*
- *What questions do you still have?*

Reach All Learners

Build Fluency Choose a section from the article for an echo reading.

- Direct a student to read the first sentence aloud. Help the student use the correct emphasis and tone to signal the end of the sentence.
- Have the next student read the next sentence. Repeat the process with the entire group.
- Repeat the activity, but during the second reading tell students to read the section more quickly and to move more smoothly from one reader to the next.

Use Small Groups Engage students with a small group activity to complete the Find It on the Page questions.

- Place students in small groups.
- Provide students with guidance on how to scan text to find specific information. For example, for the first question, students should look for the key word *paparazzi* and then read the sentence in which the word appears as well as surrounding sentences.
- Have students work together and use sticky notes to mark where they find the answers to the questions.

Assist Students Having Difficulty If students struggle to come up with prereading questions, have a brainstorming session. Brainstorm questions, not answers, about the subject of privacy and royalty. To help students generate questions, reread the first two paragraphs of the article.

WRITING JOURNAL

Extend

Write About It Students will plan and write a letter to the editor of a celebrity magazine.

- Read and discuss the Writing Prompt (Journal, p. 142). Review the Writing Rubric. Encourage students to add more points to the rubric to guide their work.
- Model how to use the organizer.
- Students should use the Check It and Fix It section and the Writing Checklist to revise and evaluate their work.

Teaching Tip If students are having difficulty avoiding sentence fragments, review as a class the sentence fragment section of the Grammar Handbook (Journal, pp. 218–219). On a transparency or a board, write a few fragments from students' writing assignments. Do not identify the authors. Then call for volunteers to explain why the sentences are fragments and how the fragments might be revised to form complete sentences.

Vocabulary Workshop Students extend their thinking about Word Bank words.

- Students can work in pairs or small groups on the Define It organizer (Journal, p. 144).
- Have students add words to the Your Choice box and their personal word bank.
- Use the Show You Know exercise to assess students' understanding.

Use a Think Aloud to model how to fill out the Your Choice box:

> **THINK ALOUD** *There were quite a few words in this article that I would like to put in a personal word bank. Unethical is one of them. From the context of the sentence, I can guess that it means something bad, but I would like to know exactly what it means. I also do not know what besieged means. I will look them up in a dictionary.*

In or Out of the In Crowd

PROGRAM RESOURCES

ANTHOLOGY pp. 156–159

TEACHING GUIDE AND RESOURCES
- Making Personal Connections Organizer **p. 147**
- Problem and Solution Map **p. 149**
- Answer Key **pp. 126–127**

REAL WORLD WRITING JOURNAL pp. 146–149

ANTHOLOGY

Preteach

Activate Prior Knowledge Have a class discussion about the subject of in crowds and cliques at school. What do students think about them? Have students complete the web in the Real-Life Connection. Students will revisit answers after they read.

Build Background *Recently, USA Today surveyed more than 120,000 students in grades 6–12. One of the survey questions was, "Are there any cliques [in your school] that get picked on?" Sixty-seven percent of respondents said* yes.

Introduce Vocabulary

- Read aloud the words, definitions, and example sentences in the Word Bank.
- Choose one of the words and use it in a sentence on the board. Ask volunteers to come to the board and continue the idea in a sentence with another vocabulary word. Continue until all the words have been used.
- *Build Academic Vocabulary* Point out the academic vocabulary in the Word Bank: *consider, distortion, individual, manipulate.* Ask volunteers to use each word in a sentence related to a school subject.

Teach

Focus on the Big Question Ask the Article BQ, *How do people persuade one another to exclude someone from their group?* Students will answer this question after reading.

- *Connect to the Unit Big Question* Write the Unit and Article BQs on the board. Discuss students' experiences with cliques. Encourage students to discuss the different perspectives of people inside and outside of cliques.

Preread the Article Model how to activate prior knowledge:

> **THINK ALOUD** *In my high school, there were jocks, preps, and nerds. I do remember that when some jocks made fun of me I felt bad.*

Have students begin to fill in the Making Personal Connections Organizer.

Conduct a Guided Reading Read the article to students as they follow along. Pause after each section to monitor students' comprehension.

- Have students create sticky notes with √, –, +, and ? marks.
- Explain that a checkmark denotes information that students already know; a minus sign is information that is different from what students thought; a question mark is information students do not understand; and a plus sign is new information.

As students read, have them attach the appropriate sticky note to sections of the text.

Reflect on the Article After reading the article, review ideas introduced before or during reading.

- Have students add words to their webs.
- As a class, discuss students' sticky notes. Answer any questions.
- Have students complete the Making Personal Connections Organizer.

Practice and Apply

Discuss the Questions Gauge students' comprehension and help them develop critical reading skills (Answer Key, pp. 126–127).

Connect to the Big Question

- Have students complete the following sentence frame: *When I was in middle school, I thought cliques were _____, but now I think they are _____.*
- Call on volunteers to answer the BQ.

Assess

Have students write a description of a *fictional* unhealthful clique and its leader. Tell them to include details about what the clique thinks is important and what the members have in common. Tell them to also include some psychological information about the clique leader based on what they have learned from the article.

Reach All Learners

Build Fluency Choose a section from the article. Read it aloud as students follow along silently. Emphasize the flow of the phrases. Tell students that part of reading fluently is to read phrases with expression rather than to read word for word.

- Direct a student to read the first sentence. Help the student approach reading the text as a series of phrases rather than separate words.
- Have the next student read the next sentence. Repeat the process with the entire group.

Use Small Groups Engage students with a small group activity to answer the second Use Clues question.

- Divide the class into small groups and give each student a Problem and Solution Map.
- Have each group use the organizer to answer the second Use Clues question.
- Invite groups to present their solutions to the class.

Assist Students Having Difficulty If students struggle to understand longer sentences, teach them how to turn long compound sentences into shorter, more understandable chunks.

- Point out a compound sentence in the selection. Read it aloud as two sentences. Ask students if they can understand the two sentences. Then read the compound sentence as one sentence. Ask students if they understand the whole sentence.
- Have students find a different compound sentence. Have them repeat the process.

WRITING JOURNAL

Extend

Write About It Students will plan and write an advice column about cliques for a middle school newspaper.

- Read and discuss the Writing Prompt (Journal, p. 146). Review the Writing Rubric. Encourage students to add more points to the rubric to guide their work.
- Model how to use the organizer.
- Students should use the Check It and Fix It section and the Writing Checklist to revise and evaluate their work.

Use a Think Aloud to model how to prewrite:

> **THINK ALOUD** *I will have to remember my audience as I write the advice column. My audience is eighth graders, so I want to make sure that I use words that they will understand. I also want my writing to be interesting and persuasive. I will use some slang to let readers know that I understand them. However, I will not use too much slang because not all the kids will know what it means. I will have to be careful about that.*

Vocabulary Workshop Students extend their thinking about Word Bank words.

- Students can work in pairs or small groups on the Define It organizer (Journal, p. 148).
- Have students add words to the Your Choice box and their personal word bank.
- Use the Show You Know exercise to assess students' understanding.

Teaching Tip If students are having difficulty figuring out synonyms for the Define It exercise, remind them to look at the definitions for clues. For example, the definition of *distortion* includes the words "twisting the truth." The opposite of truth is lie, so the synonym for *distortion* could be *lie*.

UNIT 5

The *Titanic* Tragedy

PROGRAM RESOURCES

ANTHOLOGY pp. 160–163

TEACHING GUIDE AND RESOURCES
- Venn Diagram **p. 154**
- Series of Events Map **p. 150**
- Answer Key **p. 127**

REAL WORLD WRITING JOURNAL pp. 150–153

ANTHOLOGY

Preteach

Activate Prior Knowledge Have students copy and complete the chart in the Real-Life Connection. Students will revisit answers after they read.

Build Background *In 1985, scientists found the wreckage of the* Titanic. *Studies from the wreckage showed that the ship was made of a steel that became brittle in the freezing North Atlantic waters. When the ship scraped the iceberg, the steel easily cracked.*

Introduce Vocabulary

- Write the definitions of the vocabulary words on the board. Read the words aloud.
- Have students tell you which definition on the board matches the word you just read.
- *Build Academic Vocabulary* The academic vocabulary words for this lesson are *anticipate, constant, interpretation,* and *presume.* Pass out copies of the Venn Diagram, and ask students to think of ways they might use the words in a school subject and in their own lives.

Teach

Focus on the Big Question Ask the Article BQ, *Can overconfidence lead to disaster?* Students will answer this question after reading.

- *Connect to the Unit Big Question* Have students write down both the Unit and Article BQs. Ask students to work with a partner to explain how the Article BQ is related to experience and perception.

Preread the Article Before students read, have them preview the illustration, title, and subheads. Have students write a prediction about the article. Ask them which elements of the article prompted the prediction.

Conduct a Guided Reading Read the article to students as they follow along. Pause after each section to monitor students' comprehension.

- Distribute a Web Map to students and have them write *Titanic Sinks* in the center oval.
- As you read, stop whenever the article points out a possible cause for the disaster and have students write that cause on the web.

Reflect on the Article After reading the article, review ideas introduced before or during reading.

- Have students review their answers to the Real-Life Connection. What would they change after reading the article? Ask students why.
- Ask students whether their predictions were accurate. Why or why not?
- Have students look over the word web and rate the causes from least to most likely.

Practice and Apply

Discuss the Questions Gauge students' comprehension and help them develop critical reading skills (Answer Key, p. 127).

Connect to the Big Question Draw a large T-Chart on the board to help students answer the BQ.

- Label the columns *Overconfident* and *Unprepared.*
- Discuss examples from the article that illustrate overconfidence. List them on the board. Repeat for *Unprepared.*
- Have students answer the Article BQ.
- Encourage volunteers to share their answers.

Assess

Have students write a short summary about what happened during the *Titanic* disaster.

Reach All Learners

Build Fluency Choose a section from the article for a paired reading.

- Pair students and have them read silently.
- Direct one student to read aloud while the other follows along making notes.
- The listener provides suggestions and feedback. Students then reverse roles.

Use Small Groups Engage students with a write-around activity to answer the last Use Clues question.

- Divide the class into groups of three or four. Have each student begin with a piece of paper with the question written across the top of the page.
- Have one student from each group write a response for one minute and then pass the paper to the right. The one-minute writing begins again, with a second student adding to the first student's ideas.
- Continue until all group members have written. Share responses in a class discussion.

Assist Students Having Difficulty If students have difficulty understanding what happened to the *Titanic,* help them fill out a Series of Events Map.

- Allow time after reading the article to fill out the organizer with the class.
- Go through the article and point out the different events in the order in which they occurred.

WRITING JOURNAL

Extend

Write About It Students will plan and write a list of ship's safety rules for crew members.

- Read and discuss the Writing Prompt (Journal, p. 150). Review the Writing Rubric. Encourage students to add more points to the rubric to guide their work.
- Model how to use the organizer.
- Students should use the Check It and Fix It section and the Writing Checklist to revise and evaluate their work.

Teaching Tip Before students show their work to a classmate, have them read it, slowly and carefully, aloud to themselves. Remind students that this can help them find missing words, run-on sentences, and sentence fragments.

Vocabulary Workshop Students extend their thinking about Word Bank words.

- Students can work in pairs or small groups on the Define It organizer (Journal, p. 152).
- Have students add words to the Your Choice box and their personal word bank.
- Use the Show You Know exercise to assess students' understanding.

Use a Think Aloud to help students with the Define It exercise:

> **THINK ALOUD** *The first word I am looking at is* anticipate. *How can I connect that to* constant? *Well, something that is constant always happens. Is there anything that I anticipate that always happens? Yes! I always anticipate that I will get great presents for my birthday, so that is a constant event in my life.*

UNIT 5 WRAP UP

 ## To what extent does experience determine what we perceive?

Introduce the Unit Project

Write-Around Students will participate in a write-around. Then they will summarize and present an answer to the Unit Big Question: *To what extent does experience determine what we perceive?*

- Read through the steps of the assignment with students.
- Point out the rubric so that students will know their goals for the assignment. Add other rubric points with students to guide their work.
- Allow time for students to practice and present their work. Encourage listeners to offer their feedback and advice on the presentation.

Model Use a Think Aloud to model how to give and receive feedback:

> **THINK ALOUD** *Sometimes, I dislike hearing my work criticized. When someone gives me feedback about my work, I have to remind myself to sit quietly and listen. I have to think about what people have said before I respond. When I give another person feedback, I mention at least one thing I like or am impressed by before I talk about anything that needs improvement.*

Teaching Tip Remind students that if their opinions differ they can present *all* the opinions but must come up with a unifying statement to introduce them. Help students brainstorm different statements, such as "Opinions about the effect of experience on a person's perspective may vary."

Conclude the Unit

Review Unit Objectives Return to the unit objectives and ask students to evaluate how well they mastered each one on a scale of 1 to 5, with 1 being low and 5 being high. Discuss how lower scores could be improved.

Reflect on the Learning Examine the bulletin board with students. Ask them to reflect on what they have learned. They can write or discuss with the class or in small groups. Ask questions such as these:

- *What was the most interesting article you read? What did you like about it?*
- *How did your ideas about experience and perspective change?*
- *Which topic would you like to know more about?*
- *How did the writing assignments and the write-around help you form your ideas about experience and perspective?*
- *What are other examples of two people who share one experience but might have completely different perspectives? What is one example where experience can change your perspective of an event or an issue?*

UNIT 5

Word Bank Quiz

WORD LIST A			
anticipate	constant	identity	perspective
appropriate	discipline	interpretation	presume
consider	expectations	knowledge	universal

Ten of the unit Word Bank words are defined in parentheses in the article below. As you read the article, use Word List A, above, to figure out which word best fits each definition. Write the word on the line provided. (You will not use every word on the list.) Then go on to the next page of the quiz.

Two Friends

When I was younger, I read a book about two best friends, Mira and Gabrielle. The friendship between the two girls was **(1. always there)** _____, though they came from very different kinds of families, each with a unique **(2. viewpoint)** _____ of the world. Because of this, the girls could see the same event, yet have a completely different **(3. understanding or meaning)** _____ of its significance.

Gabrielle grew up in a strict but loving home. She became a person who has high **(4. beliefs about what something will be like)** _____ of others, but who also is kind enough to **(5. believe without getting proof)** _____ that most people are good at heart. She did not **(6. expect)** _____ that people would treat her badly, and most people did not. She had a lot of **(7. ability to control her behavior)** _____ and never failed to **(8. think carefully about)** _____ her words before speaking, so she always had something **(9. right or fitting for a situation)** _____ to say to others. She used her **(10. ideas that are learned)** _____ about life to make the world better.

UNIT 5 Word Bank Quiz

WORD LIST B			
appropriate	distortion	individual	presume
background	identity	manipulate	stereotype
bias	impression	perspective	universal

Ten more Word Bank words are defined in parentheses in the rest of the article, below. As you read the article, use Word List B, above, to figure out which word best fits each definition. Write the word on the line provided. (You will not use every word on the list.)

Mira grew up in a rich but sometimes snobbish family. Their disdain for others was almost **(11. toward everyone in the world)** _____. The family had an effect on Mira's sense of **(12. set of characteristics that make a person unique)** _____. She became the kind of **(13. person separate from others)** _____ who could **(14. manage or control unfairly)** _____ any situation to suit her needs. However, she drew the line at outright lying. She tried not to tell other people a **(15. twisting of the truth to give a false idea)** _____ of the truth, and most of the time she succeeded.

Then, in high school, Mira started to choose her friends based on their **(16. education and other experiences)** _____. When Gabrielle pointed out the **(17. like or dislike that prevents her from being fair)** _____, they had a huge confrontation. Mira realized she had started to **(18. think that all who belong to a particular group have the same characteristics)** _____ other people. She realized that a first **(19. quick general idea of someone)** _____ might not be accurate. Gabrielle's friendship changed Mira's **(20. viewpoint)** _____ and behavior.

UNIT 6

 # Can anyone be a hero?

Unit Overview

The articles in this unit explore different types of heroes. Students will read and decide for themselves whether people like scientists, Native American children, female athletes, firefighters, and sport entertainment stars are heroes. Students will decide what makes someone a hero and what kind of qualities are heroic.

Launch the Unit

Connect to the Big Question Read the introduction with students and examine the illustration. Ask questions such as these:

- *What qualities do you think a person needs to have in order to be called a hero?*
- *Describe what you see in the illustration.*
- *Do you think the illustration shows a heroic act? Why or why not?*
- *Do you think society would view this person as a hero?*
- *Think of someone you consider a hero. What makes this person heroic?*

Use the prompt on the page as the basis for journal writing or for small group or whole class discussion. Students can share their ideas with partners or in small groups.

Anchor Students' Thinking Start a bulletin board on which you post the Big Question. Throughout the unit, students can add to the bulletin board. Use ideas such as the following:

- Ask students whether the people in each article are heroes and why.
- Post the sentence starter *A hero is someone who . . .* and have students add definitions after they read each article.
- Create a three-column chart titled *Words About Heroes* and label the columns *Nouns, Verbs, Adjectives.* Have students add words.
- Place exemplary writing from students' writing journal assignments on the bulletin board.
- Encourage students to post stories of heroes or heroism from newspapers, magazines, and the Internet and to connect heroes in the news with heroes in the articles.

Unit Objectives

Share these objectives with students. As you read the articles in this unit, you will:

- Evaluate whether the people described in the articles are or are not heroes.
- Determine an answer to the Big Question: *Can anyone be a hero?* Explain your answers using details from the articles and from your own experiences.
- Use content and academic vocabulary to talk and write about heroes.
- Poll the class on their answers to the Big Question, summarize their responses, and present the findings to the class.

UNIT 6

Science's Double-Edged Swords

PROGRAM RESOURCES

ANTHOLOGY pp. 168–171

TEACHING GUIDE AND RESOURCES
- Word Pyramid **p. 157**
- T-Chart **p. 151**
- Answer Key **p. 128**

REAL WORLD WRITING JOURNAL pp. 156–159

ANTHOLOGY

Preteach

Activate Prior Knowledge Take a poll of students' responses to the Real-Life Connection statements. Students will revisit answers after they read.

Build Background *Artificial intelligence, or AI, refers to a computer's ability to think intelligently, like a human being. In many works of science fiction, computers become smarter than their human creators and try to harm humankind. In reality, the uses of AI are limited. They include programs that play chess; software that monitors credit card purchases for fraud; and speech recognition software.*

Introduce Vocabulary

- Read aloud the sentences from the article in which boldface vocabulary words appear. Discuss what each word means in context.
- Have students write sentences using each word but leaving a blank in place of the word. Have student pairs exchange sentences and try to complete the sentences correctly.
- *Build Academic Vocabulary* The academic vocabulary words for this lesson are *conceive* and *responsibility*. Pass out copies of the Word Pyramid and have students complete one for each word.

Teach

Focus on the Big Question Ask the Article BQ, *How can a work of scientific genius be positive and negative?* Students will answer this question after reading.

- *Connect to the Unit Big Question* Write the Unit and Article BQs on the board. Ask students how a scientific genius might also be a hero.

Preread the Article Have students set a purpose for reading the article.

- Ask students to read the Wrap It Up questions. Explain that knowing the questions can help students focus on finding important ideas.

Conduct a Guided Reading Read the article to students as they follow along. Pause after each section to monitor students' comprehension.

- Tell students to summarize each section. Use a Think Aloud to model how:

> **THINK ALOUD** *I need to think about the most important ideas and express them in my own words. The first section describes a pro and a con of the atomic bomb. It also discusses robots. I can summarize this section like this:* In science, things like the atomic bomb and robots can be both successful and dangerous.

Reflect on the Article After reading the article, review ideas introduced before or during reading.

- Ask students to respond to the Real-Life Connection statements again. What have students learned about artificial intelligence?
- Ask students whether they found answers to the Wrap It Up questions as they read.

Practice and Apply

Discuss the Questions Gauge students' comprehension and help them develop critical reading skills (Answer Key, p. 128).

Connect to the Big Question Have students use the T-Chart to answer the BQ.

- Call for volunteers to identify a technological development and explain how it can be both positive and negative. Have them record answers in the chart.

Assess

Have students identify each of the following and write a sentence about whether each might think technological developments are mostly positive or mostly negative:

- J. Robert Oppenheimer
- Leo Szilard
- Harry S. Truman
- Kansei

Reach All Learners

Build Fluency Choose a section from the article for students to perform a radio read.

- Read the section with expression, as if you are delivering a radio or TV news report.
- Have students practice the section silently. Then call for volunteers to read it aloud.
- Assist students with the pronunciations of difficult names or terms.

Use Small Groups Engage students with a debate of the positive and negative aspects of technological developments.

- Divide the class into groups of three or four.
- Assign half the groups to argue in favor of further development of robots and half the groups to argue against.
- Give groups time to prepare their arguments.
- Ask "pro groups" to debate "con groups."

Assist Students Having Difficulty Help students interpret the pie chart and use the information to draw conclusions.

- Explain that students need to read the title of the graph in order to understand the information.
- Ask students how most people answered. Ask which answer received the fewest responses.
- Have students draw conclusions about the results shown in the graph.

WRITING JOURNAL

Extend

Write About It Students will plan and write a paragraph about the benefits and dangers of a technological development.

- Read and discuss the Writing Prompt (Journal, p. 156). Review the Writing Rubric. Encourage students to add more points to the rubric to guide their work.
- Model how to use the organizer.
- Students should use the Check It and Fix It section and the Writing Checklist to revise and evaluate their work.

Use a Think Aloud to model how to revise:

> **THINK ALOUD** *I want to be sure that I included both benefits and dangers of my scientific development and that I put them in the correct place in the paragraph. As I reread my paragraph, I see something that I listed as a benefit is actually a danger, so I need to move it. I am also going to add the transition words "Another benefit is" to make my writing easier to understand.*

Vocabulary Workshop Students extend their thinking about Word Bank words.

- Students can work in pairs or small groups on the Define It organizer (Journal, p. 158).
- Have students add words to the Your Choice box and their personal word bank.
- Use the Show You Know exercise to assess students' understanding.

Teaching Tip Create a class version of the Word Play table and see how many different responses students can generate for each word. After students have provided their responses, review how to use a thesaurus to find similar words. Point out that students can often find a word in a listing and then look up that word in the thesaurus to find even more similar words.

Buffalo Battles

PROGRAM RESOURCES

ANTHOLOGY pp. 172–175

TEACHING GUIDE AND RESOURCES
- Series of Events Map **p. 150**
- Answer Key **p. 128**

REAL WORLD WRITING JOURNAL pp. 160–163

ANTHOLOGY

Preteach

Activate Prior Knowledge Have students preview the title and subheadings and then complete the Real-Life Connection activity. Students will revisit answers after they read.

Build Background *Bison, or the American plains buffalo, provided food, clothing, and shelter for Native Americans who lived on the plains. The destruction of these animals had an enormous effect on the lives of these Native Americans. Today, there are about 200,000 bison on reserves and on ranches, where they are raised for their lean meat.*

Introduce Vocabulary

- Read aloud the Word Bank words, definitions, and example sentences.
- Write the words and definitions in random order on the board. Ask students to draw a line between each word and its definition. Then have students write a sentence for each.
- *Build Academic Vocabulary* The academic vocabulary words for this lesson are *character, integrity,* and *resolute.* Have students practice using the words by listing examples of ways they might use the words in their classes. For example, what is a character in a story? How is that meaning similar to and different from the meaning of *character* in social studies, where students might discuss the character of the American people?

Teach

Focus on the Big Question Ask the Article BQ, *Does being a hero depend on what side you take on an issue?* Students will answer this question after reading.

- *Connect to the Unit Big Question* Ask students to discuss whether they think a person whose actions they disagree with could be a hero.

Preread the Article Before students read, model how to preview and predict:

> **THINK ALOUD** *To find out what this article is about, I am going to look at the title, subheadings, photograph, and pullout quotation. The title "Buffalo Battles" makes me think this article is about conflict with these animals. I will look at the other features to find other clues.*

Model how to preview the other features. Ask students to write a prediction about the article.

Conduct a Guided Reading Read the article to students as they follow along. Pause after each section to monitor students' comprehension.

- Ask students to identify the main idea of each section.
- Ask volunteers to identify important supporting details for each main idea.

Reflect on the Article After reading the article, review ideas introduced before or during reading.

- Have students revisit their Real-Life Connection charts and adjust their notes.
- Ask students whether their predictions were accurate. Have them explain why or why not.

Practice and Apply

Discuss the Questions Gauge students' comprehension and help them develop critical reading skills (Answer Key, p. 128).

Connect to the Big Question Use free writing and class discussion to have students answer the BQ.

- Ask students to identify the differing views on the issue of wild bison and ranchers.
- Have students write for one minute about how they feel about people who have a different view from their own. Have students use responses to answer the BQ.

Assess

Have students complete the Series of Events Map to identify important events in the history of bison and the conflict with ranchers.

Reach All Learners

Build Fluency Choose a section from the article for a Paired Reading.

- Pair students and have them read silently.
- Direct one student to read aloud while the other follows along making notes.
- The listener provides suggestions and feedback. Students then reverse roles.

Use Small Groups Have students work in groups of three or four to answer the second Use Clues question (*How would you solve the conflict between supporters of wild bison and cattle ranchers?*).

- Have groups brainstorm possible answers.
- Tell groups to take notes and provide as much detail as possible showing how the proposal resolves the conflict.
- Have groups share their ideas with the class.

Assist Students Having Difficulty If students struggle to determine the importance of details and information, provide them with sticky notes to take notes on the article.

- Have students write what they think are important details on the notes as they read.
- Then ask students to review their notes, asking *Is this information important or just interesting?* Have students remove the notes next to details that are interesting but not important.
- Discuss which details are important and have students explain why the detail is significant.

WRITING JOURNAL

Extend

Write About It Students will plan and write a letter of opinion to the National Park Service.

- Read and discuss the Writing Prompt (Journal, p. 160). Review the Writing Rubric. Encourage students to add more points to the rubric to guide their work.
- Model how to use the organizer.
- Students should use the Check It and Fix It section and the Writing Checklist to revise and evaluate their work.

Use a Think Aloud to model how to preview:

> **THINK ALOUD** *To complete the organizer, I need to reread the article and find facts that support my viewpoint. The article said that in 1840 there were 60 million bison, but that only 23 survived by 1900. I know that these are facts, not opinions. I can put these facts in one of the circles on the organizer. These help support the main idea about protecting bison.*

Vocabulary Workshop Students extend their thinking about Word Bank words.

- Students can work in pairs or small groups on the Define It organizer (Journal, p. 162).
- Have students add words to the Your Choice box and their personal word bank.
- Use the Show You Know exercise to assess students' understanding.

Teaching Tip Have students take the dialogues they wrote for Show You Know and rewrite the conversations using quotation marks and dialogue tags, such as *she said*. Use the Grammar Handbook to review the rules for punctuating quotations (Journal, p. 227). Have students read their new conversations aloud.

The Youngest Heroes

PROGRAM RESOURCES

ANTHOLOGY pp. 176–179

TEACHING GUIDE AND RESOURCES
• Guess It and Check It Chart **p. 143**
• T-Chart **p. 151**
• Answer Key **pp. 128–129**
REAL WORLD WRITING JOURNAL pp. 164–167

ANTHOLOGY

Preteach

Activate Prior Knowledge Have students complete the knowledge rating in the Real-Life Connection. Students will revisit answers after they read.

Build Background *In the 1800s, conflict intensified between Native Americans and white settlers. The Cherokee were forcibly relocated from Georgia to Oklahoma in the 1830s. The conflicts continued in the 1860s and 1870s as settlers moved west and railroads were built. The U.S. government took Native American lands and forced many Native Americans onto reservations.*

Introduce Vocabulary

• Distribute copies of the Guess It and Check It Chart. Have students write the Word Bank words in the first column. Tell them to find the words in the article, look for context clues, guess the meaning, and then check the meanings against those in the Word Bank.
• Model how to complete the chart:

> **THINK ALOUD** *I see the word* consult *on page 178. First, I will read the sentence and look for context clues. I can tell that* consult *is a verb because it describes an action. I think it means "to ask an expert." I will check my guess.*

• *Build Academic Vocabulary* Ask students how they might use the academic vocabulary words for this lesson—*consult* and *irony*—in their classes. Write responses on the board.

Teach

Focus on the Big Question Ask the Article BQ, *How do oral histories preserve heroes' stories?* Students will answer this question after reading.

• *Connect to the Unit Big Question* Ask students to recall stories that family members have told about family history. Are there heroes in these stories?

Preread the Article Before students read, have them preview the article by skimming.
• Explain to students that they can quickly read, or skim, the article to get an idea of what they are going to read about.
• Have students skim the title, subheadings, caption, and first sentences of each paragraph. Have students jot down questions they have about the article's content.

Conduct a Guided Reading Read the article to students as they follow along. Pause after each section to monitor students' comprehension.
• Ask five *W*'s and an *H* questions.
• Call on a volunteer to summarize the section.

Reflect on the Article After reading the article, review ideas introduced before or during reading.
• Have students revisit their knowledge ratings from the Real-Life Connection.
• Ask students whether they found answers to the questions they wrote while previewing.

Practice and Apply

Discuss the Questions Gauge students' comprehension and help them develop critical reading skills (Answer Key, pp. 128–129).

Connect to the Big Question Refocus students' attention on the Article BQ.
• Write the Article BQ on the board. As a class, discuss the question. Have students look for ideas in the article. Write ideas on the board.

Assess

Have students create a learning log for you to assess informally. Ask these questions:

- *What are three things you learned in class today?*
- *Which things were the most interesting to you?*
- *What do you still have questions about?*
- *How could you find answers?*

Reach All Learners

Build Fluency Choose a section from the article for an echo reading.

- Read the section aloud to students, modeling how to read with accuracy.
- Have volunteers read the same section aloud, focusing on accuracy.
- Tell students to repeat the process with a partner. The first partner reads a section aloud, focusing on accuracy, and the second partner echo reads.

Use Small Groups Use a small group discussion activity to engage students in active learning.

- Divide students into groups of three or four.
- Give students a T-Chart and have them label the columns *Oral History* and *Written History*.
- Have students discuss how oral and written histories differ.
- Have groups share their observations in a class discussion.

Assist Students Having Difficulty Encourage students to make connections to understand how the children in the article might be described as heroic.

- Ask students to list words that they would use to describe heroes.
- Have students make connections between the words and the children described in the article. Which words, if any, apply?

WRITING JOURNAL

Extend

Write About It Students will interview a family member and write an oral history.

- Read and discuss the Writing Prompt (Journal, p. 164). Review the Writing Rubric. Encourage students to add more points to the rubric to guide their work.
- Model how to use the organizer.
- Students should use the Check It and Fix It section and the Writing Checklist to revise and evaluate their work.

Teaching Tip Explain to students that good interviewers listen carefully and ask open-ended questions. Explain that these are questions that cannot be answered with a simple *yes* or *no*. Have students practice using open-ended questions to interview each other.

Vocabulary Workshop Students extend their thinking about Word Bank words.

- Students can work in pairs or small groups on the Define It organizer (Journal, p. 166).
- Have students add words to the Your Choice box and their personal word bank.

Use a Think Aloud to model how to select words:

> **THINK ALOUD** *One word I want to add to the Your Choice and my personal word bank is the word reservations. I have seen this word used different ways. For example, people make dinner reservations at restaurants. Here, though, the word is used differently, to describe the lands where Native Americans lived. I will add it to my word bank so that I use it correctly.*

- Use the Show You Know exercise to assess students' understanding.

Equality on the Playing Field

PROGRAM RESOURCES

ANTHOLOGY pp. 180–183

TEACHING GUIDE AND RESOURCES
- K-W-L Chart **p. 145**
- Vocabulary Squares **p. 155**
- Answer Key **p. 129**

REAL WORLD WRITING JOURNAL pp. 168–171

ANTHOLOGY

Preteach

Activate Prior Knowledge Take a poll of students' responses to the Real-Life Connection scenario. Students will revisit answers after they read.

Build Background *In order to provide equal sports opportunities after Title IX, some schools cut funding to men's sports programs to create balance. Critics argue that males may enjoy sports more than females and forcing schools to provide equal opportunities does not recognize gender differences.*

Introduce Vocabulary

- Read aloud the Word Bank words and their definitions.
- Challenge students to see how many words they can use correctly in a single sentence.
- *Build Academic Vocabulary* All the Word Bank words except *selflessness* are academic vocabulary words. Ask students to use each word in a sentence about a school subject.

Teach

Focus on the Big Question Ask the Article BQ, *Should men and women compete on the same sports teams?* Students will answer this question after reading.

- *Connect to the Unit Big Question* Survey students about someone whom they consider a sports hero. Compare the number of male and female athletes that students identify. Use students' responses to link the Article and Unit BQs.

Preread the Article Before students read, have them preview the introductory paragraph and title.

- Distribute copies of the K-W-L Chart.
- Students should fill out the first column with what they know about sports equality and the second column with what they want to learn about gender and sports.

Conduct a Guided Reading Read the article to students as they follow along. Pause after each section to monitor students' comprehension.

- Use a Think Aloud to model how to complete the K-W-L charts:

> **THINK ALOUD** *In the third column of the chart, I will write what I learned about gender equality in sports. The first section of the article describes some great male basketball players but also describes the rise in women's pro sports. I will note that under* What I Learned.

Reflect on the Article After reading the article, review ideas introduced before or during reading.

- Have students revisit the Real-Life Connection. Have their views changed?
- Review the completed K-W-L charts.

Practice and Apply

Discuss the Questions Gauge students' comprehension and help them develop critical reading skills (Answer Key, p. 129).

Connect to the Big Question Have students answer the BQ.

- Write this sentence frame on the board: *Athletes should compete against (people of the same sex, people of the opposite sex, people of either sex) because* and have student volunteers complete it.

Assess

Have students create a learning log for you to review. Students should answer these questions:

- *What did you learn in class today?*
- *What did you find interesting?*
- *What questions do you still have?*
- *What was the point of today's lesson?*

Reach All Learners

Build Fluency Choose sections from the article for a radio read.

- Model how to read a section with expression, as a radio announcer might do.
- Have students practice reading the section silently, with expression.
- Have students read their section aloud to the class.

Use Small Groups Engage students with a writing activity.

- Divide the class into groups of three or four.
- Have each group select a female athlete and write a press release that lists her accomplishments.
- Groups can use material in the article and supplement it with what they know.
- Have groups read their press releases aloud.

Assist Students Having Difficulty If students struggle with comprehension, have them ask questions as they read.

- Explain that asking questions will help them find important ideas as they read.
- Have students write down questions before, during, and after reading.
- Ask students to answer their questions. Have students share with the class any questions they wrote for which they could not find an answer.

WRITING JOURNAL

Extend

Write About It Students will plan and write a blog entry about female athletes.

- Read and discuss the Writing Prompt (Journal, p. 168). Review the Writing Rubric. Encourage students to add more points to the rubric to guide their work.
- Model how to use the organizer.
- Students should use the Check It and Fix It section and the Writing Checklist to revise and evaluate their work.

Use a Think Aloud to model how to use the Writing Rubric:

> **THINK ALOUD** *I need to make sure my blog entry meets the requirements in the Checklist. The first point is to make sure I gave an opinion. I also supported it with ideas from the article. I do not think I included a Word Bank word, though. I need to go back and revise my blog to include one. Then I will check the grammar, usage, and mechanics of my entry.*

Vocabulary Workshop Students extend their thinking about Word Bank words.

- Students can work in pairs or small groups on the Define It organizer (Journal, p. 170).
- Have students add words to the Your Choice box and their personal word bank.
- Use the Show You Know exercise to assess students' understanding.

Teaching Tip Help students complete the All in the Family exercise. Then distribute copies of the Vocabulary Squares and help students complete a square for each All in the Family word.

UNIT 6

Our Hero!

PROGRAM RESOURCES

ANTHOLOGY pp. 184–187

TEACHING GUIDE AND RESOURCES
- Comic Strip Organizer **p. 141**
- Answer Key **p. 129**

REAL WORLD WRITING JOURNAL pp. 172–175

ANTHOLOGY

Preteach

Activate Prior Knowledge Have students complete the Real-Life Connection. Students will revisit answers after they read.

Build Background *Comic books trace their origin in the United States to comic strips that appeared in Sunday newspapers in the late 1800s. Early comic strips featured characters such as Tarzan and Dick Tracy. The first comic book, published in 1933, consisted of reprints of newspaper funnies. Called "Funnies on Parade," it proved there was a market for comics.*

Introduce Vocabulary

- Read aloud the sentences from the article in which boldface vocabulary words appear. Discuss how to use clues to figure out meanings.
- Have students practice the vocabulary words in a new context. Work with students to create new sentences for each term.
- *Build Academic Vocabulary* All the Word Bank words except *selflessness* are academic vocabulary. Ask the following questions: *What are some* inherent *human traits? Why should a presidential candidate have* integrity? *How might an athlete show that she is* resolute?

Teach

Focus on the Big Question Ask the Article BQ, *How do the powers of superheroes reflect society's concerns?* Students will answer this question after reading.

- *Connect to the Unit Big Question* Write the Unit and Article BQs on the board. Have students list the characteristics of a hero and a superhero and compare their lists.

Preread the Article Before students read, model hot to preview and predict:

> **THINK ALOUD** *I can read the first and last paragraphs to get an idea of what the article is about. The first paragraph often introduces the topic, and the last paragraph often summarizes the issues. The first paragraph asks who can stop Adolf Hitler. The last paragraph says new types of superheroes might reflect new technology. I think the article is going to be about how people who create superheroes are influenced by real-world events.*

Read aloud the subheadings. Have students make a prediction about the article.

Conduct a Guided Reading Read the article to students as they follow along. Pause after each section to monitor students' comprehension.

- Ask literal comprehension questions about each section, such as *What are the important events? Who are the superheroes?*
- Follow up with inferential questions, such as *How does this section relate to the title?*

Reflect on the Article After reading the article, review ideas introduced before or during reading.

- Review the Real-Life Connection. Do the superheroes' abilities reflect the concerns of today's society? Why or why not?
- Ask students if their predictions were accurate.

Practice and Apply

Discuss the Questions Gauge students' comprehension and help them develop critical reading skills (Answer Key, p. 129).

Connect to the Big Question Have students work in pairs to answer the question.

- Students should list superheroes, as well as the heroes' powers, described in the article and use the lists to answer the Article BQ.

Assess

Have students create a comic strip about a new superhero to show their understanding of the article.

- Give each student a copy of the Comic Strip Organizer.
- Tell students to use information from the article to think about how their superhero can be created, what powers he or she will have, and what types of situations he or she will face.
- Have students use the words and pictures in their comics.

Reach All Learners

Build Fluency Choose a section from the article for a paired reading.

- Pair students and have them read silently.
- Direct one student to read aloud while the other follows along making notes.
- The listener provides suggestions and feedback. Students then reverse roles.

Use Small Groups Engage students with a write-around activity to answer the second Use Clues question.

- Divide the class into groups of three or four. Have one member of each group write the question across the top of a piece of paper.
- The group member should then write a response for one minute and then pass the paper to the right. The one-minute writing begins again, as a new member of each group adds to the previous response.
- Continue until all group members have written on the group's paper. Share ideas in a class discussion.

Assist Students Having Difficulty If students struggle to make inferences, help them use the information in the table in the article.

- Explain that information in a table often supplements that given in the article. Ask students what new information the table provides.
- Have students examine the last column, *Source*. Ask what these sources have in common and what they tell us about the superheroes.

WRITING JOURNAL

Extend

Write About It Students will plan and write a description of a superhero.

- Read and discuss the Writing Prompt (Journal, p. 172). Review the Writing Rubric. Encourage students to add more points to the rubric to guide their work.
- Model how to use the organizer.
- Students should use the Check It and Fix It section and the Writing Checklist to revise and evaluate their work.

Teaching Tip Remind students that their purpose is to create a superhero for kids today. Discuss what kinds of qualities might be most important and relevant to today's kids. List ideas on the board.

Vocabulary Workshop Students extend their thinking about Word Bank words.

- Students can work in pairs or small groups on the Define It organizer (Journal, p. 174).

Use a Think Aloud to model how to complete the organizer:

> **THINK ALOUD** *I need to think about how two of these words are related. I know the word* attributes *can mean a person's qualities or characteristics. I also know that selflessness is a quality some people have, so I can link these two words. I will write the connection on the bottom line.*

- Have students add words to the Your Choice box and their personal word bank.
- Use the Show You Know exercise to assess students' understanding.

UNIT 6

Peacekeepers

PROGRAM RESOURCES

ANTHOLOGY pp. 188–191

TEACHING GUIDE AND RESOURCES
- Web Map **p. 156**
- Answer Key **pp. 129–130**

REAL WORLD WRITING JOURNAL pp. 176–179

ANTHOLOGY

Preteach

Activate Prior Knowledge Take a poll of students' responses to the Real-Life Connection. Students will revisit answers after they read.

Build Background *The United Nations headquarters are located in four main buildings in New York City. Countries appoint representatives to the UN, and these delegates meet in the General Assembly Hall.*

Introduce Vocabulary

- Ask students to think of synonyms for each Word Bank word. Have students substitute the synonyms in place of the boldface words in the example sentences.
- *Build Academic Vocabulary* Distribute a Web Map. Have students complete it for the academic vocabulary word *conduct* or *responsibility*. Use a Think Aloud to model:

> **THINK ALOUD** *The word* principles *goes in the center circle. I can think of several ways this word is used. In math, we talk about principles of geometry, so I will write that in one of the outer circles. In government, we talk about the principles we expect from political leaders.*

Teach

Focus on the Big Question Ask the Article BQ, *Does the United Nations uphold its original goals?* Students will answer this question after reading.

- *Connect to the Unit Big Question* Write the Unit and Article BQs on the board and discuss how an organization might be a hero.

Preread the Article Have students preview the article's title and subheadings and use them to predict what each section will be about.

- Ask students to read the subheadings and the first sentence of each section.
- Have students write a prediction about what each section of the article will discuss.

Conduct a Guided Reading Read the article to students as they follow along. Pause after each section to monitor students' comprehension.

- Have students make notes about the main ideas, concepts, and terms in each section.
- At the end of the article, ask students to synthesize their notes and write a main idea for the whole article.

Reflect on the Article After reading the article, review ideas introduced before or during reading.

- Retake the poll from the Real-Life Connection. Have answers changed?
- Ask students to compare their predictions about each section with the main ideas they wrote. Have them rate the accuracy of their predictions.

Practice and Apply

Discuss the Questions Gauge students' comprehension and help them develop critical reading skills (Answer Key, pp. 129–130).

Connect to the Big Question Have students write a response to the Article BQ.

- Have students complete the sentence frame *The original goals of the UN were to _____.*
- Then have students explain whether they think the UN upholds these goals.

Assess

Have students write self-assessments.

- Each student should write three multiple-choice and three short-answer test questions on a blank sheet of paper.
- Have students answer their own questions.
- Have each student write two to three sentences describing whether the test accurately shows his or her understanding of the article.

Reach All Learners

Build Fluency Choose a section from the article for a choral reading.

- Read the selection aloud slowly and clearly. Use as much expression as possible.
- Have students follow along silently.
- Reread the section aloud while students echo your reading. Provide feedback on student fluency and phrasing.

Use Small Groups Have groups plan a proposal about UN funding.

- Tell students they will plan a proposal to U.S. senators about whether the United States should increase the amount of money and materials it contributes to UN peacekeeping.
- Have groups discuss the topic and then take notes on their ideas.
- Ask groups to share their ideas.

Assist Students Having Difficulty If students struggle to identify main ideas in the article, have pairs work with a skeleton outline to take notes.

- Include the article title and subheads with space for notes.
- Have pairs work through the outline, recording main ideas and important details.
- Discuss completed outlines as a class.

WRITING JOURNAL

Extend

Write About It Students will plan and write an informational Web site about the UN.

- Read and discuss the Writing Prompt (Journal, p. 176). Review the Writing Rubric. Encourage students to add more points to the rubric to guide their work.
- Model how to use the organizer.
- Students should use the Check It and Fix It section and the Writing Checklist to revise and evaluate their work.

Use a Think Aloud to model drafting:

> **THINK ALOUD** *I need to make sure my first section of the Web site is factual, since my purpose is to give information. To do that, I have to make sure I do not use opinions. I also want to make sure I give information, but that I do not put so many numbers and statistics in my description that it will be hard to read.*

Vocabulary Workshop Students extend their thinking about Word Bank words.

- Students can work in pairs or small groups on the Define It organizer (Journal, p. 178).
- Have students add words to the Your Choice box and their personal word bank.
- Use the Show You Know exercise to assess students' understanding.

Teaching Tip Point out how words with the roots *duc* or *duct* often have prefixes and suffixes. Help students apply their knowledge of affixes to analyze the meaning of words like *introduction, induction, deduction,* and *reduce.* Allow students to use dictionaries for help.

Leaping into the Fire

PROGRAM RESOURCES

ANTHOLOGY pp. 192–195

TEACHING GUIDE AND RESOURCES
• Opinion and Reasons Organizer **p. 148**
• Word Pyramid **p. 157**
• Answer Key **p. 130**

REAL WORLD WRITING JOURNAL pp. 180–183

ANTHOLOGY

Preteach

Activate Prior Knowledge Have students preview the title and subheadings and complete the Real-Life Connection activity. Students will revisit answers after they read.

Build Background *Wildfires occur in most of our fifty states. They are most common in the West, where heat and drought make ideal fire conditions. Though lightning can start wildfires, four out of five are caused by humans, often from discarded cigarettes or campfires that were not correctly put out.*

Introduce Vocabulary

• Distribute copies of the Word Pyramid. Have students work in pairs to complete the organizer for each Word Bank word.
• *Build Academic Vocabulary* Ask students to rate how often they hear or use the academic vocabulary words for this lesson: *conduct, inherent,* and *devise. Students should use these ratings: often, sometimes,* or *never.* Then have students write a sentence showing how each word can be used in a class.

Teach

Focus on the Big Question Ask the Article BQ, *Can a person be trained to be a hero?* Students will answer this question after reading.

• *Connect to the Unit Big Question* Write the Unit and Article BQs on the board. Discuss with students how the Article BQ can help them answer the Unit BQ.

Preread the Article Before students read, use a Think Aloud to model how to preview and predict:

> **THINK ALOUD** *I know from previewing the title and subheadings that this article has something to do with firefighting. In the picture, I see a person parachuting into a burning forest. From the caption, I can tell that this person must be a smokejumper. I think the article is going to talk about how firefighters can be heroes.*

Model how to preview the chart.

Conduct a Guided Reading Read the article to students as they follow along. Pause after each section to monitor students' comprehension.

• Call on a volunteer to summarize each section.

Reflect on the Article After reading the article, review ideas introduced before or during reading.

• Have students revisit their charts from the Real-Life Connection.
• Ask students whether their predictions were accurate. Have them explain why or why not.

Practice and Apply

Discuss the Questions Gauge students' comprehension and help them develop critical reading skills (Answer Key, p. 130).

Connect to the Big Question Have students use the Opinion and Reasons Organizer to answer the BQ.

• Have students write the Article BQ on their organizers.
• Ask students whether they think people can be heroes when they do their jobs or whether heroes must act spontaneously.
• Have students complete their organizers.

Assess

Assess students informally by having them create an informative poster about wildfires. Have them include some of the following:

- A definition of a wildfire
- Dangers of wildfires
- Conditions that encourage wildfires
- Recent trends in wildfires or in their management

Reach All Learners

Build Fluency Choose a section from the article for a paired reading.

- Pair students and have them read silently.
- Direct one student to read aloud while the other follows along making notes.
- The listener provides suggestions and feedback. Students then reverse roles.

Use Small Groups Use a creative writing activity to engage students in active learning.

- Divide the class into groups of three or four. Have each group write a job description for a smokejumper.
- Explain that a job description usually describes the kind of work the person will do and the experience or background the person should have. Have students use information from the article to support their job descriptions.
- Compare groups' job descriptions as a class. Discuss which job sounds most appealing and why.

Assist Students Having Difficulty If students struggle to summarize the article, have them practice retelling information in their own words.

- Practice retelling one paragraph at a time. Have students read a paragraph and then close their books and tell you what the paragraph was about.
- Ask students to make notes as they go.
- Have students refer to their notes to summarize the entire article in three to four sentences.

WRITING JOURNAL

Extend

Write About It Students will plan and write a tribute to a hero.

- Read and discuss the Writing Prompt (Journal, p. 180). Review the Writing Rubric. Encourage students to add more points to the rubric to guide their work.
- Model how to use the organizer.
- Students should use the Check It and Fix It section and the Writing Checklist to revise and evaluate their work.

Use a Think Aloud to model how to revise:

> **THINK ALOUD** *Since my writing is a tribute, I want it to be descriptive and interesting. Instead of using verbs like* was *or* went, *I am going to use action verbs like* comforted *or* raced. *I am also going to change boring adjectives like* great *to something more descriptive, like* brilliant *or* talented.

Vocabulary Workshop Students extend their thinking about Word Bank words.

- Students can work in pairs or small groups on the Define It organizer (Journal, p. 182).
- Have students add words to the Your Choice box and their personal word bank.
- Use the Show You Know exercise to assess students' understanding.

Teaching Tip Compile a class list of the words students wrote for the Your Choice activity. Review different ways for students to learn new words, such as drawing pictures, identifying synonyms and antonyms, using the words in a sentence, or playing a word game.

UNIT 6

The Sport Entertainment Hero

PROGRAM RESOURCES

ANTHOLOGY pp. 196–199

TEACHING GUIDE AND RESOURCES
- Two-Column Journal **p. 153**
- Answer Key **p. 130**

REAL WORLD WRITING JOURNAL pp. 184–187

ANTHOLOGY

Preteach

Activate Prior Knowledge Have students complete the Real-Life Connection. Students will revisit answers after they read.

Build Background *Freestyle wrestling was a popular American sport in the 1800s. Several U.S. Presidents, including George Washington, Abraham Lincoln, and Theodore Roosevelt, wrestled. The goal of freestyle wrestling is to pin an opponent to the mat using a variety of grips or hand positions.*

Introduce Vocabulary

- Have students scan the article for sentences in which Word Bank words appear.
- Tell students to look for context clues about what each word means. Ask volunteers to explain what they think each word means. Then compare students' definitions to those in the Word Bank.
- *Build Academic Vocabulary* Write the academic vocabulary words *character* and the different ways the words can be used in school.

Teach

Focus on the Big Question Ask the Article BQ, *Can people look up to others who just pretend to be heroes?* Students will answer this question after reading.

- *Connect to the Unit Big Question* Have student pairs copy the Unit and Article BQs and circle similar words and ideas. Use a Think Aloud to model how:

> **THINK ALOUD** *Both questions have the word* hero *so I am circling that word. They both are also about being*

a hero or defining what a hero is. The questions are different, though, because the Unit question is general and the Article question is more specific.

Preread the Article Before students read, have them preview the article's features to make a prediction about the author's purpose.

- List purposes for writing, including to entertain, to persuade, and to inform.
- Have students predict the author's purpose for writing.

Conduct a Guided Reading Read the article to students as they follow along. Pause after each section to monitor students' comprehension.

- Give students a copy of the Two-Column Journal. Have them enter information for each section of the article.

Reflect on the Article After reading the article, review ideas introduced before or during reading.

- Have students update their knowledge ratings from the Real-Life Connection.
- Ask students the author's overall purpose for writing.

Practice and Apply

Discuss the Questions Gauge students' comprehension and help them develop critical reading skills (Answer Key, p. 130).

Connect to the Big Question Use a class discussion to answer the BQ.

- Survey students about their opinions.
- Create a two-column chart on the board with the headings *Yes* and *No*. Have students provide reasons for each position.

Assess

Informally assess students' comprehension with a quiz game.

- Have each student write one question about the article and answer it on a sheet of paper. Collect questions.
- Divide students into three or four teams. Students on each team take turns trying to answer a question you read aloud. Players should write their answers on a piece of paper and reveal them at the same time.
- The game ends when one team has scored ten correct answers.

Reach All Learners

Build Fluency Choose a section from the article for a radio read.

- Tell students that in sporting events, announcers often deliver their reports with drama and excitement. Model reading a section of the article as if you are a sports commentator. Point out your tone and phrasing.
- Have students radio read the section. Have them practice silently and then read aloud.

Use Small Groups Use a creative activity to engage students in active learning.

- Divide the class into groups of three or four and tell them they will create a WWE character.
- Tell students to use information from the article to develop their new character. They should include the costume, moves in the ring, and status (hero or villain).
- Have groups present their characters to the class.

Assist Students Having Difficulty If students struggle to comprehend the article, have them compare pro and amateur wrestling.

- Draw a large Venn diagram on the board and label the circles *Amateur Wrestling* and *Pro Wrestling (WWE)*.
- Have students add information to the diagram.
- Explain that students may need to infer some information not stated in the article.

WRITING JOURNAL

Extend

Write About It Students will plan and write a paragraph about a celebrity hero.

- Read and discuss the Writing Prompt (Journal, p. 184). Review the Writing Rubric. Encourage students to add more points to the rubric to guide their work.
- Model how to use the organizer.
- Students should use the Check It and Fix It section and the Writing Checklist to revise and evaluate their work.

Use a Think Aloud to model how to draft:

> **THINK ALOUD** *I want to be sure that I clearly state my opinion about the celebrity I have chosen. I need to make sure that all my reasons support my view and that I give specific examples to illustrate my point. I can use transitions like* first, next, *and* last *to show the different reasons I am listing.*

Vocabulary Workshop Students extend their thinking about Word Bank words.

- Students can work in pairs or small groups on the Define It organizer (Journal, p. 186).
- Have students add words to the Your Choice box and their personal word bank.
- Use the Show You Know exercise to assess students' understanding.

Teaching Tip Explain to students that there are different types of context clues they can use to figure out the meanings of unfamiliar words. Point out that it is often useful to read the sentences before and after the sentence in which an unfamiliar word appears. Tell students that it is helpful to look for synonyms, antonyms, and examples.

UNIT 6 WRAP UP

 ## Can anyone be a hero?

Introduce the Unit Project

Summary Students will survey their classmates, summarize their findings, and present to the class the answer to the Big Question: *Can anyone be a hero?*

- Read through the steps of the assignment with students.
- Point out the rubric so that students will know their goals for the assignment. Add other rubric points with students to guide their work.
- Allow time for students to practice and present their work. Encourage listeners to offer their feedback and advice on the presentation.

Model Use a Think Aloud to model how to revise the summary:

> **THINK ALOUD** *Item four of the Rubric asks whether my summary is clearly organized. In rereading my summary, I think my organization could be clearer. Since I am explaining only the positive answers to the Big Question, I need to get rid of some of the negative answers. Those go in my partner's summary. If I add a main idea sentence, I think my point will be clearer.*

Teaching Tip Explain that in a summary students retell the most important ideas in their own words. A summary is much shorter than the work it encapsulates. Have students practice summarizing by working with a familiar genre, such as a TV movie plot.

Conclude the Unit

Review Unit Objectives Return to the unit objectives and ask students to evaluate how well they mastered each one on a scale of 1 to 5, with 1 being low and 5 being high. Discuss how lower scores could be improved.

Reflect on the Learning Examine the bulletin board with students. Ask them to reflect on what they have learned. They can write or discuss with the class or in small groups. Prompt students' thinking with questions such as:

- What was the most interesting article you read? What did you like about it?

- How did your definition of a hero change as you read through the articles?
- Which topic would you like to know more about? What do you still wonder about it?
- How did the writing assignments and the summary help you form your ideas about who can be a hero?
- What other article topics do you think could be included in this unit? How would those topics explore the idea of what a hero is?

Word Bank Quiz

WORD LIST A			
attributes	courage	inherent	persevere
character	determination	irony	purpose
conceive	honor	legendary	resolute

Ten of the unit Word Bank words are defined in parentheses in the article below. As you read the article, use Word List A, above, to figure out which word best fits each definition. Write the word on the line provided. (You will not use every word on the list.) Then go on to the next page of the quiz.

A Different Breed of Hero

Some dogs serve a specific **(1. goal or aim)** _____, such as helping people after natural disasters. These dogs have **(2. part of the basic nature of something)** _____ qualities that allow them to do important work. Some dogs are bred for specific **(3. qualities or characteristics of a thing)** _____, such as their sense of smell or their agility. These dogs are able to **(4. continue even when something is difficult)** _____ in tough situations, such as digging through the snow from an avalanche. Good search and rescue dogs have **(5. mental strength)** _____ and a lot of **(6. strong desire to reach a goal)** _____ to get their jobs done. They are trained to follow a specific person's scent and are **(7. able to set a goal and stick to it)** _____ about finding a missing person. Breeds like the St. Bernard are **(8. famous or widely honored)** _____ for their ability to find people in the snow.

One **(9. difference between what is expected and what happens)** _____ about search and rescue dogs is that many were themselves rescued from animal shelters. The **(10. set of qualities that make up a person, place, or thing)** _____ of these dogs proves that they are worth rescuing.

UNIT 6 Word Bank Quiz

WORD LIST B			
conceive	devise	integrity	responsibility
conduct	honor	principles	sacrifice
consult	illustrate	resolute	selflessness

Ten more Word Bank words are defined in parentheses in the article, below. As you read the article, use Word List B, above, to figure out which word best fits each definition. Write the word on the line provided. (You will not use every word on the list.)

My Hero

When I wrote about a hero of mine, I chose someone who demonstrated **(11. act of putting someone else's needs ahead of your own)** _____.

I wrote about John Martinez, who made a big personal **(12. give up something to help someone else)** _____ to help others. My idea of a hero is a person with **(13. high moral standards)** _____. Mr. Martinez was able to **(14. make something up and figure out how it will work)** _____ a plan to get community groups involved in helping the elderly. For example, he was able to **(15. carry out)** _____ a drive to get local suppliers to donate more than 1,000 fans to senior citizens without air-conditioning. He was also able to **(16. think of)** _____ of a program to get kids to record books on tape for seniors with vision problems. His efforts **(17. give examples)** _____ how one person can make a difference. For me, the **(18. important basic truths)** _____ of helping others are what make a hero. Martinez said, "Our community needs to **(19. do what you agreed to do)** _____ our senior citizens. It is the community's **(20. duty you are expected to do)** _____ to care for each and every member."

UNIT 1

Answer Key

Unlucky Winners

Wrap It Up, Anthology, p. 7

1. The odds of winning a state lottery are four million to one.
2. He was hit by a truck.
3. Give money to their families without discussion. Donate to good causes and needy friends. Buy luxuries they cannot afford.
4. Sample response: Yes, I was surprised because I thought that everyone would be happy forever if he or she won a lot of money.
5. Sample response: Be careful with your money. Do not give it all away to everyone you know.
6. Sample response: I would buy my mother and father a house.

Connect to the Big Question

Sample response: I still think it is lucky to win the lottery but only if you are really careful with the money.

Vocabulary Exercise, Writing Journal, p. 5

I was (happy, <u>unhappy</u>) when I got home and did not have my keys. I had an (<u>important</u>, unimportant) report due. It would be (possible, <u>impossible</u>) to do without my computer. I was (<u>afraid</u>, unafraid) I would get a grade of (complete, <u>incomplete</u>). My kind neighbor (<u>politely</u>, impolitely) told me to check my pockets. It sounds (logical, <u>illogical</u>), but the keys were there the whole time!

High Flyers

Wrap It Up, Anthology, p. 11

1. Jules Leotard invented the flying trapeze.
2. Early trapeze artists were taught by family members.
3. Alfredo Codona was one of the greatest trapeze artists of all time.
4. Sample response: People enjoy learning trapeze skills because it makes them feel as if they can fly.
5. Sample response: Yes, I would go to trapeze school because it looks like a lot of fun.
6. Sample response: A good flyer would be someone who is very strong and coordinated and can stay focused on what he or she is doing.

Connect to the Big Question

Sample response: I could be a trapeze artist, because I am good at sports, work hard, and am not afraid of heights.

Vocabulary Exercise, Writing Journal, p. 9

I am afraid of heights, so I was (<u>uncertain</u>, uncertainty) about taking a trapeze class. The coach was (<u>certain</u>, certainty) that the class could help me get over my fear. Once I was on the platform, my (perceive, <u>perception</u>) of being in the air changed. I (<u>perceived</u>, perception) that this could be a lot of fun!

Going to Extremes

Wrap It Up, Anthology, p. 15

1. Richard Branson is the billionaire founder of an airline and chain of record stores.
2. They hit rough weather while floating in a balloon over the Pacific Ocean and had to make an emergency landing.
3. Sample response: Some people think that adventurers who do dangerous activities in pursuit of their own pleasure put rescuers needlessly at risk and cost the government a lot of money. Other people think that rescuing others is the right thing to do, no matter how much it costs.
4. Sample response: People might like to do dangerous things for fun because they are bored and want a new challenge.
5. Sample response: Yes, I like watching and reading about extreme sports because they are more exciting than regular sports. You never know what is going to happen next.
6. Sample response: Yes, the climbers should have known that it was more dangerous in December than at other times of year and have been prepared for the extra dangers.

Connect to the Big Question

Sample response: Yes, I think a challenge is too dangerous if it could harm a rescuer trying to help. If you are hang gliding and you fall, then only you get hurt, but the people saving the climbers in winter had to put their lives on the line, too.

Women's Wage Gap

Wrap It Up, Anthology, p. 19

1. The wage gap is the difference between men's pay and women's pay.
2. The Equal Pay Act and Title VII are two laws that help women who work.
3. Sample response: After the laws were passed, the wage gap started closing. Also, more women are working at jobs that used to be only for men.
4. Sample response: People prefer one gender over another for certain jobs because some people might be unconsciously prejudiced.
5. Sample response: If child care was provided at work, more women would go to work and more families would have more money.
6. Sample response: No, the only factor should be whether the person can do the job.

Connect to the Big Question

Sample response: I do not think women are being treated fairly in the workplace yet. They still do not get paid the same amount as men, and many people still think there are jobs women should not do.

Vocabulary Exercise, Writing Journal, p. 17

Scientists are studying the (intelligent, <u>intelligence</u>) of blue whales. Though these animals do not talk, they are not (<u>silent</u>, silence). Blue whales make many different sounds, which are (<u>dependent</u>, dependence) on the situation. A group of whales can tell the (different, <u>difference</u>) between sounds made by a member of the group and those made by other whales.

Happy Together

Wrap It Up, Anthology, p. 23

1. It is a Web site that keeps track of happiness surveys and research.
2. Lane says people are happy spending time with friends and family.
3. The top two answers were spending time with family and spending time with friends.
4. Sample response: I would have said spending time with my friends. They are more fun than my family.
5. Sample response: If people know each other, then they would look out for each other and take care of each other.

6. Sample response: No, money can buy you great things like computers and video games. All these things will be fun for the whole family and will make the whole family happy. However, computers and video games are expensive. People need money to buy them.

Connect to the Big Question

Sample response: I think having a nice family and good friends is the best way to be happy. Even if you have a lot of money, if you do not have friends and family you will be really lonely.

Winners and Losers

Wrap It Up, Anthology, p. 27

1. Most Americans think competition is good.
2. He defines competition as the ability to succeed only if others fail.
3. Sample response: It can encourage hard work, determination, and self-discipline. It can also make someone lose the desire to experiment and explore.
4. Sample response: When people moved to the United States, they had to struggle to survive.
5. Sample response: A cooperative culture might enjoy jump rope.
6. Sample response: No, competition is a bad thing. It makes some people mean by making them think that winning is the only thing that matters. It makes other people feel bad because they lost.

Connect to the Big Question

Sample response: People are not naturally competitive. People learn to be competitive. If people were naturally competitive, people all over the world would be competitive.

Vocabulary Exercise, Writing Journal, p. 25

There is no one (<u>medicine</u>, medicate) that cures the measles. That is why doctors (vaccine, <u>vaccinate</u>) children against measles. The (<u>vaccine</u>, vaccinate) prevents kids from getting the measles. Unlike the measles, the kinds of flu that are (<u>active</u>, activate) each year change, so you need to (participant, <u>participate</u>) in getting a flu shot each year.

Shark Story

Wrap It Up, Anthology, p. 31

1. Sixty people are attacked each year.
2. Five to ten people are killed each year.

3. Three endangered sharks are the grey nurse, speartooth, and northern river sharks.

4. Sample response: Sharks do not reproduce every year and have few young.

5. Sample response: Rules for swimming in shark territory include: never swim alone, leave the water when you see fish gathering together, and do not swim at dusk or at night.

6. Sample response: I think people who make movies should be able to do what they want. People should be smart enough to find out the real facts and not think that everything they see in the movies is true.

Connect to the Big Question

Sample response: Sharks are not as dangerous as they are sometimes portrayed. Even if you are swimming near to where sharks live, you probably will not get bitten by a shark.

The ABCs of Antioxidants

Wrap It Up, Anthology, p. 35

1. Oxidation turns apple slices brown.

2. Sample response: carrots, squash, sweet potatoes, tomatoes, collards

3. Sample response: Free radicals are molecules that are missing an electron. When they are in a body, they steal electrons from cell walls and other places. This causes aging and may cause cancer.

4. Sample response: Organic foods have more antioxidants than foods grown with pesticides and fertilizer.

5. Sample response: I could eat more fruits and vegetables and less fast food.

6. Sample response: Yes, one study is enough because it showed that there was a risk and people should not risk their health.

Connect to the Big Question

Sample response: Yes, if people ate better they would not have problems like obesity and diabetes.

Vocabulary Exercise, Writing Journal, p. 33

I (refer, <u>prefer</u>, confer) to ride my bike to work, but I took the bus today because it was raining. I was not sure which bus to take, so I (<u>conferred</u>, transferred, referred) with people at the bus stop. They (preferred, <u>referred</u>, inferred) me to the map of the bus routes. I had to (prefer, infer, <u>transfer</u>) from one bus to another.

Word Bank Quiz

1. evidence
2. involves
3. approach
4. subjective
5. verify
6. associate
7. uncertainty
8. consequence
9. focus
10. discern
11. objective
12. improbable
13. differentiate
14. concrete
15. crucial
16. results
17. evaluate
18. comprehend
19. perception
20. reality

Sibling Strife

Wrap It Up, Anthology, p. 43

1. Sibling rivalry is competition or confrontation between siblings for love and attention, especially from parents.
2. Children sometimes see each other as rivals for their parents' love.
3. On the positive side, sibling rivalry can be a friendly competition that pushes siblings to excel by developing their talents and skills. On the negative side, it can cause hurt and resentment between siblings.
4. Sample response: If a parent has more in common with one of his or her two children, he or she might spend more time with that child, leaving the other child feeling resentful.
5. Sample response: Be sure to give equal amounts of love and attention to your children. Also, keep a close eye on any rivalry between them and intervene if it becomes negative.
6. Sample response: Parents should step in if the rivalry begins to have a negative effect on the siblings' relationship or if the siblings cannot seem to work out a problem on their own.

Connect to the Big Question

Sample response: It is natural for siblings to feel competitive with each other for their parents' attention. That competition can spill over into other parts of their lives, such as school and activities.

Vocabulary Exercise, Writing Journal, p. 39

Few people want to have a (compromise, concession, <u>confrontation</u>). However, if you and a neighbor disagree and cannot reach a (<u>compromise</u>, concession, confrontation), you may decide to go to court. Most courts want you to work out your differences before the judge is called, so your lawyer may ask you to make a (compromise, <u>concession</u>, confrontation) or two.

Holding Parents Responsible

Wrap It Up, Anthology, p. 47

1. Parental responsibility laws punish parents for the crimes of their children. The laws may also require parental participation in punishments for the children.

2. They hope parents of young criminals, especially repeat offenders, will take more responsibility for their children's behavior and work harder to keep them in line.
3. Some say that there are cases in which parents have not done anything wrong, so they should not be punished. Also, if parents are in jail, how can they help their kids and work to support their families? Moreover, there is little evidence to prove that threats of punishment actually change kids' behavior. People against these laws also believe that parents need help, not punishment.
4. Sample response: Some kids might change to keep their parents from being punished, but many may not care or really understand the consequences for their parents.
5. Sample response: I would hold parents responsible only for being present in court and for taking part in counseling of their children. These measures might provide help instead of punishment for something parents may not be able to control.
6. Sample response: I think teens must start to be responsible for their behavior. Even if their behavior has been caused by bad parenting, they must learn to make decisions for themselves anyway, especially if they cannot count on their parents.

Connect to the Big Question

Sample response: Yes, I do, but I think parents should be responsible only for participating in court hearings and being a part of counseling. I do not think they should be punished. The legal system cannot determine their level of fault.

Identity Theft

Real-Life Connection, Anthology, p. 48

1. True
2. False
3. False
4. False

Wrap It Up, Anthology, p. 51

1. Identity theft occurs when someone uses another individual's personal information to steal from that person or someone else.

2. Spam is e-mail, especially ads, that is sent to a person who did not request it and does not want it.

3. Phishing happens when someone sends an individual an e-mail that appears to be from a trustworthy person or organization but is actually from someone trying to get information from the targeted victim or to gain access to information on that person's computer.

4. Sample response: Young people often do not realize that they could be a victim, and they are too free with their personal information, especially on their computers.

5. Sample response: Be very careful about giving out information on the computer or telephone. Use a security program on the computer, and download only from reputable sites. Also, avoid opening spam.

6. Sample response: No site is completely safe, because thieves are always finding new ways to get to information. A site from a reputable company is likely to be safe, but people should download only what they absolutely need.

Connect to the Big Question

Sample response: I will do a better job keeping the security updated on my computer. I will also delete e-mails from people I do not know and avoid downloading from sites I do not know.

Tracking Teen Drivers

Wrap It Up, Anthology, p. 55

1. A GPS is a tracking system that uses a satellite to show where a vehicle is at any time.

2. They reduce insurance expenses and give parents peace of mind about where their children are.

3. Some kids feel that the GPS is an invasion of privacy and shows a lack of parental trust. They also find it distracting when a parent calls, signals, or sends a text message about their driving while they are behind the wheel.

4. Sample response: Teens are not always the safest drivers and do not always use the best judgment, so parents find the tracking systems helpful to make teens accountable.

5. Sample response: You could compare the number of accidents between drivers with tracking systems and those without.

6. Sample response: I probably would not like it, because I want my parents to trust me. However, I am their responsibility, so I understand it. It is also a small price to pay for driving privileges.

Connect to the Big Question

Sample response: I think they are probably both. However, I think most teens would rather have their privacy invaded than have a deadly accident, so I think the devices are a good idea.

The Greed Game

Wrap It Up, Anthology, p. 59

1. U.S. teenagers spend about $100 billion a year.

2. Teens tend to feel insecure, so marketers try to exploit those weaknesses and make kids believe that they need some item to be popular or accepted.

3. A credit card is like taking out a loan; the card owner has to pay the bill and the interest on it. Interest can be high, and if the card owner cannot or does not pay the bill, the person's credit rating can be hurt.

4. Sample response: Ads show only thin, beautiful women in the latest fashions.

5. Sample response: I would probably ask myself if I really need it and if I can afford it. I should also ask myself why I want it, to make sure that I am not just being taken in by the advertising.

6. Sample response: Some teens are like the ones in ads, but not all are, and the ads make a lot of teens feel as if they should be like the teens pictured.

Connect to the Big Question

Sample response: I think advertising takes unfair advantage of teens and lowers their self-esteem. However, teens have to learn from their mistakes and be responsible.

Learning from Crime Victims

Wrap It Up, Anthology, p. 63

1. About 41 percent of criminals are likely to become repeat offenders.

2. One purpose is to make offenders change their behavior by realizing the toll their crimes took on their victims.

3. The victim expresses feelings about the crime and asks the offender questions. The offender answers the questions and explains how the crime happened and how he or she feels about it.

4. Sample response: The victim may need to meet the offender either to confront or try to forgive the offender in order to move on from the experience.

5. Sample response: You could keep track of how many offenders were arrested again after completing a program. You could then compare that number to the number of offenders who repeat crimes and did not complete a program.

6. Sample response: No, a victim may not want to see the offender, and that should be the victim's choice.

Connect to the Big Question

Sample response: No, victims should not be forced to go through that experience if they do not want to.

Preparing for the Flu

Wrap It Up, Anthology, p. 67

1. A flu pandemic occurred.
2. "Bird flu" is a flu virus that infects birds and may be transmitted to people, for whom it is very deadly.
3. Storing enough of the vaccine would ensure that people are vaccinated in case of a pandemic. However, this would be very expensive, and it may not even stop the spread of the bird flu if the virus changes. Also, it is difficult to decide who should get the vaccine first.
4. Sample response: A quarantine occurs when authorities like the police or government do not allow people who are infected with a contagious disease freedom to travel from a certain area. The purpose of a quarantine is to limit the spread of disease.
5. Sample response: Life would change drastically. People might be quarantined, and most towns would probably close schools and businesses. Supplies of necessary items might become low or completely depleted. People would probably be very frightened and would tend to stay indoors.
6. Sample response: Yes it would, because it would be very important to keep the flu from spreading. A person could be spreading the virus and not even know it.

Connect to the Big Question

Sample response: No, we need to keep studying ways to cure the disease, but we also need to spend time and money preparing for severe outbreaks. A pandemic could kill many people, so we need to be educated about what to do if one occurs.

The Development Debate

Wrap It Up, Anthology, p. 71

1. Six million acres of farmland were lost to development between 1992 and 1997.
2. Open space is undeveloped, natural land. People value open space because they use it for recreation or simply for enjoying the outdoors and wildlife.
3. New residents require expansion of public resources that must be paid for. In addition, infrastructure must be built, and that must be paid for also.
4. Sample response: The air would probably become more polluted because of the building process and the loss of trees that help keep the air clean.
5. Sample response: I would want to know how they planned to use existing resources and whether they would be leaving much of the natural landscape intact.
6. Sample response: Yes, people in a community should be a part of the discussion, along with public officials and businesses. People should have a say, because development will affect their quality of life and the value of their property.

Connect to the Big Question

Sample response: Yes, I think people could do a much better job of planning how growth should occur. This way, we could take advantage of existing resources and make better use of our land. We could also preserve open space to enjoy in the future.

Vocabulary Exercise, Writing Journal, p. 67

Each group of science students formed its own study (<u>unit</u>, unify). They wanted to find out if an (<u>acid</u>, acidify) can be made from something else. First, the members of each group had to (unit, <u>unify</u>) their efforts. They discussed how to (pure, <u>purify</u>) their equipment. Then they added a (<u>pure</u>, purify) form of one liquid to another. The mixture had a (<u>horrid</u>, horrify) smell! Though the process might (horrid, <u>horrify</u>) anyone walking past the lab, the students did indeed find that the ingredients began to (acid, <u>acidify</u>).

Word Bank Quiz

1. change
2. radical
3. reveal
4. unify
5. resolve
6. inclined
7. debate
8. defend
9. oppose
10. discuss
11. adversity
12. confrontation
13. struggle
14. compromise
15. progress
16. produce
17. negotiate
18. conclude
19. inestimable
20. motive

Sixth Sense Survival

Wrap It Up, Anthology, p. 79

1. The sixth sense is an intuition that alerts people to possible danger.
2. Rensink identified conscious sight and mindsight.
3. Sample response: Rensink showed people pictures that had small differences in them. Between the photographs, he quickly showed people a gray field. People anticipated changes in the pictures before they were shown, perhaps as a result of unconsciously seeing the gray field.
4. Sample response: People might notice another car before they could "see" it.
5. Sample response: People on bikes would be safer using their sixth sense. People could use their sixth sense walking alone late at night.
6. Sample response: Yes, Rensink is a scientist and he knows what he is doing. If he believes that there is a sixth sense, then he may be right.

Connect to the Big Question

Sample response: I think there is a sixth sense, but I think people still do not know exactly what causes it or how it works.

Vocabulary Exercises, Writing Journal, p. 73

For my science report, I plan to (<u>investigate</u>, investigation) how quickly people (<u>react</u>, reaction) when playing a video game. I will use a common (distract, <u>distraction</u>), such as (<u>loud</u>, loudness) sounds to test the players' (aware, <u>awareness</u>) of the game. I will make a (predict, <u>prediction</u>) that people will do better in a (<u>quiet</u>, quietness) environment.

Looking over Your Shoulder

Real-Life Connection, Anthology, p. 80

1. True
2. False
3. True
4. True

Wrap It Up, Anthology, p. 83

1. A Global Positioning System is a device that gets geographic, or positioning, information from satellites orbiting Earth.

2. A GPS uses images from the satellite to show a driver's location and the best route to a destination.
3. Sample response: GPS has been used to find lost hikers, help cab drivers, and keep track of soldiers and people on parole.
4. Sample response: People are against GPS technology because it can invade a person's privacy.
5. Sample response: GPS could be attached to dogs in case they run away or to personal electronic devices in case they got stolen.
6. Sample response: Yes, it is wrong. The company should be able to tell in other ways whether the person is doing a good job.

Connect to the Big Question

Sample response: Yes, teenagers need their freedom. They are close to being adults and should not be followed by their parents.

Dressing by the Book

Wrap It Up, Anthology, p. 87

1. Seventy-five percent of respondents were in favor of bans on gang symbols.
2. Sample response: The following is a list of items that may be banned in a dress code: gang colors, tattoos, piercings, tight or short clothes.
3. Sample response: Dress codes make students safer. They help students concentrate. They help students prepare for being in the business world. They make students take school more seriously.
4. Sample response: Schools might ban certain clothes because they may insult another student or conflict with that student's beliefs.
5. Sample response: No, students know how to dress for work. They have probably had to dress formally for a special occasion before.
6. Sample response: Yes, I do, because parents know what clothes cost and students should have some say in their own lives.

Connect to the Big Question

Sample response: Apart from gang colors and symbols, kids should be able to wear what they want to school. It is one way they express who they are. If a student's clothing is not appropriate, the parents should be the ones who tell the student not to wear something.

Textbook Technology

Wrap It Up, Anthology, p. 91

1. An e-text is an electronic text.

2. Sample response: E-texts would weigh a lot less than my textbooks.

3. Sample response: Most e-texts do not let you write notes or highlight. They can be uncomfortable to read. They are expensive.

4. Sample response: E-texts are read on laptops, and most schools do not have enough money to give every student a laptop.

5. Sample response: E-texts would make learning more fun. Even kids who do not like to read like technology, so e-texts would get them interested.

6. Sample response: Yes, I like computers and feel comfortable using them.

Connect to the Big Question

Sample response: Yes, e-texts would get students interested because they could include things like movies, which are more interesting than just words. Because the texts will be more interesting, more kids will pay attention to what they are reading and will therefore learn better.

Vocabulary Exercises, Writing Journal, p. 85

I read a book about how animals (<u>adapt</u>, adapting) to their environment. For example, chameleons (<u>change</u>, changing) their color. (Blend, <u>Blending</u>) in with plants helps them stay safe. This way of (hide, <u>hiding</u>) is like camouflage clothing that military people wear. The difference is that chameleons do not (<u>have</u>, having) to wear clothes.

The Witness Dilemma

Wrap It Up, Anthology, p. 95

1. They are asking for a postponing of the trial to a later date.

2. Sample response: The witness is frightened because the criminal would know who the witness is and might want revenge. Also, the witness may not want to miss work.

3. The person can be required to travel back to the place he or she was visiting as many times as an appearance in court is required.

4. Sample response: Hotlines are anonymous, so no one will know who reported the crime.

5. Sample response: I would be willing to testify if someone got hurt because no one should be allowed to hurt someone else.

6. Sample response: The justice system would probably be weakened if witnesses did not have to testify. More people would refuse to testify, and without eyewitness testimony it could be harder to convict criminals.

Connect to the Big Question

Sample response: I think that witnesses should be forced to testify in court because more people who are guilty of crimes will probably be convicted.

Instant Friends

Wrap It Up, Anthology, p. 99

1. A blog is a web log where people with similar interests post messages to each other.

2. About 120,000 blogs are posted each day.

3. Sample response: In the past, teens made friends by doing sports, joining clubs, or living in the same neighborhood. Today, teens make friends online.

4. Sample response: You can meet more people from all over the world. If you are different from the people in your school or your neighborhood, you can meet people who are like you.

5. Sample response: No, I have not, because my mom does not let me do that.

6. Sample response: You cannot tell for sure if someone is lying to you online, but you can try to find out by asking other people online if they know the person in question.

Connect to the Big Question

Sample response: No, I think that the Internet is letting more people get to know each other. I can meet someone who lives thousands of miles away and learn about how the person lives. I can meet someone who lives close by, but because we do not have the same circle of friends I never would have talked to the person if we had not met online.

Vocabulary Exercises, Writing Journal, p. 93

1. The **incoming (not coming, <u>coming in</u>)** freshman class at our high school has to attend a special assembly.

2. Joe gained weight when he was **inactive (<u>not active</u>, active within).**

3. You should always **inspect (not look at, <u>look carefully into</u>)** a used car before buying it.

The Newest Newcomers

Real-Life Connection, Anthology, p. 100

1. True
2. False
3. True
4. True

Wrap It Up, Anthology, p. 103

1. About 2,000 different religious groups are in America.
2. The five freedoms are freedom to worship, freedom from oppression, freedom from want, freedom from fear, and freedom to create.
3. Sample response: Immigrants face challenges such as encountering unfamiliar foods, learning a new language, and adapting to a new culture.
4. Sample response: People think their lives will be better in the United States than in the country in which they currently live.
5. Sample response: Everyone would be able to find a job, but many jobs would be left open because they pay too little.
6. Sample response: Immigration should be encouraged because people deserve the chance at a better life.

Connect to the Big Question

Sample response: America offers immigrants a chance to be part of a democracy and to have a job.

Hip-Hop: Keeping It Real

Wrap It Up, Anthology, p. 107

1. Sample response: Hip-hop is the popular culture of many young people today. It includes urban styles of clothing, music, and dance.
2. Sample response: A Jamaican recited rhymes over a break in popular records.
3. Sample response: MCing, DJing, and break dancing are some major elements.
4. Sample response: Advertisers think using rap is a good thing because most young people listen to hip-hop.
5. Sample response: Kids will buy something that they connect to hip-hop because they think hip-hop is fashionable.
6. Sample response: Hip-hop music and culture are great because the music is fun to listen to and to dance to and because it talks about real life.

Connect to the Big Question

Sample response: Hip-hop is real when it is about music and real life and not about selling merchandise.

Word Bank Quiz

1. growth
2. ignorance
3. awareness
4. reaction
5. empathy
6. reflect
7. question
8. influence
9. insight
10. enlighten
11. subject
12. understanding
13. argument
14. concise
15. technique
16. imitate
17. process
18. modified
19. adapt
20. revise

UNIT 4

Answer Key

Ooooh, Scary!

Wrap It Up, Anthology, p. 115

1. A horror movie is a film that is supposed to scare viewers.

2. Chaney played characters such as the Phantom of the Opera and the Hunchback of Notre Dame, frightening characters made to look ugly with special makeup techniques. Chaney often played characters that were lonely and isolated from society.

3. Today's horror movie characters are even more frightening because of advanced makeup techniques and computer-generated effects. The characters are also portrayed as less human and more monstrous.

4. Sample response: Chaney's Phantom seemed more human. His Phantom was driven by a need for love and self-expression. Englund's Phantom was so shocking and disgusting that he seemed more like a monster than a human being.

5. Sample response: They all have an important role, but the sound effects are the most important. Some horror movies do not have much of a story or great actors, but the music and sound effects build anticipation and create thrills anyway.

6. Sample response: Yes, horror movies can tell great stories and teach lessons, as well as scare people.

Connect to the Big Question

Sample response: Yes, I think some horror movies are too bloody and realistic. The best horror movies leave more to the imagination.

Up a Tree

Wrap It Up, Anthology, p. 119

1. She wanted to save Luna and other trees in that forest from loggers.

2. Hill had to deal with terrible weather, frostbite, and blisters from forest fires.

3. Pacific Lumber agreed to spare Luna and the trees nearby for $50,000. The state and federal governments bought 10,000 acres of forest to keep it from being logged.

4. Sample response: The media covered the story because Hill went to such extremes in support of her beliefs.

5. Sample response: I think many people would be without jobs, and the lumber industry would sue the government. Also, things made of wood would be too expensive for anyone to afford.

6. Sample response: I would support a partial ban to protect forests with endangered plants and wildlife or in places with few remaining forests. I do think that we need some logging to provide jobs as well as lumber and other materials made from wood.

Connect to the Big Question

Sample response: Yes, protests can get out of hand, but sometimes people have to take extreme action to get large businesses and the government to pay attention to important issues.

As Big As All Outdoors

Wrap It Up, Anthology, p. 123

1. The company used a series of signs placed a few hundred feet apart along the roadside. The signs formed a funny rhyme about shaving cream.

2. The Highway Beautification Act was intended to reduce the number of billboards on highways.

3. For skywriting, a plane uses a special oil to create a white, smoky trail from the exhaust of the airplane. For skytyping, five planes fly in a line and let out little puffs of vapor. The dots form letters.

4. Sample response: Some people think outdoor advertising is dangerous because it is distracting to drivers.

5. Sample response: I would research the accident rate in a certain areas, then see if the accident rate increased after placing outdoor advertising in the areas.

6. Sample response: No, I would not trust it completely, because the organization may be biased. It may have more interest in keeping business alive than in keeping the public safe.

Connect to the Big Question

Sample response: Yes, I think that ads with personalized messages or those that contact drivers' mobile phones are too distracting and should be outlawed.

UNIT 4 Answer Key

Put Me In, Coach!

Wrap It Up, Anthology, p. 127

1. A life coach is someone who is paid to help people set goals and reach them.

2. A life coach can help people improve their job performance, find a new occupation, develop skills, or work on relationships.

3. Some people worry that teens already have too many people giving them advice, so more might be confusing. Also, some people think that teens need to learn how to work through problems, deal with stress, and learn from their mistakes. Life coaches might get in the way of this process.

4. Sample response: Teens might want to become more organized, work on study skills, define their goals, and deal better with stress.

5. Sample response: They should be knowledgeable, honest, and skilled at listening.

6. Sample response: I think teens should definitely have goals in order to be working toward something and improving. However, teens should also be flexible enough to change goals if they discover new talents, interests, or opportunities.

Connect to the Big Question

Sample response: No, I think teens need to find role models and mentors to help them set goals. I also think they need to seek the advice of many people instead of depending too much on one person.

Longing to Be Like Mike

Wrap It Up, Anthology, p. 131

1. For every professional athlete, there are 9,999 who do not achieve at that level.

2. Young people might miss out on other opportunities or fail to develop other talents by focusing too much on sports. They also might not study or be prepared to do something else if their dream does not come true.

3. Sample response: Emmit Smith, Jerry Stackhouse, Antawn Jamison, and Juwan Howard all went back to school.

4. Sample response: Some people think that there is an overemphasis on sports in minority communities. The media make the problem worse by so often portraying black and Latino men as athletes and musicians. Rarely are minority men portrayed as professionals in other fields.

5. Sample response: It would help if minority men in business and other professions would be mentors to young men of color and provide other role models. I also think that people need to put pressure on the media and those in the entertainment industry to stop providing such a narrow view of people in the African American and Latino communities.

6. Sample response: Yes, I think they feel more comfortable with sports than they do in school or jobs. Most of my friends spend a lot of time playing sports. It is a good way to relieve stress, but my parents think I should finish school.

Connect to the Big Question

Sample response: Yes, I think the media glamorize sports careers and make it seem as if a career in sports is all that a young man of color can aspire to. They also show success stories and rarely show the many athletes who do not make it or struggle to get by in a sports career.

Time to Serve

Wrap It Up, Anthology, p. 135

1. A military draft requires young men to serve in the armed forces if the country needs them. They can be excused only for approved reasons.

2. The United States first drafted men for the Civil War in the 1860s.

3. Volunteers could help in schools, serve in hospitals, provide disaster relief, help with security at airports and other places of transportation, or provide care for senior citizens.

4. Sample response: Some people think that "volunteer" work should not be forced upon people. They also worry that the plan will be too costly and will take jobs away from people who need the pay.

5. Sample response: People could pick up litter and clean up graffiti. They could also help out in community centers and volunteer to mentor young people.

6. Sample response: Yes, I think it is important for people to learn the value of serving others. I also think such a plan might help young people learn about talents and skills they may not realize they have. This might help them find rewarding careers.

Connect to the Big Question

Sample response: I think it would send the message that serving others is something everyone should do. It also reminds people that the country believes in giving something back.

Hip-Hop into Hall of Fame

Wrap It Up, Anthology, p. 139

1. Rhythm and blues and country helped form rock and roll.

2. The Hall of Fame looks for people "who have made rock and roll the force that it is in our culture." This includes people who may not be rock and roll musicians but who have influenced rock and roll in an important way.

3. Sample response: Chuck Berry, James Brown, Elvis Presley, Aretha Franklin, and Miles Davis have been inducted into the Rock and Roll Hall of Fame.

4. Sample response: Some people think that rap is not music but rather words and rhythms made on a turntable. They think rap is just a fad and should have its own Hall of Fame.

5. Sample response: I think rock and roll stars have incorporated some of the beats and rhymes from rap into their own music. They have also adopted some of the hip-hop style.

6. Sample response: They are all Hall of Fame inductees who play music that is not rock and roll. However, the Hall of Fame chose them anyway because they have strongly influenced rock and roll.

Connect to the Big Question

Sample response: Yes, I do if they have had a strong influence on rock and roll. Music genres like rock and roll are constantly changing, and rap is as much a part of that change as country, jazz, or any other genre.

Texting on Trial

Wrap It Up, Anthology, p. 143

1. Text messaging is sending short typed messages using the keypad of a cell phone.

2. Text messaging is a quick and easy way to stay connected with friends.

3. Cyberbullying is using technology like the Internet, e-mail, and cell phones to threaten or intimidate people.

4. Sample response: Teachers and parents think it is a distraction during class and at other times when students should be sleeping or doing something else important.

5. Sample response: I would begin by cancelling the text messaging feature completely and making the child earn it back. Then I would put a monthly limit on it that would turn off the feature after a certain number of texts.

6. Sample response: You should not respond to it. Keep a record of what happened and tell your parents.

Connect to the Big Question

Sample response: Yes, I think it can be, but there should be reasonable limits set by parents. If text messaging is abused, it should be taken away.

Word Bank Quiz

1. define
2. meaning
3. convey
4. verbal
5. language
6. tone
7. continuum
8. possible
9. frequently
10. confusion
11. isolation
12. emotion
13. connection
14. explanation
15. discourse
16. self-expression
17. misinterpret
18. interact
19. pattern
20. respond

Answer Key

Pros and Cons of Protest

Wrap It Up, Anthology, p. 151

1. The right to free speech and the right to free assembly are guaranteed by the U.S. Constitution.
2. A "walkout" occurs when people refuse to go to their classes as a form of protest.
3. Walkouts can shut down an entire campus and keep *all* students from attending classes even if they do not agree with the protest. Parents also complain that they pay a lot of money to have their children in college and expect their kids to be able to attend classes.
4. Sample response: Some college officials believe in free speech but worry that protests can force one group's perspective on the entire campus.
5. Sample response: If school officials work with student protesters, the officials show that they believe in the rights of freedom of speech and freedom of assembly.
6. Sample response: Yes, I do, because students who protest are doing something important. They are learning about the world and learning how to be active citizens.

Connect to the Big Question

Sample response: If student protesters and school officials work together and keep open minds, then students can have protests without disregarding anyone's rights. Protests could also be scheduled at times when there are not any classes, so that even the protesters will not have to worry about missing class.

Royal Rights to Privacy

Wrap It Up, Anthology, p. 155

1. Paparazzi are aggressive freelance photographers.
2. Princess Diana died in a car accident.
3. Some people blame the paparazzi for Diana's death because the photographers were chasing her car and forcing the driver to go too fast in order to avoid them.

4. Sample response: People might be interested in the private lives of royals because royals are rich and famous. People may also have dreams of being like the royals.
5. Sample response: If laws were passed to prevent unauthorized photographs of celebrities, people would get interested in other things like books.
6. Sample response: I believe the public is more responsible for the princes' dilemma because if the public did not buy the magazines, the paparazzi would not have any work.

Connect to the Big Question

Sample response: No, I think the royals are just people; the public does not have a right to know about royals' private lives. The royals should be left alone to do their jobs.

In or Out of the In Crowd

Wrap It Up, Anthology, p. 159

1. A clique is small groups of friends or associates that exclude other people.
2. Cliques may have rules about how members look, talk, and act.
3. Clique leaders may use flattery, humiliation, and the threat of gossip to keep members from leaving.
4. Sample response: Since clique leaders cannot easily control self-confident people, they form a group of people that they feel they can control.
5. Sample response: I would stand up to a clique member trying to bully an outsider. I would tell the person that he or she is not better than anyone else and should leave people alone.
6. Sample response: There will always be unhealthy cliques. There needs to be one student leader who can stand up to them.

Connect to the Big Question

Sample response: I used to want to be in the popular clique, but now I know that the people in that clique are just really lame.

Vocabulary Exercise, Writing Journal, p. 149

My neighbor got my (divided, <u>undivided</u>, individually) attention when he said that he was moving to Spain and wanted to (<u>divvy</u>, division, divisible) up his video games before he left. (Divide, Divisible, <u>Division</u>) has never been my favorite kind of math. Since there were four friends and nine games, the games were not evenly (<u>divisible</u>, indivisible, individual) among the friends. We decided that each (division, divvy, <u>individual</u>) would choose two games, and we would flip coins for the last one.

The *Titanic* Tragedy

Wrap It Up, Anthology, p. 163

1. The *Titanic* sank in 1912.
2. The officer in charge was unable to stop the ship in time because it was going too fast and it was too big to stop quickly.
3. Sample response: If the captain had reduced the ship's speed and changed the ship's course to avoid the ice, the disaster might have been prevented.
4. Sample response: Safety rules were not strict enough at the time the *Titanic* sank.
5. Sample response: Had the crew of the *Titanic* been fully trained in emergency procedures, it may have been able to alert nearby ships to come to *Titanic*'s aid.
6. Sample response: Yes, I think the captain was responsible for the *Titanic* disaster because it was his decision to make the ship go too fast and to go into an area full of icebergs.

Connect to the Big Question

Sample response: Yes, I believe overconfidence can lead to disaster because the captain believed that the ship could not sink. He was overconfident about how strong the ship was, so he was not as careful as he should have been.

Word Bank Quiz

1. constant
2. perspective
3. interpretation
4. expectations
5. presume
6. anticipate
7. discipline
8. consider
9. appropriate
10. knowledge
11. universal
12. identity
13. individual
14. manipulate
15. distortion
16. background
17. bias
18. stereotype
19. impression
20. perspective

UNIT 6

Answer Key

Science's Double-Edged Swords

Real-Life Connection, p. 168
1. False
2. True
3. False
4. False

Wrap It Up, Anthology, p. 171
1. McCarthy defines *artificial intelligence* as the "science and engineering of making intelligent machines, especially intelligent computer programs."
2. Kansei is a humanoid robot capable of imitating human facial expressions.
3. People are concerned that robots could be programmed to learn the way humans do and teach themselves things people do not want them to know. People are also afraid that robots might do harmful things to humans.
4. Sample response: Nuclear energy might be viewed as good because it provides us with energy and power. It might be viewed as bad because it can be used in weapons that could destroy the world.
5. Sample response: The humanoid robots that are being researched often have the same human features and characteristics as their creators.
6. Sample response: I think there should be some limits on AI research. If AI researchers are allowed to learn and do anything they want, humans might end up in a situation similar to a science fiction movie.

Connect to the Big Question
Sample response: Technological developments can be positive because they help people live longer and better lives. They also provide us with things like electricity. They can be negative because sometimes they are used for harmful purposes, such as fighting wars. Scientists also may not fully understand or be able to control what they have created, leading to unintended consequences.

Buffalo Battles

Wrap It Up, Anthology, p. 175
1. It is estimated that there were 60 million bison in 1840.

2. Robert Conger predicted that no law would be able to save the bison from eradication as settlers moved across North America.
3. Sample response: Conger's prediction that Congress could not pass a law to save the buffalo became true, since most bison were killed. The survival of a few bison was not a result of protection from a law but of a few lucky bison living in a remote area.
4. Sample response: Ranchers might support killing bison but not elk because elk may not share the same grazing land as cattle. Also, elk may not infect cattle with disease as easily as bison may.
5. Sample response: To solve the conflict between supporters of wild bison and cattle ranchers, I would restrict cattle ranching in the areas around Yellowstone.
6. Sample response: Both sides have good arguments. Ranchers are right to be concerned with their cattle's safety and food supply. Bison supporters, however, also have a point. Bison have a right to live on lands that they traditionally roamed.

Connect to the Big Question
Sample response: I think people generally have a positive opinion of someone if that person's views are the same as their own.

The Youngest Heroes

Wrap It Up, Anthology, p. 179
1. The government set up Native American schools to try to integrate Native Americans into "white" society.
2. Some Native American parents sent their children to the schools willingly in the hopes that the children would have a better future.
3. Sample response: Among the sacrifices children made at the boarding schools were giving up their native languages; giving up their traditional styles of dress; and, for the boys, cutting off their hair.
4. Sample response: I can conclude that not consulting Native American leaders about the boarding schools meant that the planners did not value or respect Native American traditional ways of life.

5. Sample response: If I could change one thing about the way the U.S. government treated Native Americans, it would be to abolish the boarding schools. Parents have a right to care for, raise, and teach their own values and language to their children.

6. Sample response: I think the boarding schools were cruel. Children should not be taken from their parents and thrown into a situation away from everything they know and love.

Connect to the Big Question

Sample response: Oral histories preserve the stories of heroes by passing on stories that otherwise would be lost. Mainstream society did not value Native Americans, so their stories were not seen as being worth telling. By passing stories along orally, Native Americans preserved important parts of their history.

Equality on the Playing Field

Wrap It Up, Anthology, p. 183

1. Title IX is a law that says schools receiving federal money must provide equal opportunities for male and female students.

2. The WNBA was first organized in 1997.

3. Sample response: Reasons for the lack of mixed-gender teams include the fact that women and men are built differently. In sports that require strength, men are usually stronger than women.

4. Sample response: Research shows that women may be stronger than previously believed, so in sports that require strength and skill, women may someday be able to compete.

5. Sample response: One result of mixed gender sports teams might be that women make a lot of money as professional athletes, get a lot more media exposure, and become more likely to be role models for girls.

6. Sample response: I think that TV sports shows do cover women's professional sports adequately. There are not as many women's as men's pro sports. Also, if there were a larger following for women's sports, TV sports shows would cover the sports because of the demand.

Connect to the Big Question

Sample response: I think male and female athletes should compete against others only in sports requiring skill rather than strength or in which women might have equal abilities compared to male athletes.

Our Hero!

Wrap It Up, Anthology, p. 187

1. Superman first appeared in comic books in 1938.

2. Superman fights for "truth, justice, and the American way."

3. Bruce Banner and Peter Parker are similar in that both are educated and both became superheroes as a result of radiation or radioactive materials.

4. Sample response: Superman may have been popularized in the United States by Americans' fear of entering a world war.

5. Sample response: New technologies like computers, cloning, and genetic engineering might inspire a new superhero. This character might have computer chips and might be able to process information like a computer, have a cloned twin, and be able to assume attributes of plants or other animals.

6. Sample response: People might enjoy reading about the feats of imaginary superheroes because they distract people from worries and show the triumph of good over evil.

Connect to the Big Question

Sample response: Superheroes do seem to reflect society's concerns. They have changed historically, adapting to new circumstances and reflecting new technology and the uncertainty that comes with it.

Peacekeepers

Wrap It Up, Anthology, p. 191

1. The League of Nations formed the basis for the United Nations.

2. The mission of the UN is to bring all nations of the world together to work for peace and development, based on the principles of justice, human dignity, and the well-being of all people.

3. UN peacekeeping forces help keep peace during a civil war and assist in world anti-terrorism work.

4. Sample response: The death and destruction of World War I might have made countries want to avoid future conflicts.

5. Sample response: If there were no United Nations, there might be more violence and conflict within and between countries and possibly another world war or escalation of nuclear weapons.

6. Sample response: I do not think the United Nations should have a larger military force. The purpose of the UN is not to fight; it is to keep the peace. If the UN had a larger military force, nations may lose trust in the UN's neutrality.

Connect to the Big Question

Sample response: Yes. I think the UN is upholding its original goals. While conflicts may have become more complex and difficult to solve, the UN continues to make an effort at solving them.

Vocabulary Exercise, Writing Journal, p. 179

The repairman said he had to (<u>conduct</u>, conductor, conduction) an inspection of our house. He found that the electrical system was old and that the process of electricity (conduct, conductor, <u>conduction</u>) was not working properly. He suggested that we replace the wiring and the main supply (conduct, <u>conductor</u>, conduction).

Leaping into the Fire

Wrap It Up, Anthology, p. 195

1. A wildfire is an "unwanted or unplanned fire burning in forests or wild land areas that threatens to destroy life, property, or natural resources."

2. Smokejumpers parachute from planes and hike through rugged terrain in order to fight wildfires.

3. Firefighters can contain wildfires by clearing brush from the edge of a fire and by lighting backfires.

4. Wildfires might help keep the land healthy by enriching the soil with ash and by clearing out tall trees and letting new plants grow.

5. Sample response: The government could reduce the danger to people and property by regulating how land in forested and overgrown areas is developed and by not allowing people to live in high-risk areas.

6. Sample response: The number of people living in areas where wildfires often start should be limited. The damage caused by wildfires costs money and lives.

Connect to the Big Question

Sample response: I think that people can be trained to be heroes and that being paid to do a job does not mean that someone is not a hero.

The Sport Entertainment Hero

Wrap It Up, Anthology, p. 199

1. The Undertaker is a professional wrestler who dresses in black and acts the part of "bad guy."

2. WWE stands for World Wrestling Entertainment.

3. Owners wanted to classify pro wrestling as entertainment rather than sport so that they were not bound by rules and could therefore make more money.

4. Sample response: WWE is so popular because it has good and bad characters that battle one another and many people find it highly entertaining to watch.

5. Sample response: If WWE followed amateur wrestling rules, there would not be the outrageous costumes and personalities. The moves would also have to be real rather than scripted, since it would be a sport. There probably would not be as much interest in the WWE, so it would not be very profitable.

6. Sample response: I think sport entertainment like that promoted by the WWE is fine. If people enjoy watching this type of entertainment, they should be allowed to do so.

Connect to the Big Question

Sample response: No. I do not think that people who pretend to be heroes can be considered real heroes. A real hero risks his or her life. Pretend heroes are just acting and may not be heroic in a real-life situation.

Word Bank Quiz

1. purpose
2. inherent
3. attributes
4. persevere
5. courage
6. determination
7. resolute
8. legendary
9. irony
10. character
11. selflessness
12. sacrifice
13. integrity
14. devise
15. conduct
16. conceive
17. illustrate
18. principles
19. honor
20. responsibility

USING THE GRAMMAR, USAGE, AND MECHANICS HANDBOOK IN THE WRITING JOURNAL

The Grammar, Usage, and Mechanics Handbook combines explanations with practice exercises. Therefore, it can be used for review as well as reference. More specifically, you might use the Handbook to do the following activities.

Peer Evaluations In the Check It and Fix It section for each writing assignment, students are directed to use the Handbook to look up principles of grammar, usage, and mechanics. Model how to use the Handbook table of contents. On the chalkboard, write in lowercase letters the name of a landmark building (for example, *empire state building*), and ask students to look up how to capitalize the name. Direct students to scan the table of contents on page 189 of their Writing Journal to find the section titled Capitalization. Together, turn to page 223 and find the capitalization rule that applies (No. 2: Capitalize the proper name of a place). Use the rule to capitalize the name correctly.

Individual, Partner, or Group Review As you evaluate student writing, list the kinds of errors each student makes. Use the list to help the student make a personalized proofreading list so that he or she knows the areas on which to focus. Help students set priorities. If a student has several areas of difficulty, select two or three important principles to work on. Follow up by assigning pertinent review exercises. You might ask students to complete exercises individually as homework or to do exercises in class with a partner or in a small group. If you wish, make answer keys available to students so that they can evaluate their own answers. Then review the principles that give difficulty.

Mini Lessons As an alternative, use the Handbook to do mini grammar lessons a few days each week. Pose a frequently asked grammar question to the class, and use the Handbook to answer it. The following Student FAQs may used to plan mini lessons.

NOUNS		
When do I need to add an *-s* to a noun?	Regular Plurals	190
Which is right: *citys* or *cities? Lifes* or *lives?*	Special Noun Plurals	191
Should I say *two women* or *two womens?*	Irregular Plurals	192
What is the difference between *'s* and *s'?*	Possessive Nouns	192
PRONOUNS		
Should I say *I* or *me? My* or *mine?*	Subject and Object Pronouns Pronouns in Compounds Possessive Pronouns	193 194 194
Which is right: *this, that,* or *them? These* or *those?*	Demonstrative Pronouns	195
Should I use *their* or *his* or *her?*	Indefinite Pronouns Pronoun-Antecedent Agreement	195 196
VERBS		
When do I need to add an *-s* to a verb?	Present Tense Verbs	199
Should I use *has* or *have? Do* or *does? Is* or *are?*	Tricky Present Tense Verbs Agreement with Compound Subjects Agreement in Questions	200 201 201

WRITING JOURNAL GRAMMAR HANDBOOK
Answer Key

Regular Plurals, p. 190

1. many <u>camps</u>
3. several <u>things</u>
4. Riding . . . , clowning, and juggling are <u>skills</u>
5. Kids
6. five <u>days</u>
9. Most <u>parents</u>
10. equipment

Special Noun Plurals, p. 191

1. lunches
2. policies
3. tomatoes
4. Sandwiches
5. dishes
6. loaves
7. lives
8. boys

Irregular Plurals, p. 192

1. people
2. women
3. men
4. children

Possessive Nouns, p. 192

1. <u>Lynn's</u> parents
2. a few <u>friends</u> went
3. <u>David's</u> cell phone
4. <u>men's</u> hands
5. <u>climbers'</u> relief

Subject and Object Pronouns, p. 193

1. <u>they</u> are
2. to <u>them</u>
3. confuse <u>us</u>
4. for <u>us</u>

Pronouns in Compounds, p. 194

1. friend and <u>I</u> split
2. between him and <u>me</u>
5. <u>he</u> and I

Possessive Pronouns, p. 194

1. mine
2. yours
3. theirs
4. my
5. hers

Demonstrative Pronouns, p. 195

1. That
2. this
3. those
4. These

Indefinite Pronouns, p. 195

1. All *P*
2. Nobody *S*
3. Many *P*
4. Anybody *S*
5. Most *P*
6. Each *S*
7. Somebody *S*
8. Both *P*

Pronoun-Antecedent Agreement, p. 196

Sample responses:
1. class project, <u>it</u>
2. everyone, <u>his or her</u>
4. sugar maples, <u>their</u>
5. red maples, <u>their</u>
7. anybody, <u>his or her</u>

Relative Pronouns, p. 197

Sample responses:
1. Folk tales are traditional stories that change over time.
2. Urban myths are folk tales that often reflect social problems.
3. Urban myths are created by imaginative people, who make them up for many reasons.
4. Jan Harold Brunvand, who is an expert on urban myths, has written several books about them.
5. Some urban myths are cautionary tales, which are stories that warn people about a potential danger.

Action Verbs and Linking Verbs, p. 198

1. depend
2. hang
3. shoot
4. fly
5. is
6. teaches
7. are
8. can be

Present Tense Verbs, p. 199

1. grandfather takes
2. Damian and his grandfather prefer
3. Damian catches
4. He and his grandfather travel
5. fish run
6. They return
7. season begins
8. It ends

Tricky Present Tense Verbs, p. 200

1. parents do not know
3. I am not
4. problems are
5. computer has
6. we have
7. parents were

Agreement with Compound Subjects, p. 201

2. Favian has
3. teacher knows
5. Samantha and I are

Agreement in Questions, p. 201

1. Are, you
2. does, Peter Parker
3. Do, you
4. Have, superpowers
5. do, Parkers

Past and Perfect Tenses, p. 202

1. Jeremy has wanted
2. he watched
3. firefighter rescued
4. they had
5. Everyone called
6. Jeremy and his parents visited

Irregular Verbs: Past and Perfect of *To Be*, p. 203

1. I was
2. We had
3. visit was
5. it had
6. she wasn't
8. I have

Irregular Verbs 3: Past and Perfect That Change Vowels, p. 204

1. knew
2. forgotten
3. rang
4. seen
5. knew
6. sat
7. come
8. saw

GRAMMAR HANDBOOK Answer Key

Irregular Verbs 4: Past and Perfect That Change Completely, p. 205

1. bought
2. taught
3. did
4. sold
5. found
6. thought
7. caught
8. told
9. bought
10. brought

Verbs as Describers, p. 206

1. old-fashioned barbeque
2. grilled chicken
3. baked potatoes
5. freshly picked strawberries

Future Tense, p. 206

1. will take
2. will give
3. will register
4. will get
5. will consider
6. will do
7. will try
8. will go

Progressive Tenses, p. 207

Sample responses:
1. I am reading *Bless Me, Ultima*.
2. I was watching *Summer Days*.
3. I will be eating dinner at 6 o'clock.

Modals, p. 207

1. should spend
2. could ride
4. can drop
6. might meet
7. will call

Articles, p. 208

1. an aquarium
2. a neon
3. The colors
4. a kick
5. an angelfish
6. the tetras
7. the water

Adjectives That Compare, p. 209

1. tallest
2. younger
3. older
4. oldest
5. most famous
6. more dangerous
7. braver
8. more adventurous

Irregular Adjectives, p. 210

1. worse
2. worst
3. more
4. best
5. least

Double Comparisons, p. 210

1. better
3. worst
4. harder

The -ly Adverb Ending, p. 211

1. gracefully
2. wildly
3. quickly
4. happily
5. joyously
6. repeatedly
7. usually
8. really

Good and Well, p. 212

1. well
2. well

Double Negatives, p. 212

1. didn't have any OR had hardly any
2. couldn't afford to buy anything
3. didn't have any OR had no

Prepositional Phrases, p. 213

1. for class president
2. from my friends
3. in the school hallways
4. After school
5. about my plans
6. without their help
7. to them
8. of my friends

Coordinating Conjunctions, p. 214

1. but
2. or
3. and
4. yet
5. nor
6. for
7. so
8. and

Subordinating Conjunctions, p. 215

1. Though Janelle is my twin
2. whereas she likes music
3. When she sings
4. as if she is the worst singer on earth
5. because she is my sister

Correlative Conjunctions, p. 215

1. Both . . . and
2. not only . . . but also
3. Neither . . . nor

Run-on Sentences, p. 217

Sample responses:

1. Charlie Nagreen sold meatballs at a fair, but they did not sell well.
2. They rolled off the bread; it was too hard to eat them.
3. Charlie flattened the meat, and he created the first hamburgers!

Fragments, p. 218

Sample responses:

1–2. Though we think of heroes as fearless, heroes often feel fear.
4–5. When the opportunity arises, they may be unwilling to help others.
7–8. Even though they are afraid, they may react quickly to rescue another person.
9–10. In fact, their acts may seem even more heroic because they are willing to put their fear aside.

Fragments Missing Sentence Parts, p. 219

Sample responses:

1. I always enjoy dancing.
2. It is fun to perform.
3. I enjoy dancing in front of an audience.
4. The audience members are clapping for me.

Paragraph Focus and the Topic Sentence, p. 220

Topic sentence: Even though there are laws to protect women in the workplace, discrimination still exists.

Sentence off topic: Unfortunately, disabled people are also sometimes discriminated against.

Paragraph Development, p. 221

Sample responses:

1. sending and receiving written messages over a cell phone
2. fast
3. distracting them from their studies
4. kids may text message when they should be paying attention in class

GRAMMAR HANDBOOK Answer Key

Paragraph Coherence and Transitions, p. 222

Sample responses:
2. Therefore,
3. First,
4. Later,

Capitalization, p. 223

1. Uncle
2. Chicago
3. Tower
4. Then
5. *Is Only*
6. Korean

End Marks, p. 224

Sample responses:
1. pie?
2. class.
3. oven.
4. everywhere!
5. happen."

Commas, p. 225

1. handball, Matthew? (direct address)
2. two, three, or four players. (series)
3. Really, (introductory word)
4. One player serves the ball using a hand or a fist, and the opponent tries to return the serve. (main clauses joined by a coordinating conjunction)
5. June 10, 2008, in Hightown, California. (date, address)
6. Carey, my handball partner, (group of words that explains)
7. Detroit, Michigan, to (address)
8. When the audience cheers, it (introductory clause)

Apostrophes, p. 226

1. Bill's favorite sport
2. It's
3. he's
4. parents' plans

Semicolons, p. 227

1. sport; it
2. homemade; therefore,
3. simple; in fact,
4. surfing; therefore,
5. way; it's

Quotation Marks, p. 227

1. "Did you practice playing your guitar?" Mickey asked.
2. "I started to," Mauricio replied, "but then I decided to watch TV."
4. "Wishful Thinking"
5. "Play Guitar Like a Pro"

Italics and Underlining, p. 227

1. *Gone with the Wind*
2. *Teen Magazine*
3. *The Wizard of Oz*
4. *Wicked*

Spelling, p. 228

1. receive
2. supplies
3. neighbor
4. sloppily
5. amazed
6. dazzling
7. players
8. guys
9. craziest
10. winners

GRAPHIC ORGANIZERS

Organizers guide vocabulary development, support comprehension strategies, bolster students' preparation for reading, or assess students' learning of key concepts related to the Big Questions.

Cause and Effect Map

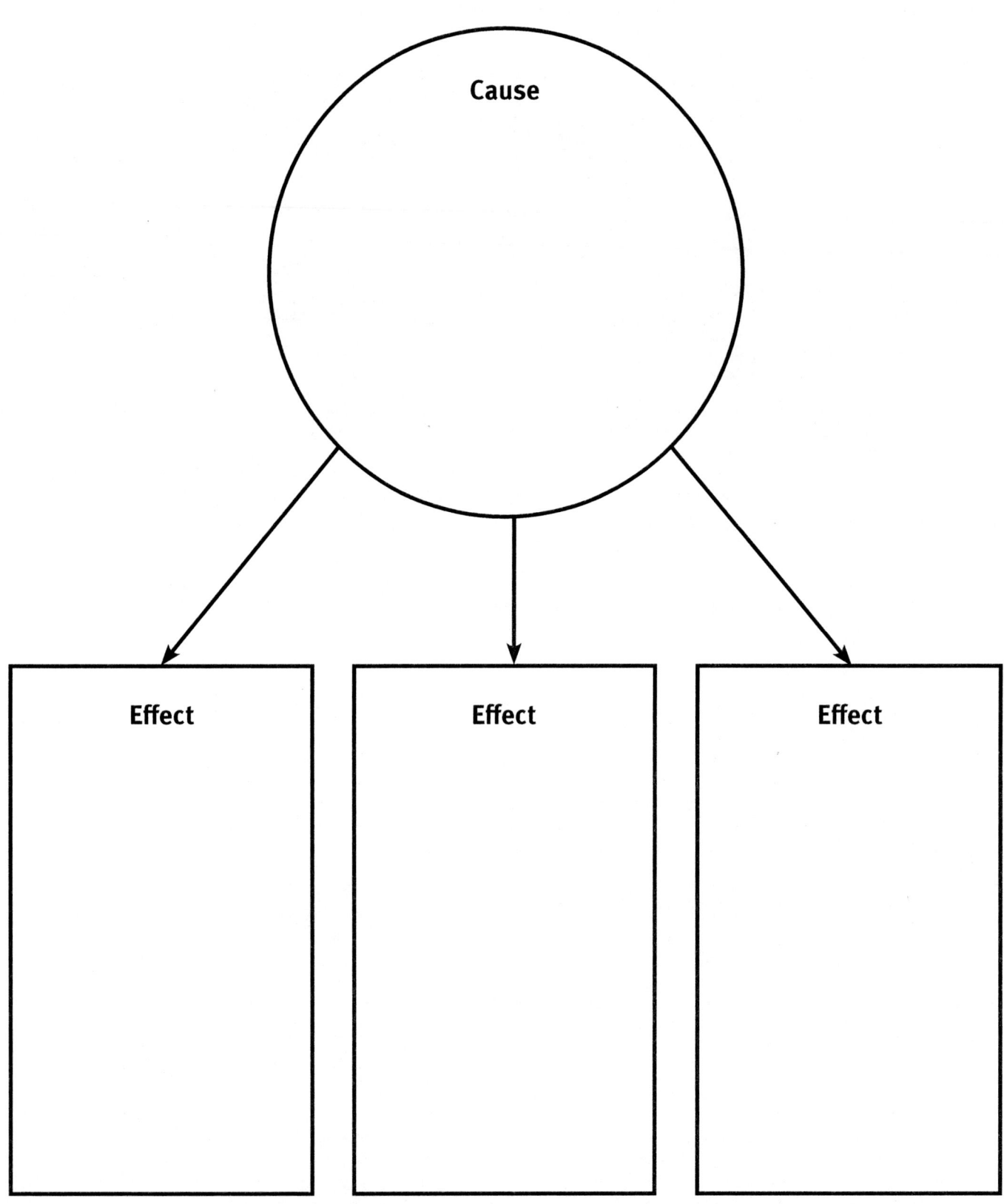

Comic Strip Organizer

Draw-Define-Use Organizer

Word Definition: _____

_____

Sentence: _____

_____

Word Definition: _____

_____

Sentence: _____

_____

Guess It and Check It Chart

Word	Context Clues	Guess	Check

Inference Map

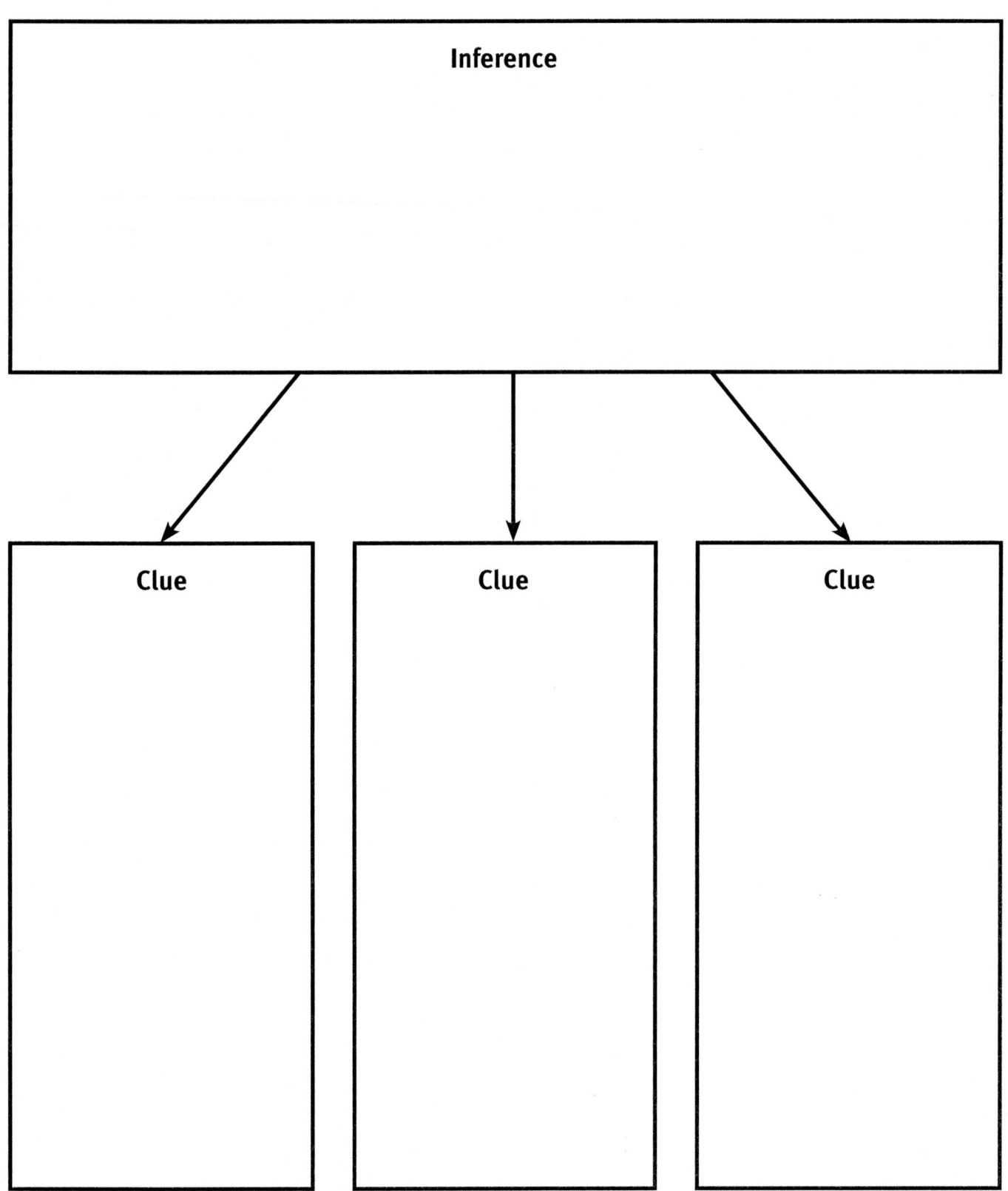

Inference

Clue

Clue

Clue

K–W–L Chart

K: What I Know	W: What I Want to Know	L: What I Learned	Questions After Reading

Main Idea Map

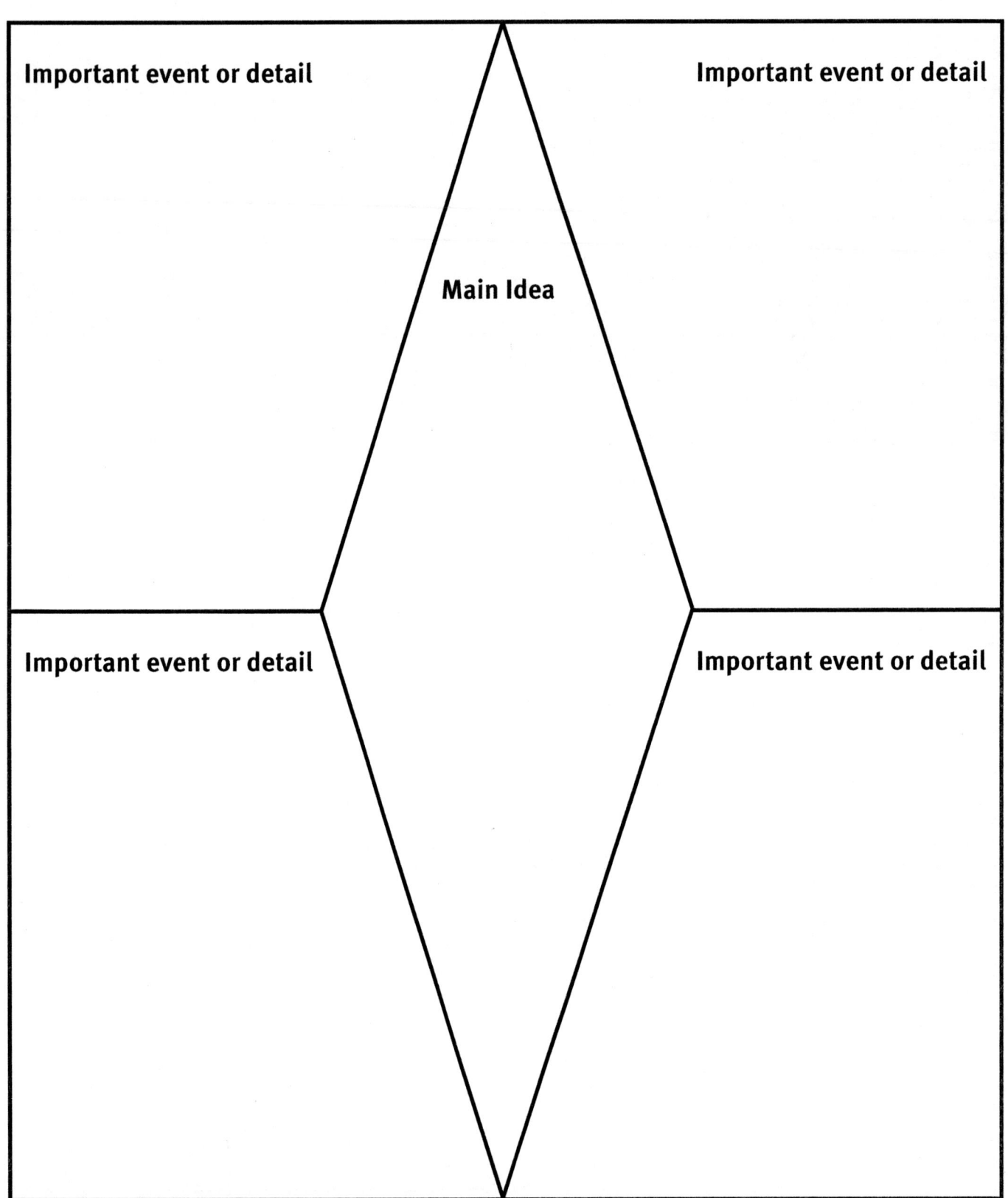

Important event or detail

Important event or detail

Main Idea

Important event or detail

Important event or detail

Making Personal Connections Organizer

<table>
<tr><td colspan="2">What is being explained or described in the text:</td></tr>
<tr>
<td>Connection to
My Personal Experiences</td>
<td>Connection to Other Things
(movies, books, other people)</td>
</tr>
<tr><td>1.</td><td>1.</td></tr>
<tr><td>2.</td><td>2.</td></tr>
<tr><td>3.</td><td>3.</td></tr>
</table>

Opinion and Reasons Organizer

Opinion

Reasons

Problem and Solution Map

Problem

Solution	Response

End Result

Series of Events Map

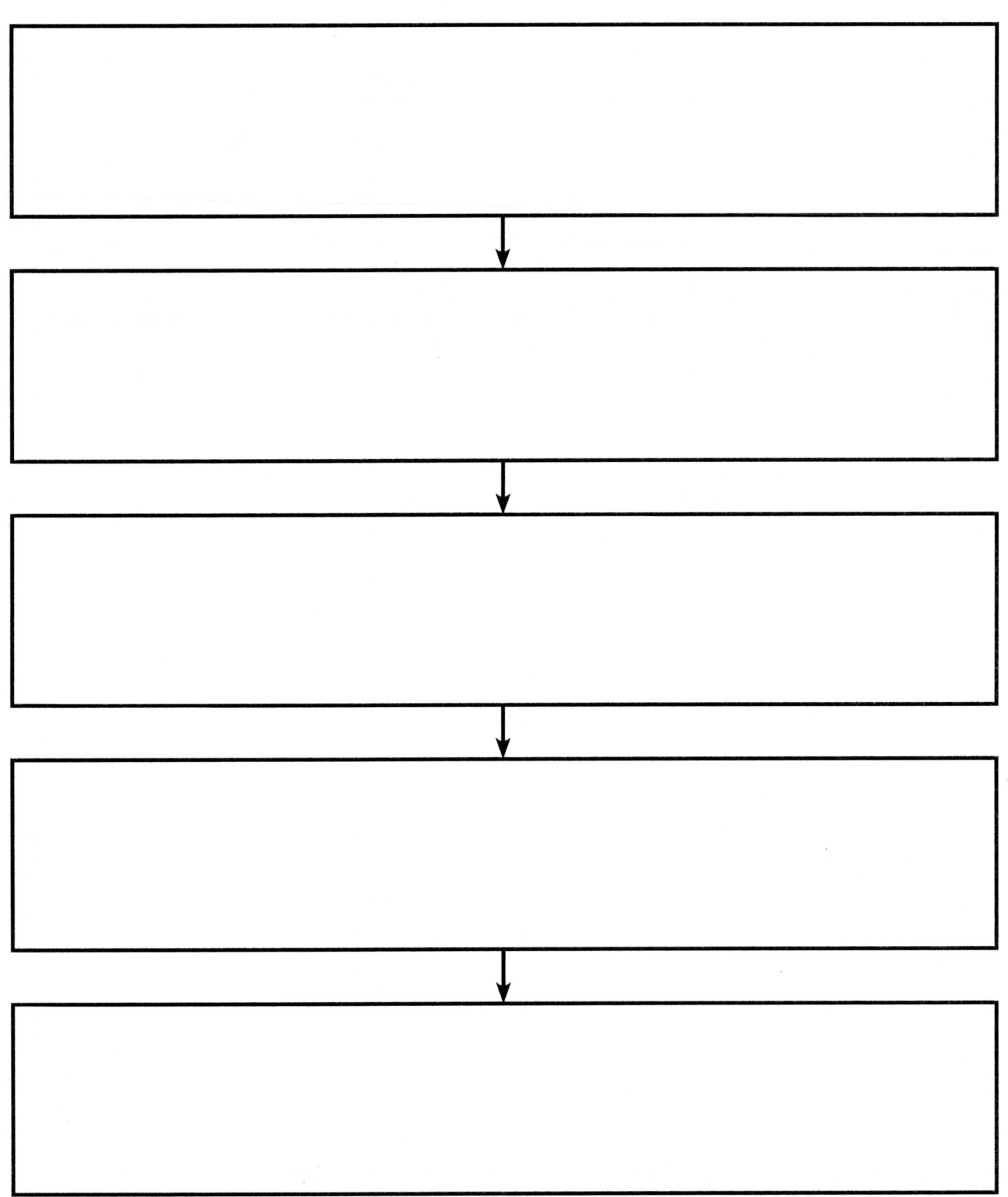

T-Chart

Three-Column Chart

Two-Column Journal

Ideas from the Article	My Thoughts

Venn Diagram

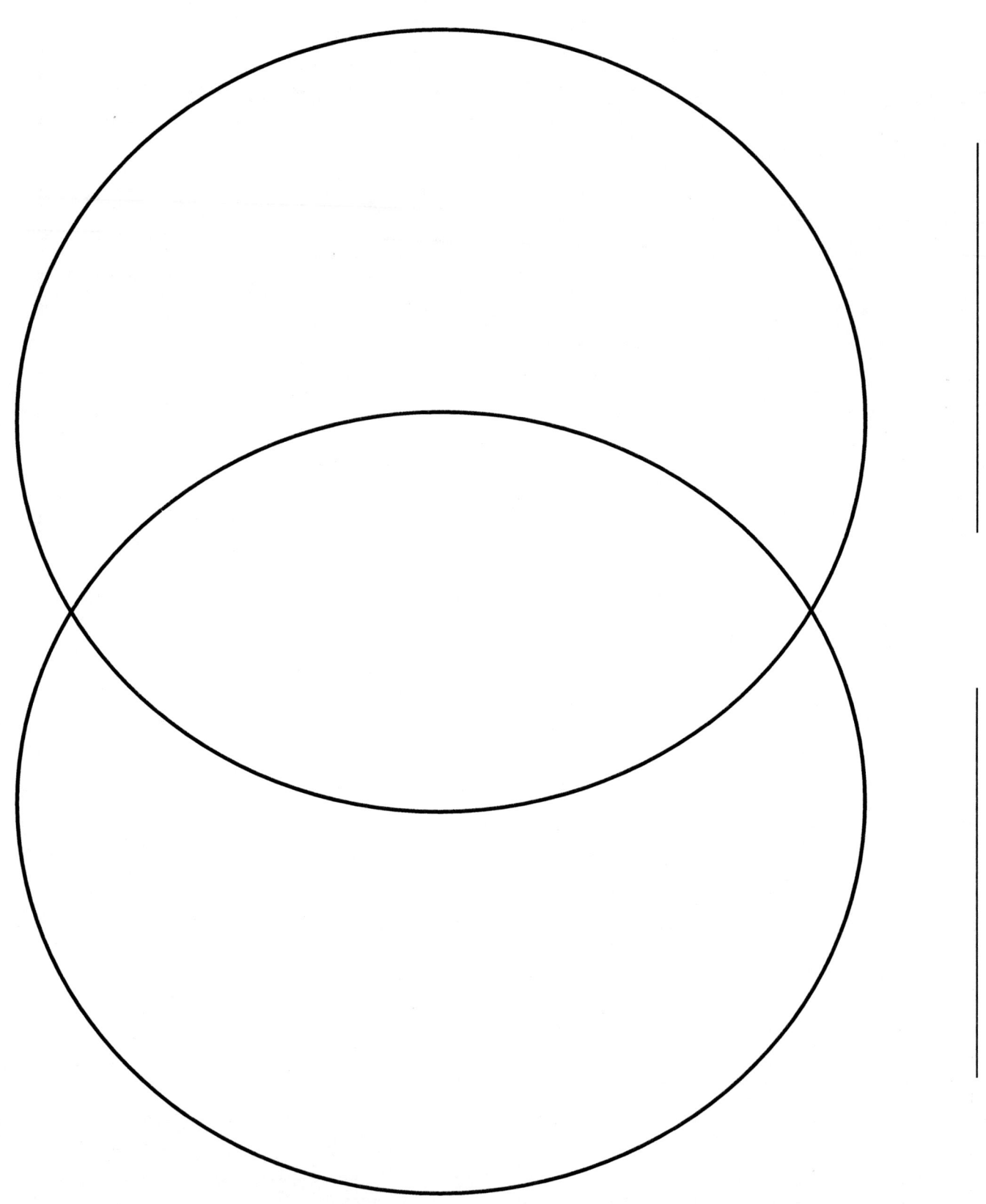

Teaching Guide and Resources

Vocabulary Square

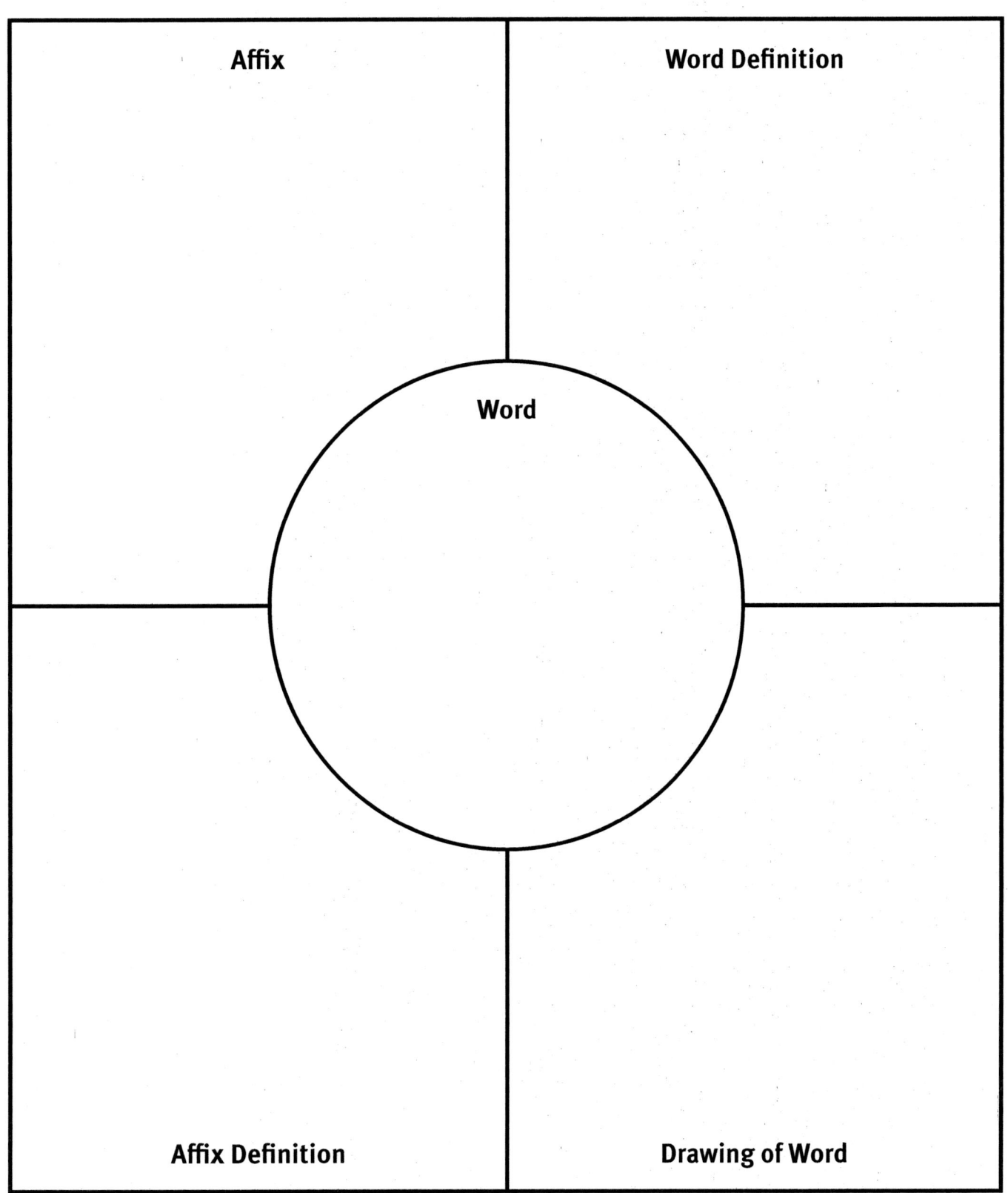

Affix

Word Definition

Word

Affix Definition

Drawing of Word

Web Map

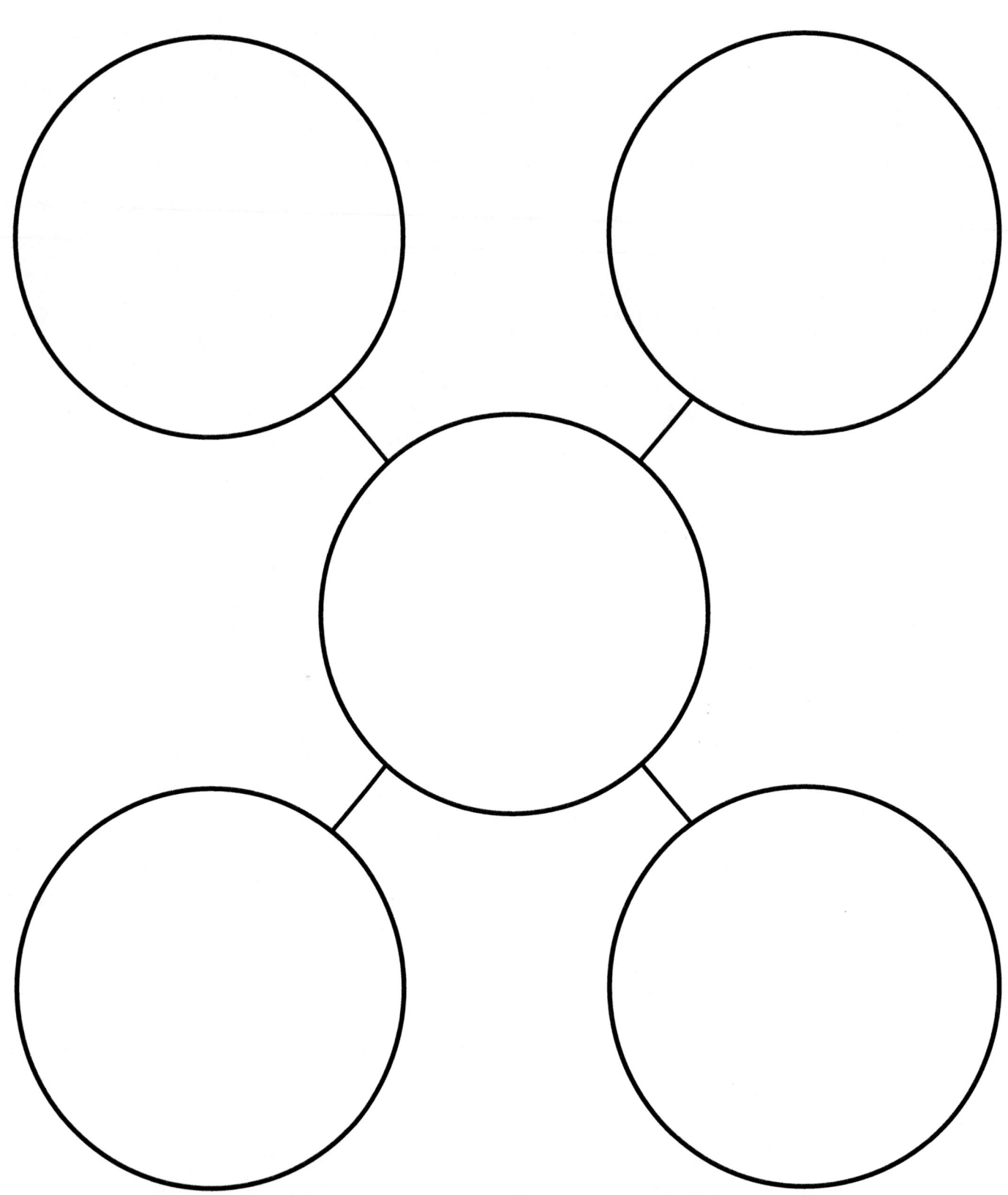

Word Pyramid

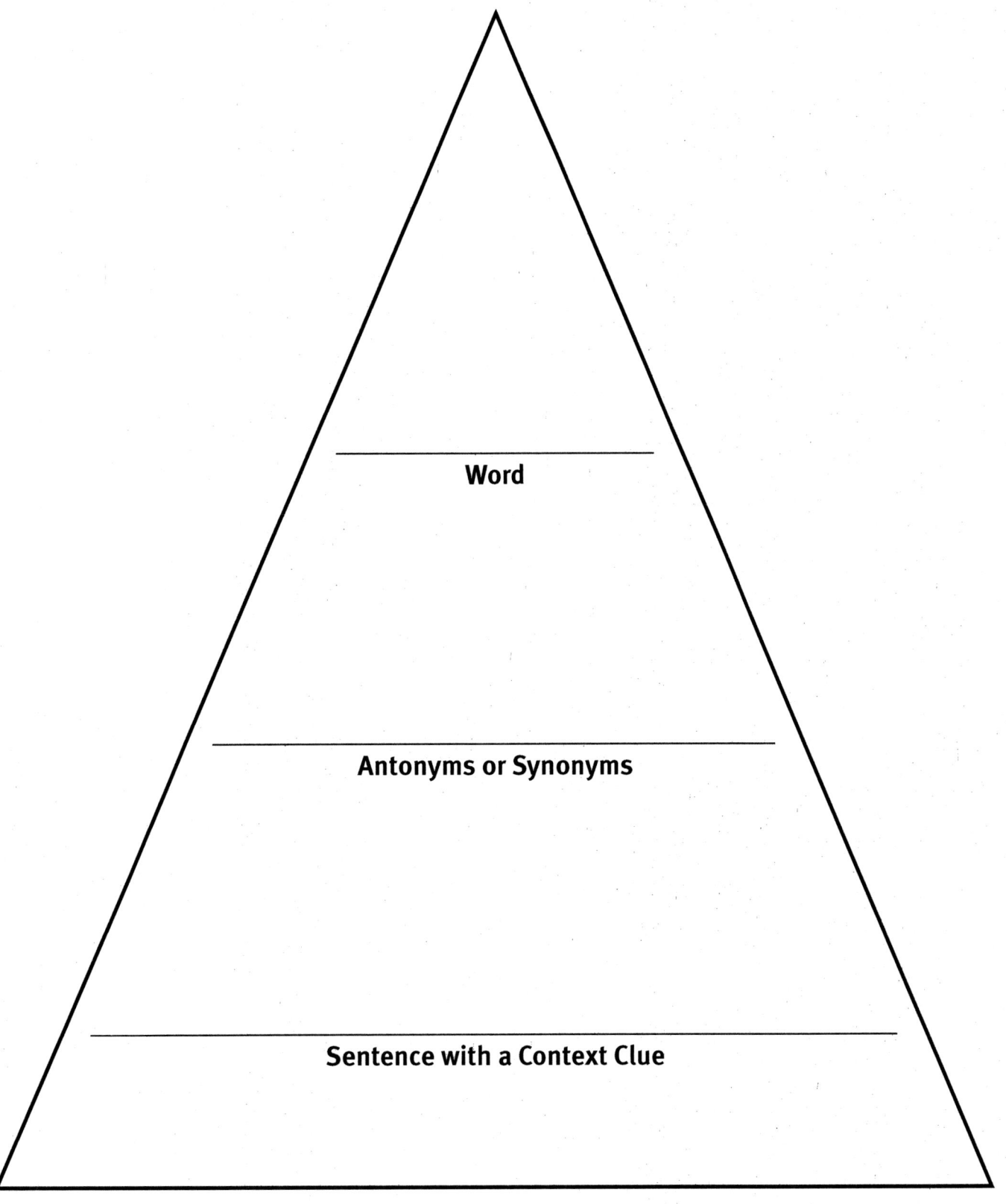

Word

Antonyms or Synonyms

Sentence with a Context Clue

Reality Central **Strategy Bookmarks**

Reality Central Strategy Bookmark

Ask Questions

BEFORE you read, ask:
- What clues does the title give me about the text?
- What do I already know about this topic?
- What predictions can I make?

WHILE you read, ask:
- What is the main idea?
- What details help me visualize?
- What do I need help to understand?

AFTER you read, ask:
- What predictions were confirmed?
- What connections can I make to this text?
- What do I still wonder about?

Reality Central Strategy Bookmark

Use Fix-Up Strategies

For an unknown word:
- Skip the word and read on.
- Use a new meaning. Ask, "Does this make sense?"
- Use connections to understand the words.
- Reread the text.
- Study the graphics.
- Use reference sources.
- Keep a word list. Refer to it often.

For new or difficult ideas:
- Figure out what the author is trying to tell you.
- Put a sticky note near important ideas or details.
- Remember your purpose for reading.
- Think about what you already know about the topic.
- Create images in your mind.
- Adjust your reading rate.

Reality Central Strategy Bookmark

Summarize

BEFORE you read:
- Preview the title and headings.
- Think about what you will read.

WHILE you read:
- Mark key words with sticky notes.
- Mark main ideas with sticky notes.

AFTER you read:
- Use the key words and main ideas to create a summary.

Remember, a summary includes:
- your words, not the author's.
- only the most important ideas, not all the ideas.

Reality Central **Strategy Bookmark**

Make Inferences

An inference is based on:
- background knowledge
- clues from the text

List what you **know** about the topic:

_____

_____

_____

_____

List **clues** from the text:

_____

_____

_____

_____

What **inference** can you make?

_____

_____

_____

_____

Reality Central **Strategy Bookmark**

Preview, Predict, and Set Purposes

Preview Before you read, look at:
- the introduction
- the title
- photographs
- captions
- heads and subheads
- boldface words
- graphs, charts, and other visuals
- the questions at the end

Predict Answer these questions:
- Why did the author write this?
- What will I learn as I read it?
- What will the author tell me?

Set Purposes
- Am I reading for entertainment, to hear a message, or to find out information?
- Finish this sentence:
  As I read, I expect to find out

_____.

Reality Central **Strategy Bookmark**

Make Connections

Connect to Your Own Experiences
- What does the text remind you of from your own experiences?
- How are these situations alike?
- How does the connection help you understand the text?

Connect to the World
- How does the text remind you of something you have seen or heard about?
- How are these situations alike?
- How does the connection help you understand the text?

Connect to Other Texts
- What other text (print or media) does this article remind you of?
- How are the texts alike?
- How does the connection help you understand the text?

Reality Central **Strategy Bookmarks**

Reality Central **Strategy Bookmark**

Visualize

Use images to create a picture in your mind as you read. Mark words that create powerful images with sticky notes.

What can you **see**?

What do you **hear**?

What can you **feel**?

What might you be able to **smell**?

Can you **taste** anything?

How do these images help you understand the text?

_____

_____

_____

_____

_____

Reality Central **Strategy Bookmark**

Read Fluently

Fluent reading is about reading rate, accuracy, and expression.

Reading Rate:

✓ Slow down for difficult passages and text full of facts.

✓ Speed up for text that is familiar or easy to read.

Accuracy:

If you are unsure of a word:

✓ "Try out" several words to see which one fits.

✓ Look for clues around the word.

✓ Reread or read on.

Expression:

✓ Use punctuation as clues to stop, slow down, or alter your voice as you read.

✓ Read short sentences with "power punch."

✓ Longer sentences sound smooth and flowing.

✓ Think about the right tone of your voice for the text.

Reality Central **Strategy Bookmark**

Determine Importance

Strategic readers can differentiate between important information and less important information. Important information is **relevant.** Information that is less important is **irrelevant.**

As you read, mark relevant information with sticky notes.

Use the relevant information to write a statement of main idea.

_____

_____

_____

_____

_____

_____

_____

TABLE OF CONTENTS

Assessment Tools

Use the assessment tools at various points as you work with *Reality Central*. Assessments are designed to help inform your instruction. The results of assessments will help you plan how best to work with each student.

Retelling Rubric

Ask the student to retell you the important parts of a piece of expository text. Use this rubric to assess understanding of ideas, text structure, and key vocabulary.

Student Name: _____

Passage/Text: _____

Date: _____

4	• Accurately retells important concepts from the text in own words. • Organizes information using appropriate text structures throughout the retelling (such as sequential order, classification, cause and effect, compare and contrast, and so on). • Appropriately uses key vocabulary. • Synthesizes concepts from the text, using textual evidence and prior knowledge to draw inferences and generate original conclusions.
3	• Explains the main ideas and supporting details from the text in own words. • Organizes the information using appropriate text structure (such as sequential order, classification, cause and effect, compare and contrast, and so on). • Utilizes some key vocabulary. • Attempts to draw inferences/generalizations and supports them with textual evidence and prior knowledge.
2	• Demonstrates a partial understanding of the text, randomly restating facts/concepts, or relying heavily on the author's words. May copy some material from the text. • Organization is less defined; text structure is weak. • May utilize some key vocabulary. • May include inaccuracies or omissions.
1	• Relates a limited amount of information, conveying little or no understanding of the text. May copy extensively from the text. • May include some inaccuracies, omissions, or confusions. • May include information that is off-topic.

Phrasing and Fluency Checklist

Use this checklist to record oral reading behaviors.

Student Name: _____

Passage/Text: _____

Date: _____

When the student read orally, phrasing and fluency were:

_____ appropriate for the text, combining short and long phrases and considering punctuation

_____ in longer phrases

_____ in short phrases

_____ word by word

The student's reading rate was:

_____ adjusted properly to match text

_____ inconsistent

_____ too fast for the text

_____ too slow for the text

The number of correct words per minute _____

Recommended oral reading rates (Good, Kaminski, Barr, and Rasinski)

Grade	Oral Correct Words Per Minute
6	110–150
7	150–180
8+	180–200+

The student used the following strategies when encountering difficulty:

_____ rereading up to point of difficulty

_____ reading ahead

_____ using visual clues such as illustrations

_____ breaking words into syllables

_____ sounding out words letter by letter

_____ other. Describe:

_____

The student self-corrected when the miscues were the following:

_____ semantic (interfered with meaning)

_____ graphemic/phonemic (did not match the text)

_____ syntactic (did not sound like correct language)

Other observations that inform instruction:

_____

_____

_____

_____

Collaboration Rubric

Use this checklist to assess students' work in groups. Students can use this tool to assess their own participation in group activities.

Student Name: _____

Date: _____

CATEGORY	4	3	2	1
Focus and Participation	Stays focused on the task and what needs to be done. Self-directed and contributes to the group.	Focuses on the task and what needs to be done most of the time. Can be counted on by other group members.	Focuses on the task some of the time. Other group members need to remind the person to stay on task.	Lets others do the work. Rarely focuses on the task and what needs to be done.
Dependability	Follows through on tasks that are assigned and does not depend on others to do the work. Shares responsibility for tasks.	Follows through on most assigned tasks.	Does not follow through on most assigned tasks. Sometimes depends on others to do the work.	Depends on others to do the work. Does not follow through on assigned tasks.
Discussion Skills	Respectfully listens, interacts, discusses, and poses questions to all members of the team and helps to direct the group in reaching consensus.	Listens respectfully, interacts, discusses, and poses questions to others during discussions.	Has some difficulty respectfully listening and discussing.	Has great difficulty listening, may argue during discussions, and does not listen to others' opinions. May keep group from reaching consensus.
Solving Problems	Looks for and suggests solutions to problems.	When others suggest solutions, improves the solutions.	Does not suggest or improve solutions, but is willing to try out others' solutions.	Does not try to solve problems or help group members solve problems.
Teamwork	Has a positive attitude about working with the team in collaboration.	Usually has a positive attitude about the work of others on the team.	May be critical of the work of others.	Critical of the work of other group members.
Sharing Information	Gathers research if necessary and shares useful ideas with the group.	Provides some useful research and ideas to the group in discussion.	Sometimes provides useful research and ideas with the group.	Seldom provides useful ideas to the group or contributes research to the project.

Independent Reading Rubric

Use this rubric to periodically assess students' behaviors as independent readers.

Student Name: _____

Date: _____

Category	4	3	2	1
Frequency of Independent Reading	Student reads daily.	Student reads most days.	Student reads occasionally.	Student seldom reads independently.
Difficulty Level of Books Selected	Student chooses books at or beyond independent reading level.	Student chooses books at independent reading level.	Student chooses books at and below independent reading level.	Student chooses books below independent reading level.
Variety of Genres Represented in Independent Reading	Student chooses texts from a wide variety of genres.	Student is willing to try reading texts from a variety of genres.	Student does little experimentation in reading various genres.	Student does no experimentation with genres.
Completion of Books Started	Student completes most books initiated independently and completes class reading.	Student completes many of the texts initiated independently and completes class reading.	Student completes less than half of the reading initiated independently and completes some of the class reading assignments.	Students fails to complete many books chosen independently and read as a class.

Writing Rubrics

Share with students these rubrics for expository, persuasive, and narrative writing. Remind students that:

- **expository writing** relates information.
- **persuasive writing** tries to convince readers of something.
- **narrative writing** tells a story.

Encourage students to add points to these rubrics to guide their writing. Extra space is provided in each rubric.

CATEGORY	4	3	2	1
Expository Writing	* My paper is well-developed. I have more than enough information to inform the reader about the topic. The information is presented clearly, with many details. * I have a clear pattern of organization. I use the same pattern throughout the writing. * I thought about the audience. * I frequently use language choices to maintain a style or a tone.	* My paper is fairly well-developed and I have enough information to inform the reader about the topic. The information is presented clearly, and there are some details about the topic. * I have a pattern of organization, and I try to stick to it. * I thought about the audience. * I use language choices to maintain a style or a tone.	* My paper has a small amount of information. The information does not clearly explain the topic. * I used details, but they may be the wrong details or they may not help to explain the topic. * I thought about the audience. * I do not have a clear style or tone.	* I did not tell enough about the topic. * I have only a few details. * It's hard to follow the organization. * I may not address the intended audience. * I do not have any style or tone.

CATEGORY	4	3	2	1
Persuasive Writing	* My stand on the issue is clear. * Numerous specific details support my stand. * My organization is logical. * I understand the type of audience I am writing for, and I use language that makes sense for persuasive writing. * I thought about my audience and how to persuade them.	* My stand on the issue is clear. * I have chosen enough specific details to support my stand. * My organization is logical. It strays only a little. * I use some persuasive language. * I have included ideas that will persuade my audience.	* My stand on the issue could be clearer. * There are some details, but they are general or may not really help to explain my position. * I tried to organize, but my writing jumps around. * I tried to understand the audience I was writing for. * I needed to use more persuasive language.	* I do not present a stand on an issue. * I have few details. * I have no real pattern of organization. * I did not try to write for the audience. * I used little persuasive language.

CATEGORY	4	3	2	1
Narrative Writing	* My paper is well-developed and complete. * I have a clear organization that makes sense for telling a story. * I meet the audience's needs. * I used language that makes sense for narrative writing.	* My paper has gaps or uneven parts. * I have an order that makes sense for telling a story. * I tried to meet the audience's needs. * I use language that for the most part makes sense for narrative writing.	* I tried to develop my ideas, but the paper is not whole or complete. * My order may get off track. * I tried to understand the audience I was writing for. * Not all my language "works" for narrative writing.	* I did not develop the ideas in a logical way. * My order is confusing. * My audience may not understand my ideas. * My language choices do not help tell the story.

Beautiful
BAVARIA

Klaus-Jürgen Vetter (Editor)

CONTENTS

◄◄ **THE DANUBE GORGE.** Between Kelheim and Weltenburg Abbey are the "Weltenburg Narrows", a nature reserve. Here the Danube river cleaves its way through the Jurassic limestone rock.

◄ **VITAL TRADITION.** On festive occasions, the people in Bavaria are proud to wear their traditional costume. The cultivation of heritage and tradition is of high interest here.

"If I was to travel, nowhere would I rather tour than through Swabia and Bavaraia, for they are friendly and good natured, accomodating and awaiting the wayfarer, and they do good work for their money."

Martin Luther

WHERE TO BEGIN, what to highlight when talking about Upper Bavaria, a swathe of land, whose sheer mention makes people romanticize?

Southern Bavaria is one-of-a-kind. Every region has its own special feature: there are the grandiose Alps, with Germany's highest peak, the Zugspitze, the magnificent alpine uplands and the breath-taking landscape around Berchtesgaden, Tegernsee and around Chiemgau, there is a charming landscape of rivers, and of course, historical cities, such as Regensburg, Augsburg and Munich, Bavaria's lively, culture-rich capital. There is something wonderful to be discovered on every scale, from picturesque hideaways to grandiose scenic views, such as the Ramsauer Pfarrkirche in the area Berchtesgaden as pictured here – one of the most photographed scenes in Bavaria.

There is water everywhere – nestled in magnificent scenery, the inviting lakes are perfect for swimming, sailing or for a ride on a steamboat. Chiemsee is considered to be the "ocean" of Bavaria. From relaxing in nature to mountain climbing, hiking, sailing, downhill or cross-country skiing, the possibilities are endless.

Bavaria even offers an array of activities for those who wish to be inspired. Countless enchanting castles, such as Neuschwanstein and Herrenchiemsee, never cease to amaze. There are many famous churches and cloisters to tour and there are world-renowned art galleries, such as those in Munich, to visit. Those who prefer fun and excitement will certainly find it at Oktoberfest, the largest fair in the world.

▼ "KÖNIGSSEE" – KINGS LAKE AT BERCHTESGADEN. An entire valley envelops the so-called cleanest lake in Germany. The lake is 8 km/5 m long and up to 1.2 km/0.7 m wide. It is like an emerald green rhinestone, surrounded by mountain peaks, such as the Watzmann (2713 m/8900 ft) and the Jenner (1874 m/6148 ft).

The majestic lake was formed by glaciers during the ice age. Today, the lake forms the heart of Berchtesgaden National Park, which was established in 1978. The park was created to preserve this beautiful area.

▼ ▶ ST SEBASTIAN – THE RAMSAUER PARISH CHURCH. One of the most popular Christmas card scenes is the small, but world renowned church in the area of Berchtesgaden. It stands out beautifully against the mountain scenery. It is no surprise that Joseph Mohr, the writer of "Silent Night" was once a priest here.

▼ ▼ THE BERCHTESGADEN MARKETPLACE. Wonderfully restored buildings encompass the health resort's marketplace. A fountain from the year 1558 can be found in the middle of the marketplace.

▼ ▼ GLÜCK AUF! Although it is still fully functioning, the salt refinery in Berchtesgaden is visited by about 400,000 people a year. The mining railroad travels 700 meters deep into the mountainside. Along the way there is salt grotto and a salt lake, which can only be crossed by raft. A salt museum provides additional information.

▶ ST. BARTHOLOMÄ. The building complex on the Hirschau Peninsula, on the west coast of "Königssee", is mainly made up of a small church and a former hunting castle. It is easiest to reach Bartholomä by ship.

◄◄ **SYMBOLS OF BERCHTESGADEN.** The Watzmann is a mountain range with various ridges, rock faces and spectacular peaks, such as the 2713 m/8900 ft high Grand Watzmann, the Watzmannfrau, and the Watzmankinder. There are many sayings and legends related to the Watzmann. It is also notorious for the famous 1,800 m/5,900 ft high East Wall, which rises over Kings Lake. The East Wall should only be attempted by experienced climbers. Everyone else should take the path from the Watzmann house up to the peak.

◄ **MAJESTIC VIEWS** (top picture, this page). The view from the Jenner over Kings Lake and the beautiful mountainous landscape reminds most hikers of the words of Josef Ganghofer – "Lord, let those you love be placed in this land!" The Jenner train, which goes from Schönau up to the almost 1,874 m/5,900 ft high peak, allow non-hikers to view the spectacular scenery. Various paths lead from the mountain and Jenner central station throughout Berchtesgaden National Park. With a little luck, you might see an ibex (wild goat), a chamois (antelope), or even Edelweiss (alpine flowers) along the way.

◄ **ROYAL NAVIGATION.** A ship tour on the crystal-clear lake of fairytales, Königssee (Kings Lake), is exceedingly worthwhile. Electric boats provide an introspective journey as they glide through the water. In 1908, these boats were introduced to the lake in order to help preserve the water's natural beauty. The boats travel from the Königssee district to St. Bartholomä and Salet.

◄ **FAMOUS ECHO.** During the trip, the ships' captains blow a melody on their trumpets, which rings out from the steep rock faces, creating the famous Echo of Kings Lake.

◄ **OBERAMMERGAU.** About 20 km/ 12 m north of Garmisch-Partenkirchen, in the area of Werdenfelser is the small village of Oberammergau, famous for its passion-plays, which take place every ten years (also see page 39).

The famous buildings with Lüftlmalerei facades, a variant of the Trompe-l'òeil, are a must-see. The Fresco technique is used for these paintings; watercolors with a mineral basis are applied to fresh plaster so that the colors sink deep into the stucco and conjoin to form a water-insoluble layer that lasts. Well-to-do farmers or traders displayed their wealth through these house facades. The symbols are mostly of a religious nature and in Oberammergau, they are often scenes from the passion-plays. The most beautiful facades of this type can be found on the Pilatus, Forst and Mußldoma Houses.

▼ **SKI OR WOODCARVING COURSES.** Oberamergau has a lot to offer. On one side it is a winter sport and health resort, on the other side, it the center of the fine art of woodcarving.

In as early as the 12th century, monks began to pursue this craft. In the 18th century, the Oberammergau production houses and their various branches emerged. Here, the door-to-door sale of items was organized. Today in Oberammergau there are about 60 wood carvers, who produce both holy and profane figures. Those fond of the wood craft should take a little detour to the Pilatus House. Here you can watch a wood carver at work in his shop. There are also vacation courses available for those who would like to try their own hand at the craft.

Woodcarving has been practiced in Oberammergan for over 500 years. So quite naturally this is also the main focus of the Oberammergau museum. The museum has a rich selection of fine woodcarving on display from the gothic to modern times. A special section is devotetd to cribs. On display there is the historical church crib, which Ludwig II was very fond of. In the museum visitors also get information about the local history .

▶▶ THE TOWERS — A SYMBOL OF MUNICH. The symbol of Munich is the two round domes of the Frauenkirche. Due to the fact that buildings in Munich's inner-city mustn't be built over 100 m/330 ft high, the 99 m/325 ft meter high towers, certainly stand out. The foundation of the late gothic church was laid in 1468. Just 20 years later, the church was fully completed. The "Devils Footstep" in the entrance way has become a legend. The church suffered heavy damages in World War II, when a large portion of the interior was destroyed and looted. After the war, the church was continuously reconstructed and finally fully restored in 1994.

▶ MUNICH. Marienplatz is the heart of the city. The U- and the S-train lines run directly below ground and above ground is the square where the Christmas market (Christkindlmarkt), political assemblies, concerts and FC Bayern's major parties take place. The old Town Hall, which is now a toy museum, can be found at the end of the square.

▶ THE GLOCKENSPIEL IN THE NEW TOWN HALL. At 11 o'clock sharp, the glockenspiel chimes in the tower of the new town hall on Marienplatz (also at noon and 5 pm in the summer). Accompanied by 43 chimes, 32 life-sized figures present a jousting tournament and a dance of coopers. This beautiful neo-gothc style building was constructed between the years 1867 and 1908. The 100 m/110 yd long facade is richly decorated and covered with many figures. An 85 m/280 ft high middle tower topped-off with the Munich mascot also houses an observation deck. Constructed in 1638, the Marien Column can be found directly in front of the new town hall. On the corners of the column, cherubs fight against the plagues of mankind; war, pest, hunger and disbelief.

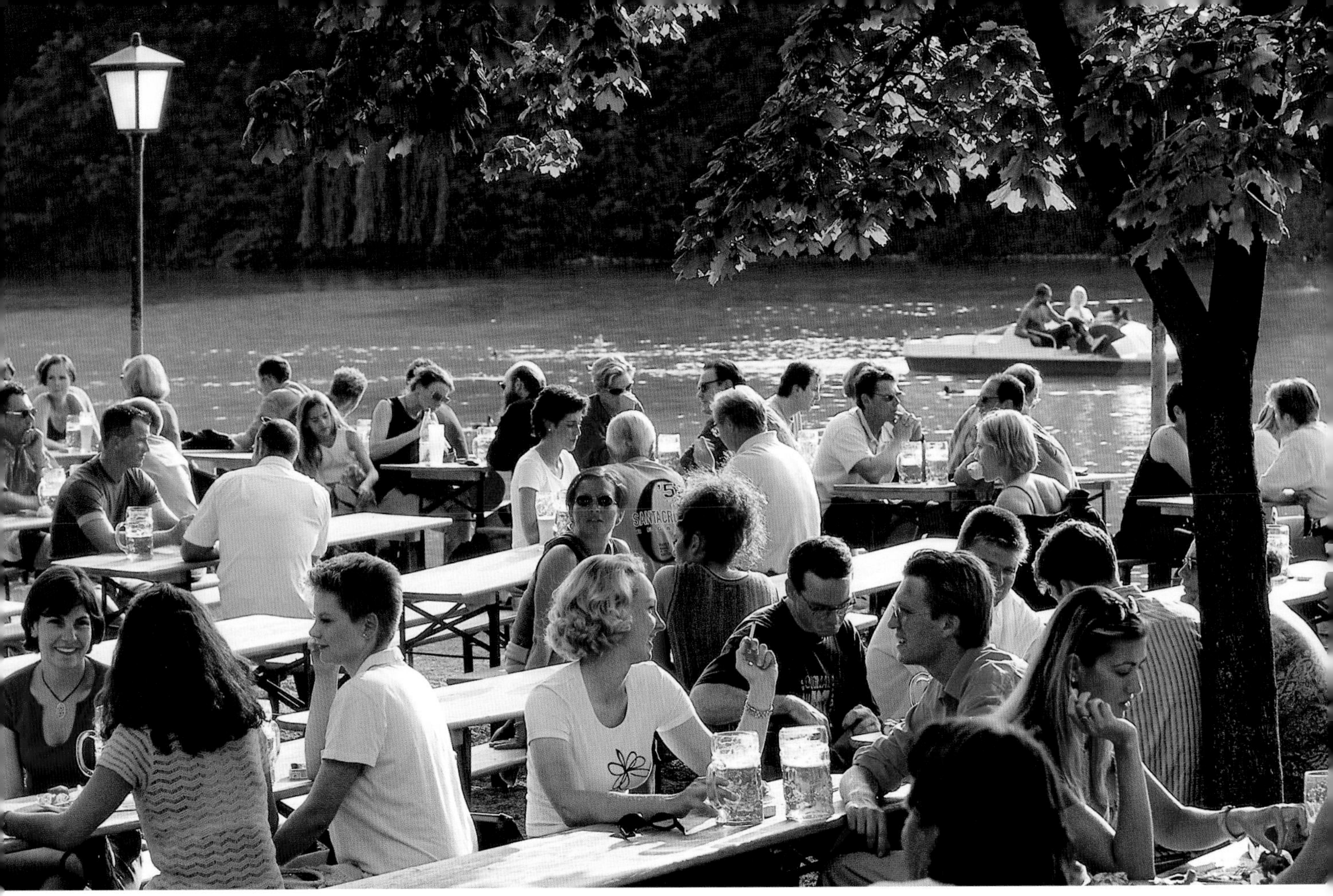

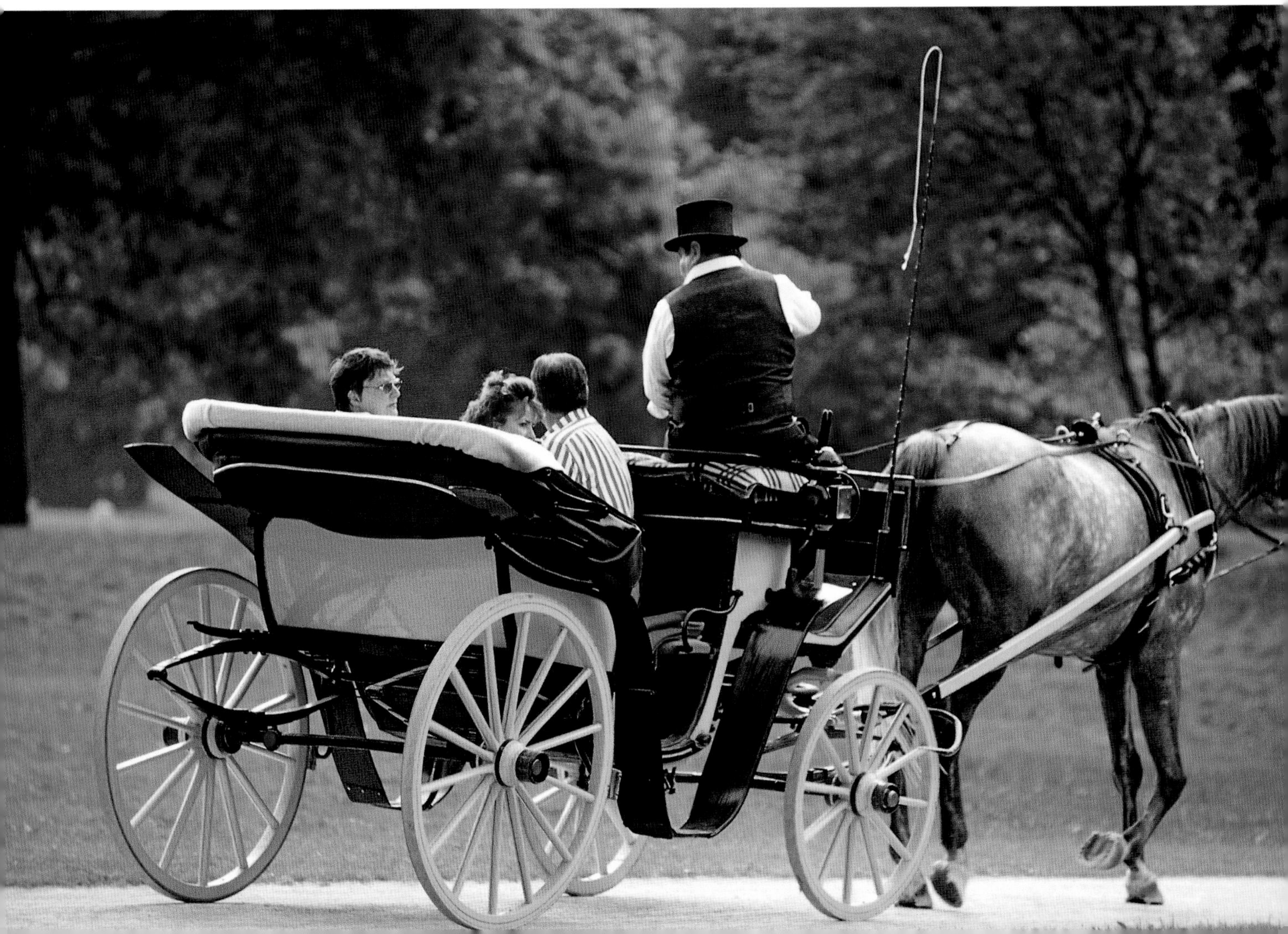

◄◄ RELAXING IN THE ENGLISH GARDEN. The Kleinhesseloher Lake is located in the heart of the English Garden. Here you can watch the ducks or enjoy a liter (Mass) of beer at the Lake House. The English Garden is, in the true sense of the term, a park for the people. From dog owners, parents and children, cyclists, sunbathers, horseback riders, to students or athletes, the park is a place of relaxation for everyone.

◄◄ COACH RIDES IN THE PARK. Just like in the 19th century, you can enjoy a leisurely coach ride through the park. More than 200 years old, the park is large enough for such rides – measuring around 3.7 square kilometers, it is even bigger than Central Park in New York City. The 78 km/48 m long pathway is certainly lengthy enough for an extensive trip.

◄ SUMMER IN THE CITY. On beautiful summer days, the English Garden is a retreat for locals and tourists, who can't or don't want to drive to one of the many lakes around Munich. On days like these, ice cream consumption is especially high. By the way, people nowadays don't make such a fuss about the nudists that can be found everywhere in the park.

◄ THE CHINESE TOWER IN THE ENGLISH GARDEN. The beer garden at the Chinese tower offers another way to cool down. The 7,000 seats and the Bavarian brass band make this beer garden one of the liveliest in Munich. The 25 m/82 ft high tower was modelled after a Pagode from the "Kew Gardens" in England, which was itself, built according to a Chinese model. The original tower was built in 1789/90, but burnt down several times. It was, however, always rebuilt again.

▼ **"Eisbach"-pleasures.** Summers can be very hot in Munich. The Eisbach (ice creek) – which is not as cold as it sounds – in the Englische Garten offers a refreshing dip.

▶▼ **Bavarian Cooking at Platzl** (top right picture, this page). Whoever wants to get to know the Munich restaurant culture and local culinary delights a little better should head to Ayingers am Platzl. The traditional restaurant is in the middle of the old city, next to the Hofbräuhaus.

▼▼ **Viktualienmarkt.** Not much is left of the old Farmer's Market. Today, Vitualienmarkt, also known as "the good parlor of Munich" is a market for the gourmet. It is perfect for those in search of exotic fuit, an exclusive type of cheese or a rare spice.

▼▼ **"In Munich there is a Hofbräuhaus ..."** 35,000 Visitors drink 10,000 liters of beer a day at the world's most famous taproom. The freestate is glad because the Hofbräuhaus in Munich is a state owned establishment. A brass band entertains the guests in the "Schwemme", the rustic beer hall on the ground floor. On the upper floor there are even more party halls. When the weather is nice, it is especially nice to have a drink in the neighboring beer garden.

▶ **The Victory Gate "Das Siegestor".** The Victory Gate marks the end of Ludwigstrasse and the beginning of Leopoldstrasse. Built under Ludwig I, the gate was modelled after the Arch of Constantine in Rome and was dedicated to the Bavarian armies. After it was heavily damaged in World War II, it was rebuilt in a more simple style and was inscribed with the words "Dedicated to victory, destroyed by war, a reminder of peace".

◀ THE OLYMPIC PARK IN NORTHERN MUNICH. The barren three square kilometer area in northern Munich was transformed into an exciting landscape of athletics for the 1972 Olympic Summer Games.

The 1972 games were the largest yet, setting records in many categories. But one event will always cast a shadow over the Games of Peace: In the early morning of 5 September palestinian terrorists broke into the Olympic village. They killed two members of the Israeli team and took hostage of members of the team. In an ensuing battle another 9 Israeli, 5 terrorists and one policeman were killed. The Olympics were suspended and a memorial service was held. In defiance of the terrorists the International Olympic Commitee decided to resume the games after 34 hours.

Today the Olympic Park is very alluring to both locals and tourists. Each day, thousands of people come to go for a walk, to do exercise, to go to a concert or a festival, or to enjoy the extraordinary architecture of the park buildings. In the center of the the Olympic Park is the stadium with its exciting pavilion roof. The 75,000 square meter construction is made out of plexi-glass sheets that hang from 58 steel poles and span across the stadium and the Olympic and Swim Halls. Many concerts and big events take place in the 75,000 seat stadium or in the hall where there are 14,000. The 291 m/955 ft high Olympic tower offers a fascinating view of the area and its surroundings.

▼ THE ALLIANZ ARENA. Since May, 2005, The Munich National Soccer Club's new stadium can be found in Fröttmaning. There are enough seats for 70,000 people. For FC Bayern, the dream of a proper soccer arena has come true. It all began in 2001 with a public vote in which the majority of the Munich population voted for the construction of a new stadium. The 340 million Euro stadium was then built in record time. The outer shell is especially impressive. 2760 air pockets light up red, white or blue, according to which team is playing. The 2006 FIFA World Cup was opened in the Allianz Area.

▶ WELCOME TO THE WIESN'. The Oktoberfest in Bavaria, playfully called the "Wiesn", is the largest and probably the most popular fair in the world. Each year it takes place at the Theresienwiese (Theresien Field) and runs for 16–18 days in September and beginning of October. It all began in the year 1810, when on the occasion of their wedding, Crown Prince Ludwig and Princess Therese held a fair that lasted for several days. It was so well received, that the fair developed into a permanent tradition. Today there are almost 200 carnie companies with 80 carnival rides at the Wiesn. Many of them are sentimentally old-fashioned, while others are true thrillers – just like the 14 large and 16 smaller beer tents. Roughly six million visitors celebrate together at the Theresienwiese.

▼ FESTIVE BEGINNINGS (bottom picture, this page). Every Oktoberfest begins with the Parade of the Wiesn Hosts. Accompanied by a marching band, the parade of splendidly decorated horse carriages and host and carnie coaches is lead to the pavilions by the Münchner Kindl and the Lord Mayor.

▶▶ "EIN PROSIT DER GEMÜTLICHKEIT". The beer doesn't stop flowing after the Lord Mayor taps the first barrel and calls out the traditional "Ozapft is" (It's tapped!). Around 6 million Mass (=1 Liter mugs) are drunk ever year. This also explains the hilarious mood in the beer tents! Very often, the mood is so great that the tents become too crowded and the entrance doors have to be temporarily closed. Traditional brass music is played until 6:00 pm but afterwards, pop music sparks up the mood and after a while just about everyone dances on the benches!

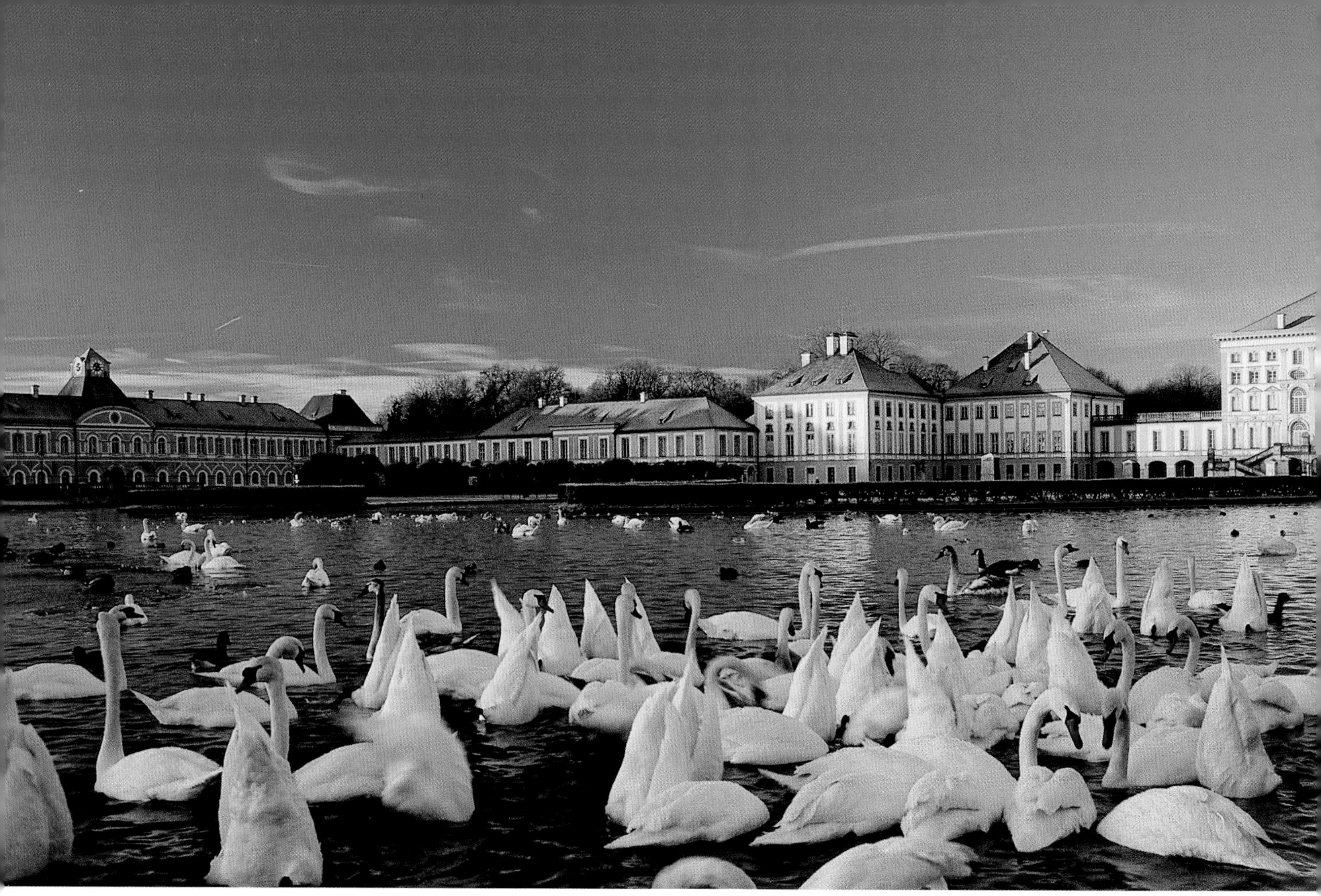

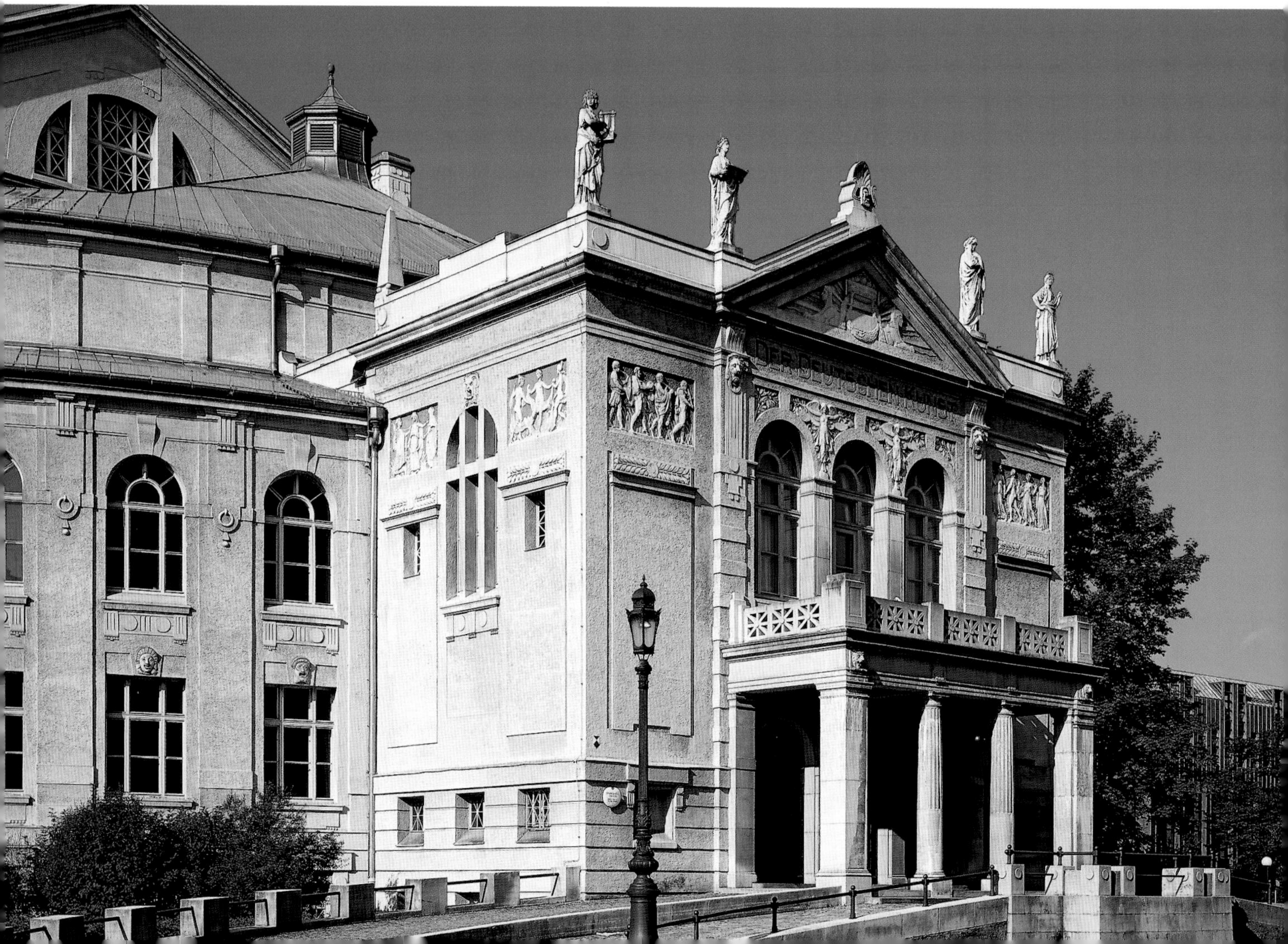

◄◄ **NYMPHENBURG PALACE.** The former summer residence of the noble Wittelsbacher family is popular with locals and tourists alike. The palace is not only in the middle of the city, but also in the middle of a beautiful park that the Nymphenburg Canal flows through. The baroque palace houses King Ludwig I's "Gallery of Elegance", the "Marstall Museum" and the Museum of Man and Nature, which is especially recommendable to children.

◄◄ **"RAISE THE CURTAINS!".** Munich has many distinguished stages, but The Prinzregenten Theater is one of the most loved playhouses amongst them. It was constructed in 1900–1901 and was modelled after the Richard-Wagner-Festival House in Bayreuth. Today, the "Prinz" (Prince) houses the Bavarian Theater Academy of August Everding.

▲ **THE GALLERY IN THE LENBACHHAUS** (top picture, this page). Amongst other collections, the former Villa of the "Painter Prince", Franz von Lenbach houses the one-of-a-kind collection of the group of painters known as "Blaue Reiter" ("Blue Riders"). Exhibits of classic, modern and contemporary art are shown in the attached complex.

◄ **ANTIQUE AND MODERN ART.** The paintings and sculptures that are on display in the New Pinakothek range from Classic to Art Nouveau. The most prominent art collections of the 19th century can be found here. Directly across the way is the Old Pinakothek, which houses one of the most significant painting collections in the world. European pieces from the middle ages up to the end of the Rococo period are on exhibit here.

◄ **CONTEMPORARY ART.** The Contemporary Pinakothek, which was opened in 2002, houses one of the largest collections of art from the 20th and 21st centuries. It conjoins four various art museums; art, graphic arts, architecture and design.

▼ "All Wrestlers – ready – pull!". In Bavaria, finger wrestling is more than entertainment; it is actually an organized sport with competitions, championships and organization of various age groups and weight classes. Not being much practised anywhere else in the world it will probably never be an Olympic discipline – alas!

▼ ▼ The Maypole Tradition. In Bavaria, the custom of putting up a maypole can be dated back to the 16th century. Local clubs, fraternities or fire departments usually take on this task. Many helping-hands are required to heave up the maypoles with the two trusses called "Schwaibln".

▶ ▼ The Stealing of the Maypole. One of the most popular customs according to young people is the stealing of a maypole. A few days before the pole is set-up, a delegation from the neighboring village tries to steal it. Therefore, the maypole must be well protected and watched over, especially at night. If it gets stolen anyway, it must be rescued somehow. Usually it is bartered for with snacks and lots of beer. The entire group then eats and drinks together.

▼ ▼ May Celebration. The celebration begins as soon as the maypole is solidly anchored. The white and blue flag is raised, the brass band starts to play and the May Dance begins.

▶ The Maypole. Traditionally, the maypole is a symbol of the affluence of a village community. The tallest tree is always selected – very often it is over 30 m/100 ft high! The maypoles in Upper Bavaria are usually spiralled and painted white and blue. They are then decorated with a green tree top, colourful banners, a wreath and the guild symbol of the local craftsmen.

◄◄ **CLOISTER ANDECHS.** The bavarian cloisters transformed the area not only through their churches and buildings, but also through their economic, political and cultural influences. Cloister Andechs was built on Holy Mountain on the east coast of the Ammersee during the 15th century. The cloister churches, St. Nikolaus and St. Elisabeth house famous relics and is a popular pilgrimage destination. Over 500 years ago, the Benedict monks began to brew beer here. Today, the famous "Andechser" is on tap at the Cloister bar.

◄ **BENEDICT ABBY ETTAL** (top picture this page). This cloister is located about 10 km/6 m north of Garmisch-Partenkirchen. It was founded in 1330 by Kaiser Ludwig IV in order to secure the commerce route between Augsburg and Verona. The miraculous image of the Ettal Madonna in the cloister church of St. Mariä Himmelfahrt (St. Mary's Ascension) is venerated by pilgrims. Amongst other things, a few inns, a brewery and a boarding school belong to the cloister.

◄ **CLOISTER REBDORF.** Cloister Rebdorf can be found embedded in the beautiful countryside of the Altmühl Valley. It was founded in 1165 as an Augustine Canon monastery. The convent, with its 183 m/200 yd long right side, faces Altmühl and the prestigious arcade courtyard.

◄ **CLOISTER BENEDIKTBEUERN.** Not far from Kochelsee (Kochel lake) lies the oldest cloister in Upper Bavaria (established in 739). The story says that the Holy Bonifatius himself consecrated the first cloister church. Today the cloister is in possession of Salesianer Don Boscos and is the home of many educational institutions.

▶ THE BAVARIAN OCEAN. Not only does Bavaria have mountains, but it also has an "ocean" – Chiemsee. Measuring 80 square kilometres, the Chiemsee is the biggest lake in Bavaria and the third largest in Germany. You can even sit and watch the turn of the tides here. The lake formed during from a melting glacier during the last ice age. All of its islands are famous, but the most well-known of all are the Fraueninsel and the Herreninsel, with the Herrenchiemsee Palace. The lake and the circumjacent Chiemgau are beautiful vacation destinations. The Chiemgau Mountains, the Hochfelln, the Hochgern and the Kampenwand also contribute to the beauty of the area. In this area, the possibilities are endless; you can climb mountains, relax on the beach, participate in water sports, go hiking, take a bike tour or check out the culture attractions.

▶ TOUR OF THE LAKE WITH THE SALON STEAMBOAT. One of the greatest ways to get to know the Chiemsee area is by taking a ride on one of the 11 boats that travel between the Chiemsee community and the islands. A ride on the old paddle wheel steamer, "Ludwig Fesler", which was built in 1926, is especially fun. A journey at the stern of the Salon takes the passengers back in time.

▶▶ FRAUENCHIEMSEE ISLAND (aerial view, opposite page). The Fraueninsel can be reached by ship all year round. After the Herreninsel, it is the second largest island on Chiemesee. Roughly 300 people live on the car-free island. The Benedictine abbey, Frauenwörth, which the island was named after, was established here in as early as the 9th century. The church buildings were built in the 11th century, but stand on older Carolingian foundations. Today, seminars and days of reflection take place in the cloister.

▼ **THE CAROLINGIAN GATE HALL.** The gate on the north side of the cloister stems from the beginning of the Frauenwörth period, around 850 AD. It is a one-of-a kind in the Bavarian area.

▼▼ **KAMPANILE AS A SYMBOL** (top right). Today, the free-standing bell tower from the 11th century is the symbol of Chiemgau.

▶▼ **HERRENCHIEMSEE.** A large portion of the Herreninsel is covered with forest and is, for the most part, uninhabited. However, the largest island on Chiemsee offers a brilliant attraction; the New Herrenchiemsee Palace.

King Ludwig II built it as a smaller version of The Palace of Versailles. Due to the king's death, the palace was never fully completed and some parts were even torn down again. The spacious park with its fountains and gardens were also modelled after Versailles.

▼▼ **GRANDIOSE ROOMS AND MUSEUM.** The absolute highlights of the palace are the hall of mirrors with the corner rooms, the Peace Hall and the War Hall (shown in the picture here). The 98 m/320 ft high, grandly arranged hall with its 17 huge mirrors and 17 arched windows, towers above the

entire west side of the palace. The unfinished section of the south wing houses the King Ludwig II's Museum.

▶ **THE FAIRYTALE KING.** Today in Bavaria, Ludwig II (1845-1886) is playfully called "Kini" (King), even though he was everything but close to his people. To be precise, he was quite egocentric and afraid of people. As a result of his extravagant lifestyle and his pricey palace projects, he was highly in debt. The Bavarian government incapacitated him and forced him to resign. He then drowned mysteriously in Starnberger Lake.

LUDOVICUS II.
BAVARIAE REX.
MDCCCLXV.

◄ **REIT IM WINKL** is the ideal vacation place with guaranteed Good Weather. In the middle of the Bavarian Alps in Chiemgau lies this small village. There may only be 3,500 residents, but there are 5,000 beds available for vacationers. At an altitude of 695 m/2280 ft, this climatic paradise is protected by the mountain in three cardinal directions – it is only exposed on the west side. Thanks to its location and special climatic conditions, you can, in the truest sense of the word, breathe deeply. Long hours of sun during the warm season and plentiful snow for the winter sport fanatics are both guaranteed. The Winklmoosalm, which belongs to Reit im Winkl, is a first class ski and hiking

area. St. Pankratius Parish Church, located in the middle of town is also worth seeing. The neo-baroque construction stems from the years 1912/1913 and is currently listed as a preserved landmark.

▼ **THE PASSION PLAYS.** In 1633 in the middle of the Thirty Years War, the plague ravaged through Oberrammergau. The residents vowed to perform regular passion plays if the plague would end. Afterwards there were no more plague victims to mourn and the passion plays were performed every ten years, up until today (the next will be in May 2010) There are over 100 performances each season. Two thousand lay actors, who must have been born in or have lived in Oberrammer-

gau for at least 20 years, contribute to the plays. Over 520,000 people attended the plays during the 2000 season. The play tells the story of the last five days of Jesus' life and takes up to six hours to perform. The Passion Theater is located on the northern edge of the town and has enough seats for up to 4,200 guests. The stage is open and the surrounding scenery acts as the setting.

The Oberammergau Passion Play depicts the last five days in the life of Jesus Christ, beginning with his entry into Jerusalem till his crucification and eventually the Resurrection.

Since 2002, the Passion Play House is also used for operas and other theatrical performances.

◀◀ **Mittenwald and Violin Construction.** On the foot of the Karwendel Mountain lies Mittenwald, a village that flourishes on tourism. For a long while, however, the village's main source of income was violin construction. A Mittenwälder, Matthias Klotz learned the craft in Italy and introduced it to his hometown in 1679. Violin making is still a well maintained tradition in Mittenwald. Many of the local violin workshops carry out century old family traditions. Since the mid 19th century, there has been a world renowned violin making school and a violin museum there.

▲ **The Vacation Spots Around Tegernsee.** Whether on land or on the water, the area around Tegernsee is certainly worth a visit. A ride on a row boat or on the excursion steamboat provides an impressive view onto the Tegernsee valley and its beautiful towns with their countless spa facilities and clinics.

In Bad Wiessee, the iodine-sulphur sources offer a place of healing and relaxation and a casino also is there for those who need a change of pace!

◀ **The Tegernsee Train.** From 1883 to 1998, the small Tegernsee Train serviced the 12 km/7.5 m route between Schaftlach and Tegernsee. Today it is a special occasion when the royal blue, coal driven steam locomotive, TAG 7 returns to the track for a rare tour!

◀ **Walchensee.** The Untouched Alpine Lake, the beautiful Walchensee, lies in the middle of the Bavarian Alps near Kochel am See. Its coast is barely tilled, motorboats are forbidden. There is also a beautiful natural beach whose waters are perfect for sailors, surfers and divers. The mountain lake is framed by forested mountains, such as the Benediktenwand and the Jochberg.

▶ NATURAL MONUMENT PARTNACH-
KLAMM. In the Rein Valley near Garmisch-
Partenkirchen lies the 800 m/870 yd long
Partnachklamm, one of the most beautiful
gorges in the entire alpine area. The
stream has carved a depth of 80 m/260 ft
into the mountain. In earlier years, it was
used to transport timber into the valley.
The gorge can be accessed all year round.
The Partnach certainly impresses with its
whirlpools, rapids and wild waterfalls.
Those without a fear of heights can also
venture onto the iron bridge that is
68 m/220 ft above the gorge.

▶ TAKE THE TRAIN TO THE PEAK. Exploring
the Zugspitze doesn't have to be exhaust-
ing! The Bavarian Zugspitz train comfort-
ably takes visitors from Garmisch, through
Grainau and up to the 2,599 m/8,530 ft
high Zugspitz plateau. The Glacier Train
Station can also be found here. In 1930,
after only two years of construction, the
cog railroad began operation. It over-
comes a 250 percent incline over a 19
km/12 m long distance, 4.9 km/3 m of
which are through tunnels.

▶▶ THE ZUGSPITZE. Germany's highest
mountain lies in the Wetterstein Mountains. At 2962 m/9,718 ft, it has the highest
elevation of all mountain peaks in Germany. The Zugspitze also forms a mountain border with Austria. Just under the
peak is the Alpine Club Hut "Münchener
Haus" and a fully manned weather station.
Originally, the west peak, where the golden
summit cross can be found, was a meter
lower than the west peak, but the Nazis
demolished it. Germany's one and only
glacier ski area can be found about
400 m/1,300 ft below the summit of the
Zugspitz (called the Zugspitzplatt)

▼ **Farchant – "Bergdorf" in the Golden Land.** In the Loisach Valley, or "Golden Land", not far from the Zugspitze, lies the beautiful village of Farchant (700 m/2,300 ft above sealevel). In the 18th century, the village profited largely from its location on one of the most important trade routes in Europe. Murals which are painted on the various grand farm houses, often depict this scene. Today, the breathtaking panoramic views and the gorgeous area between Wetterstein and the Ammer and Ester Mountains are especially awe-inspiring.

▼▼ **High House (Inn).** Skiing makes you very hungry, so stop in at the Sonn-Alpin at the top of the Zugspitze for a bite to eat (picture top right). Here you can also find the "highest" post office in Germany.

▼ **The Esterberg Pasture** (below left). At an altitude of 1,265 m/3,800 ft, the Esterberg is the summer pasture for the Farchanter or Partenkirchen cattle. Located in the middle of a luscious meadow, this pasture is also open all year round for those in seek of rest, relaxation or a place to reflect on the meaning of life.

▼▼ **Up to the Summit in Ten Minutes.** Although the Eibsee cable car was already fully functioning in the year 1963, today it is still considered to be a technical masterpiece. It goes from the Eibsee Station to the Summit station.

► **Wildbad Kreuth** is located near Tegernsee and is just two kilometres from the Kreuth health resort. The former bathhouse was built in 1511 and was frequented by illustrious guests such as Kaiser Franz Joseph I and Czar Nikolaus I. Now a conference and education center, the CSU holds its annual convention here every January.

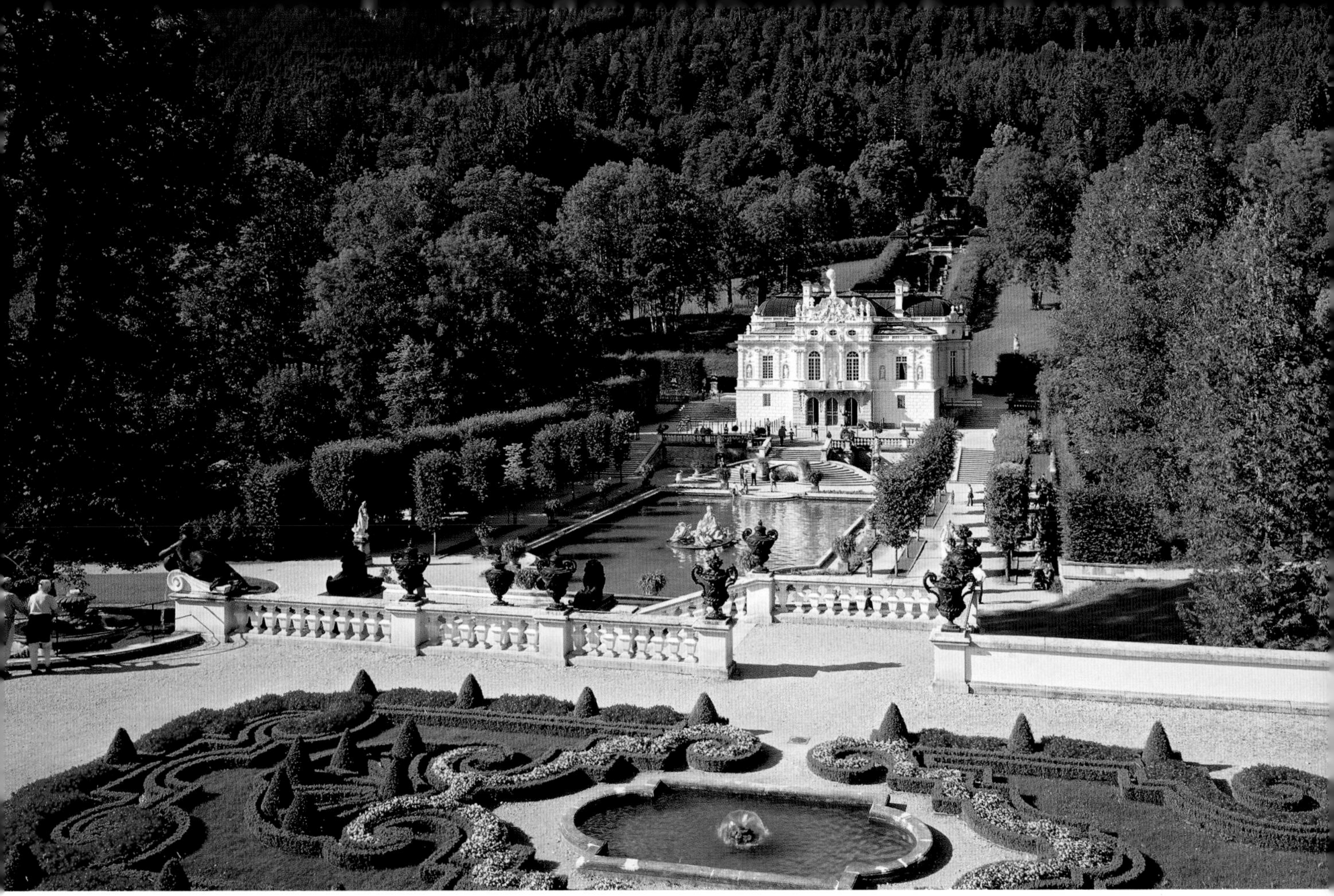

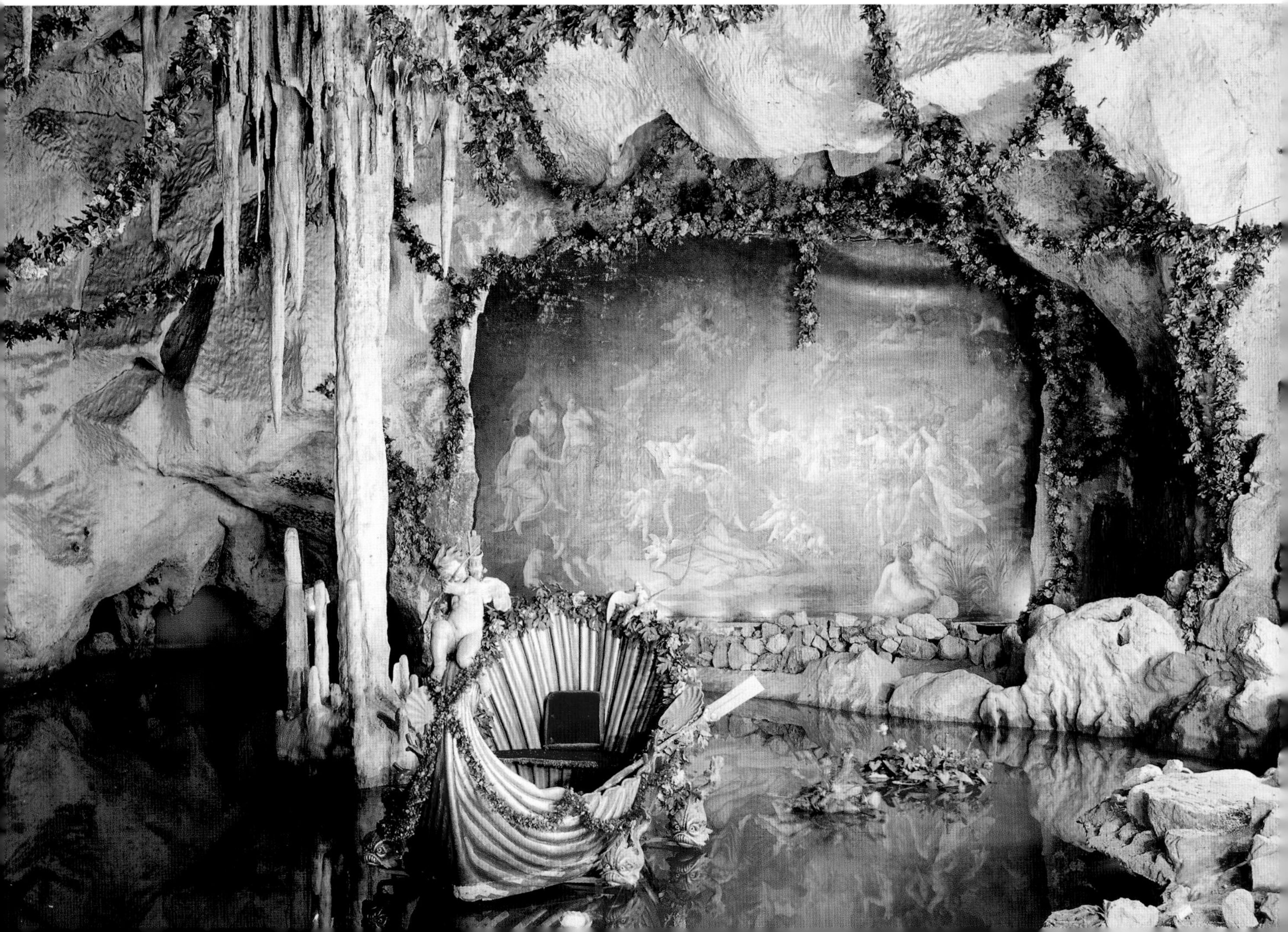

◄◄ ROYAL VILLA – LINDERHOF PALACE is another magnificent building which belonged to Ludwig II. It was built between 1874 and 1878 in place of a small hunting castle. The palace and its pompous interior have been maintained in its Rococo style. Linderhof became the Kings preferred residence and it was, in fact, the only one of his palaces that he ever saw fully completed.

◄◄ THE KINGS LITTLE REFUGE. The buildings in the park add to the special charm of Linderhof Palace. Visitors here are especially impressed by the artificial stalactite cave that is based on the Venus Grotto from the Wagner Opera "Tannhäuser". Lights, rainbows, waterfalls and waves could all be found here when the king paddled over the little lake.

▲ THE WIESKIRCHE – A JEWEL IN PFAFFEN-WINKEL (top picture this page). In an area that is rich with churches and cloisters, you can also find the Wieskirche. Built between 1745 and 1754, it is one of the most extraordinary displays of Bavarian Rococo that exist. UNESCO declared the pilgrimage church as a World Heritage Site and stated that it is "a masterpiece of human creativity and an unprecedented example of a lost culture".

◄ NEUSCHWANSTEIN. According to Ludwig II's letter to Richard Wagner, the medieval castle should have been called "The Schwangau Palace". However, the palace, which is nestled in the grandiose mountain scenery, has become known throughout the world as the "Fairytale Castle". Construction began in 1869 and continued for 15 years, but was never fully completed. Today, Neuschwanstein is on the list as a possible addition to the new Seven Wonders of the World.

◄ ST. KOLOMAN. Not far from Neuschwanstein is the small church, St. Kolomon. This church served as a place of pilgrimage, especially during the plague of the 17th century.

▼ Füssen. In East Allgäu, at the end of "The Romantic Street", lies the beautiful village of Füssen. The old city with its houses from the late middle ages, the castle with its painting collections and the former Benedictine Cloister, St. Mang are all worth seeing.

▼▼ Kempten in Allgäu. The former Roman city, with its Italian flair, is an attractive vacation destination. You shouldn't miss the archaeological park, Cambodnum, the grandiose rooms of the Residenz or the Museums. The picture (top right) shows the Orangerie in the "Hofgarten".

▼ Nördlingen in Ries (below left). The former free imperial city lies in Nördlinger Ries, a meteor crater. It is decreed as the only German city with a full-standing, well-maintained, accessible city wall. There is still a tower keeper there and in the evening you can even hear the watchman's call.

▼▼ Lindau – "Bodensee" (Lake Constance). The classic vacation question – mountains or water? – can be confidently answered with "Lindau". In this medieval city you will find the old city hall, which was used by the parliament in 1496. The six meter high

lion monument watches over the old harbour and the lovely Wang Tower.

► Augsburg. The history of Augsburg is long and eventful. There are not only traces of the Romans here, but also of the Fugger and Welser merchant dynasties. Both of these families were responsible for the economic booms of the 15th and 16th centuries. There are many things worth seeing here. Don't forget to stop and see the city hall, which was built by Elias Holl between the years of 1615 and 1624 – the most significant building from the Renaissance period north of the Alps.

▶THE BAVARIAN KITCHEN. Hearty and rich with calories, Bavarian food is exceptionally delicious. The main dish usually consists of meat, preferably pork, but also venison, duck and goose are favourites. A selection of dumplings, called Knödel, cabbage and sauerkraut are served as side dishes. As a visitor, you should simply treat yourself to a "Schweinshaxn" with bread dumplings!

▶ALLGÄU'S EMMENTHALER. Cheese made in the Allgäu enjoys good sales far beyond the region itself. The local dish of Käsespatzen (cheese dumplings) has become an accepted dish beyond the confines of Bavaria. Flour, milk, eggs, onions and, natch, a hefty lacing of cheese, such are the ingredients for this most traditional of the Allgäu's recipes.

▶▶LORD PRESERVE HOPS AND MALT. Bavarian beer is the best – or so say the Bavarians. The oldest brewery in the world, Weihenstephan, is located in Freising, a city in the heart of old Bavaria. Although the monks have probably been brewing beer since the eight century, it did not become official until the year 1040. In Bavaria, the "purity standards" are strictly adhered to. These rules prohibit the use of any product other than water, malt, hops and yeast. Tapped into one liter mugs, the favourite beers are wheat and pale ale.

◄ "FRANCONIA IS LIKE A MAGIC CUP-BOARD; new drawers keep opening to reveal colorful sparkling gems..." the poet Karl Immermann once wrote, and today still his words hit the mark. The swathe of land in the north of Bavaria reveals 15 wholly different travel landscapes, each with its own character and all of them a perfect dream. Whether one revels in the pristine nature of the Franconian Lake District, the Franconian Forest or the Franconian Suisse, to name but a few – one is never far from the historic towns with their medieval centers, castles, fortifications and eminent churches. There are the world-renowned sites like Nuremberg, Würzburg or Bamberg as well as the smaller towns, in which one feels as if one has gone back in time. They all too have the special flair that makes a visit worthwhile. In Bamberg, the Old Town is on the UNESCO list of World Heritage Sites, in Würzburg the Residence. Also one of the magnificent monuments of Franconia is the Würzburg Fortress Marienberg. Towering on a plateau rock above the river Main, this mighty stronghold, which dates back to the year 1000 and was the prince-bishops' see from 1253, features a spectacular view over Würzburg. Yet, among all the beauty and cultural highlights, one must not neglect one's physical well-being. Those who have ever gotten to know the good wines or the savory local beer only need to have some Nuremberg sausages, and they will rave about their visit to Franconia forever.

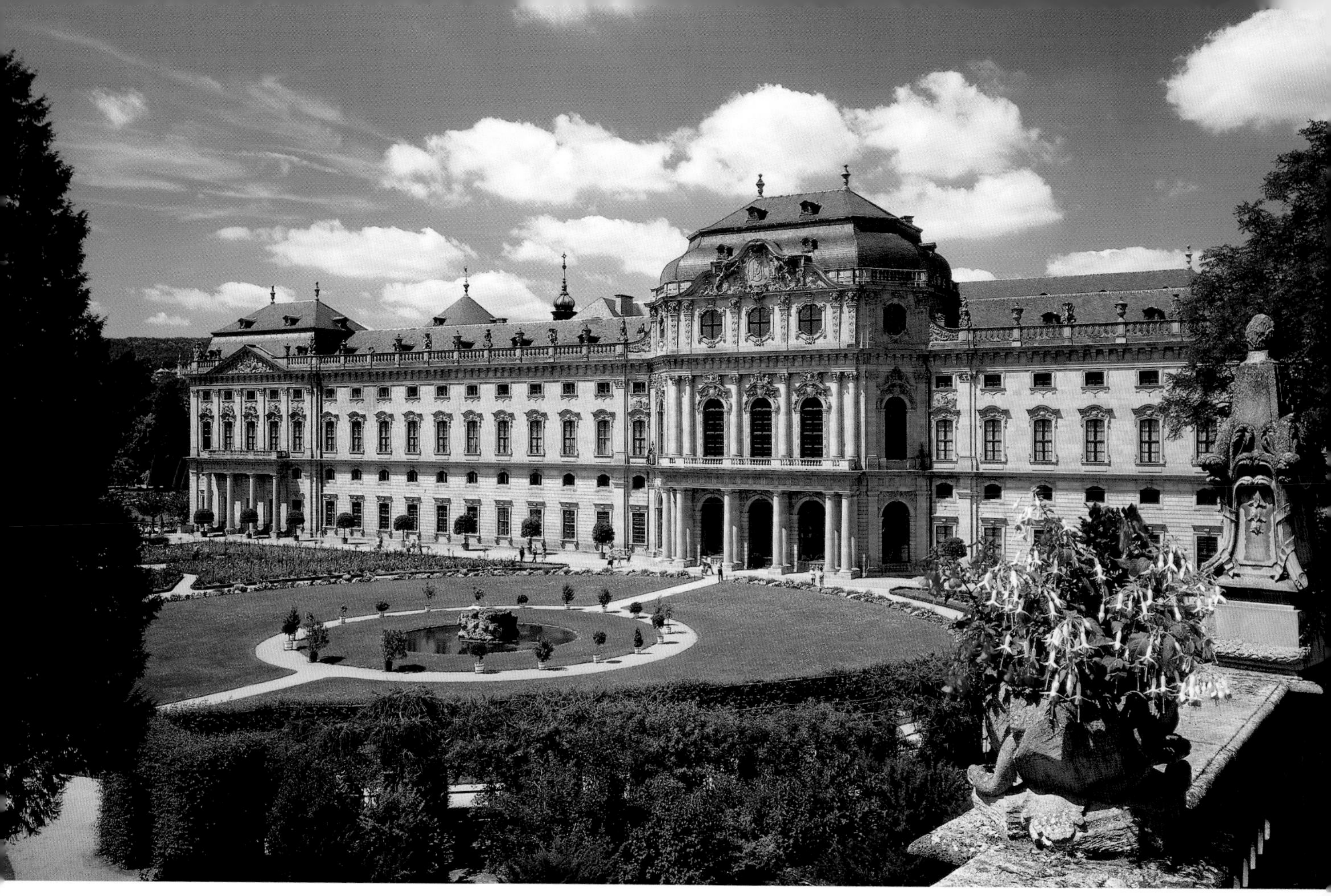

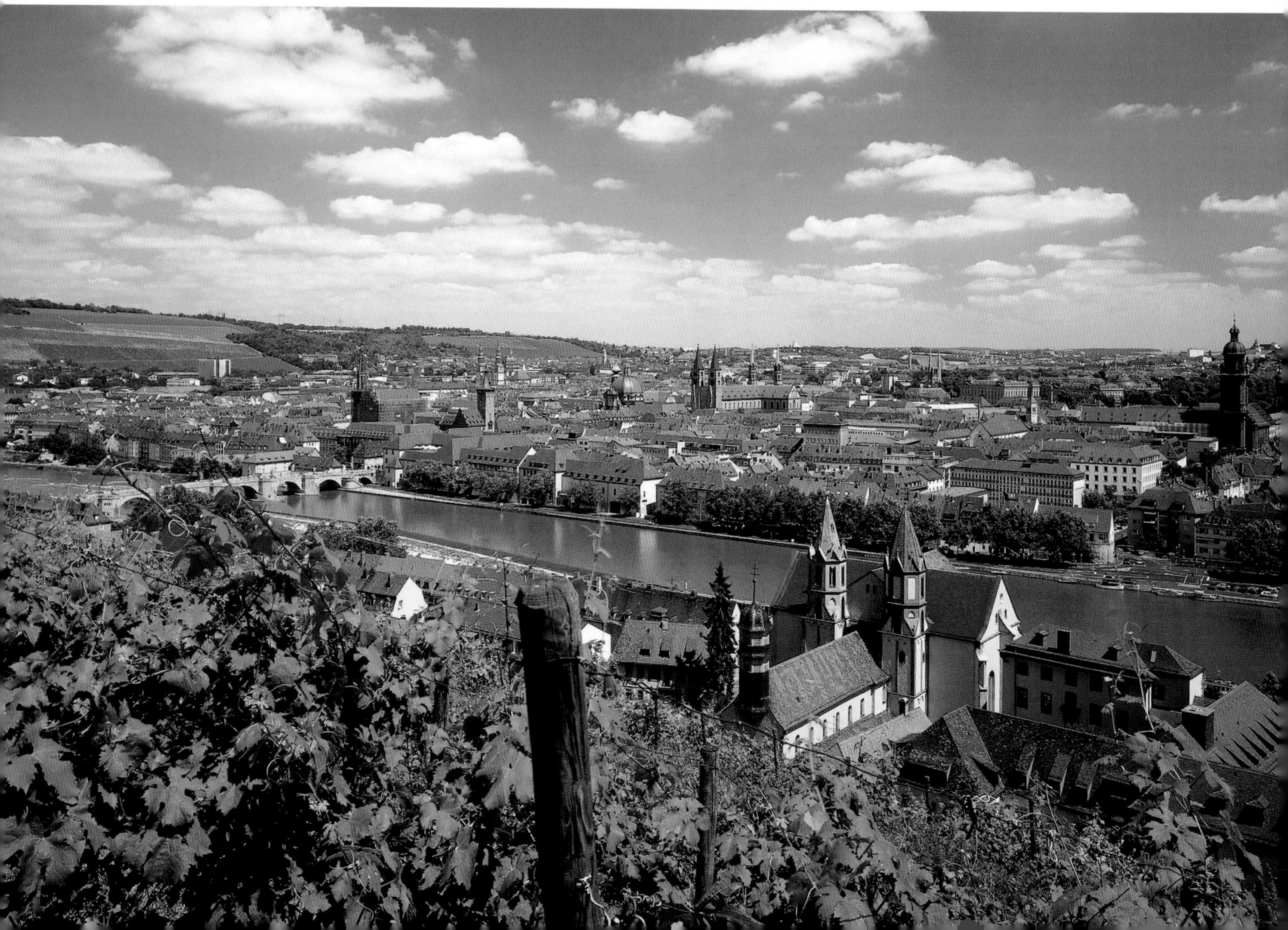

◄◄ **WÜRZBURG – RESIDENCE.** The Residence, formerly the see of the Würzburg prince-bishops, is considered the main work of Southern German Baroque. It was built between 1720 and 1744. UNESCO, which in 1981 declared the castle a World Heritage Site, describes it as "the at once most homogeneous and the most extraordinary of the Baroque palaces". Famous above all is Balthasar Neumann's staircase with its 600 square meter unsupported vault and the magnificent ceiling fresco by Giovanni Battista Tiepolo.

◄◄ **WÜRZBURG VISTA.** The Baroque city with its 1,300 years of city history lies on both sides of the river Main amidst idyllic vineyards. From the Fortress Marienberg, one gets a wonderful view over the river and the town with its churches, like St. Kilian Cathedral (Dom St. Kilian), St. Mary's Chapel (Marienkapelle), Neumünster Church or the Pilgrimage Church, Käppele.

▲ **CENTER OF FRANCONIAN WINE.** Visiting one of the many wine taverns is a must in Würzburg. Also a real highlight: a tour of a winery, like the Staatlicher Hofkeller, with guided tour of the wine cellar and wine tasting. Even Goethe is said to have cherished the Hofkeller-Riesling.

◄ **POMPEJANUM AND JOHANNISBURG CASTLE.** Amidst a vineyard near Aschaffenburg lies the Pompejanum, a copy of a Roman villa built by Ludwig I. Not far away is Johannisburg Castle, which houses a branch of the Bayerische Staatsgemäldesammlung (Bavarian State Painting Collection).

◄ **WÜRZBURG'S "GRINZING".** Within the so-called Main triangle in front of the gates of Würzburg lies Randersacker. The winemakers' village with its 1,200 year old winegrowing tradition is a popular place for excursions. Worth seeing are the Balthasar-Neumann-Pavilion and the Romanesque tower of the village church.

▼ Ochsenfurt. On the southern tip of the Main triangle lies surrounded by lovely vineyards the small town Ochsenfurt. Worth seeing are the medieval Old Town, the restored half-timbered houses and the Gothic New Town Hall (Neues Rathaus) with its lance-shaped turret, the figure clock and the "Narrenhäuschen" (Fools' Cot), which used to serve as a detention and sobering-up cell.

▼▼ Reminiscent of Medieval times. In Prichsenstadt (bottom left) in the Franconian wineland, one feels sent back to the Middle Ages not only at the sight of the mighty city gate or the half-timbered houses, but also when the night-watchman during his evening patrol serenades the visitors. Top right: pumkins for sale.

▼▼ Wine town Sulzfeld am Main. Quietly and peacefully lies the little town with its more than 1,000 years of history. It is hard to believe that in the year 1266, on St. Cyriac's day, one of the largest cavalry battles of Medieval times was raging here ("Cyriakusschlacht"). Today, the visitor can enjoy the medieval atmosphere taking a tour of the defense wall with its towers and gates, the narrow alleyways and the old burgher houses.

▶ Escherndorf – vineyard on the river Main. The vines here grow on steep slopes. Franconian white wine is traditionally bottled in a "Bocksbeutel", a bottle in the form of a flattened ellipsoid. The Franconian wine region offers numerous settings for wine tasting, wine dinners with local cuisine and special guided tours to vineyards and wine cellars. Some wineries offer as a special treat seminars dedicated to wine and cheese – two delicacies that go together well.

◄◄ **"The Spessart Inn"**. Mespelbrunn Castle lies hidden away in a Spessart valley between Frankfurt and Würzburg. In 1957 it served as backdrop for the famous movie with German actress Lilo Pulver. When the construction of the moated castle was begun in 1427, its tower and moat were meant to improve security. Later, when the castle was remodeled in the Renaissance style, they added to the romantic sight.

◄ **Pilgrimage in the vineyard**. On a rise near Volkach lies, amidst vineyards, the church Maria im Weingarten (Our Lady in the Vineyard). The pilgrimage to the wooden miraculous image of the dolorous Mother of God started in the 14th century. Another treasure of the church is the floating Madonna in the Rosary ("Madonna im Rosenkranz") by Tilman Riemenschneider. She was stolen from inside of the church in 1962 and only returned after Henri Nannen, editor of the magazine "Stern", voluntarily paid a ransom. Also notable is the gorgeous view over the Main valley.

◄ **Volkach Main river loop** (Volkacher Mainschleife). A cruise around the Main river bend near Volkach is an excellent way to enjoy the beautiful Main landscape with its meadows and wine slopes. For those folks suffering from seasickness, a ride on the Mainschleifenbahn is recommended. Getting active and hiking up one of the slopes is rewarded with a panoramic view.

◄ **Miltenberg**. On the left bank of the river Main, between Spessart and Odenwald forests, lies the historic Old Town of Miltenberg. Well worth seeing is the market square, the so-called "Schnatterloch", with its red sandstone Renaissance fountain from 1583 and the surrounding half-timbered houses. High above the market square, on Greinsberg mountain, sits enthroned Mildenburg castle, built around 1200 and formerly seat of the archbishop's burg graves. Today, its inner courtyard displays some remarkable stone monuments.

▼ **ROTHENBURG OB DER TAUBER.** Situated on an escarpment above the Tauber valley lies Germany's most romantic town – say its countless visitors from around the world. For, on the whole, the Old Town still looks much like it did in the Middle Ages. Idyllic, half-timbered houses, the labyrinthine alleyways, high towers and strong fortifications send the visitor on a trip back into the past. At the market square stands the Town Hall with its older, Gothic block with tower and the younger part from the Renaissance era.

▼▼ **EVERY YEAR AT CHRISTMAS TIME** (picture bootom left). Is there a more magnificent backdrop for a Christmas market than this half-timbered town? It takes place on the Reiterlesmarkt and attracts friends of mulled wine from everywhere. Whoever does not make it to Rothenburg during Advent season can always visit the Christmas stores in Herrngasse.

▼ **THE RÖDER TOWER (RÖDERTURM).** Apart from the Town Hall Tower, only the Röder Tower is accessible. The walls facing out of town are distinctly more stout than the ones facing the city. The tower was an important sentry post during wartimes.

▼▼ **THE HOLY BLOOD ALTAR (HEILIG-BLUT-ALTAR).** The city church St. Jacob is the most prominent in Rothenburg. The two towers of the Gothic church significantly shape the townscape. Inside can be found the precious Holy Blood Altar, which was carved by Tilman Riemenschneider.

▶ **TOWN LANDMARK.** The so-called Plönlein, a small, triangular city center square with the pillar fountain (Säulenbrunnen) and Siebers Tower is a well-loved photo motif.

► **Nürnberg – St. Lawrence's Church (Lorenzkirche).** On Lorenzer Platz rises the biggest and artistically most prominent church of Nürnberg, the Gothic St. Lawrence's Church with its two towers and western façade decorated with rosettes. In its interior, the 18 meter high, tower-like tabernacle (Sakramentshäuschen) is just as worth seeing as the wooden sculpture "Annunciation" in late Gothic style. St. Lawrence's Church was badly damaged during the Second World War; especially the roof truss had to be rebuilt entirely.

► **Craftsmanship and conviviality.** In 1971 the Crafts Yard (Handwerkerhof) was established in the place of the former Nürnberg armory yard. Since then it is highly esteemed by tourists and locals due to the versatile craftsmanship and culinary treats on offer there. In little workshops, one can watch goldsmiths, glass painters, pewterers, doll makers, potters, gingerbread bakers and others at work and purchase the manufactured artifacts in the stores.

►► **Nürnberg – 1,000 years of history.** Since its first documentary mention in 1050, the second largest city in Bavaria, with 500,000 inhabitants, can look back on a 1,000 year history. Having become rich through trade and craft, the city was made Imperial City, seat of parliament, medieval metropolis, cultural hub, industrial center, railway city, but then also city of the "Party Rallies" and place of the "Nürnberg Trials". At every corner traces from past eras can be found, which constitute Nürnberg's richness today. Its pretty townscape the city on the river Pegnitz owes to the burgher houses, the prominent churches, the fountains and its landmark, the Imperial Castle (Kaiserburg).

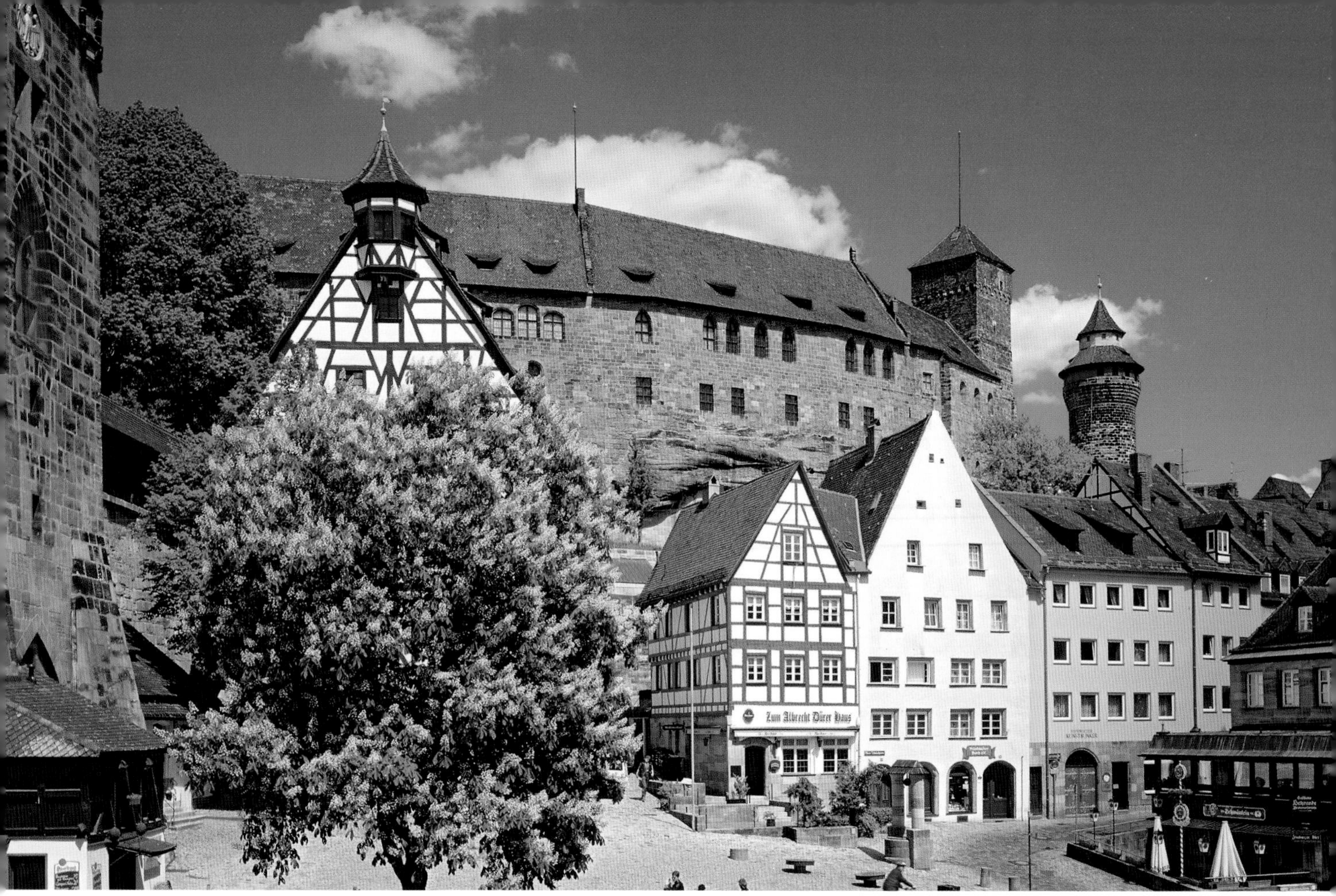
Zum Albrecht Dürer Haus

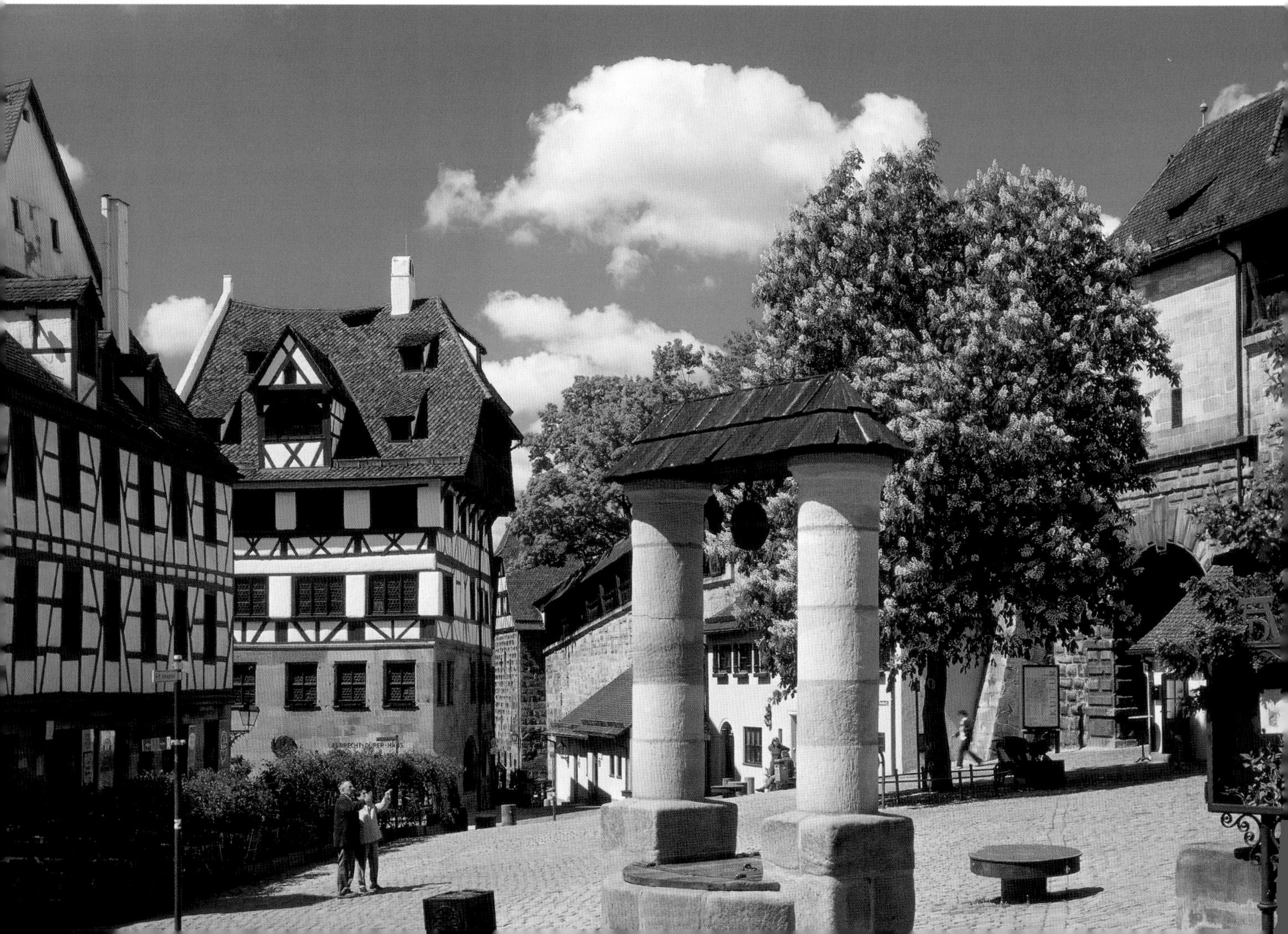

◄◄ **Nürnberg's castle**. The famous medieval palatinate saw many a crowned head, for all the emperors between 1050 and 1571 resided here at least for some time and continued to expand the formerly Salian royal castle. Particularly worth seeing are the double chapel with choir tower and the imperial residential and state rooms.

◄◄ **"Back to Dürer"**. The painter Albrecht Dürer (1471–1528) is probably the most distinguished son of Nürnberg. In his honor, a museum was established in his residential house. The visitors are guided by Agnes Dürer herself (either via headset or impersonated by an actress), who tells about everyday life with her famous husband. Dürer's artistic techniques are demonstrated in the painting and graphic workshop. In front of the house stands Tiergärtner Tor. The gate, part of the city fortification, today is a popular photo motif.

◄ **Variety of fountains.** There are about 180 fountains in Nürnberg, historic ones as well as modern ones. Most famous are the Beautiful Fountain (Schöner Brunnen), the Marriage Carousel (Ehekarussell) and the Gooseherd Fountain (Gänsemännchenbrunnen), all of them designed around a theme and richly decorated.

◄ **Railway and mail.** The Nürnberg Traffic Museum houses both the German Railway Museum and the Museum of Communication. Because of its large "experience area", a visit is worthwhile especially for families. Many a railroader's heart warms looking at the historic rail vehicles and the model collection.

◄ **Nürnberg Christmas Market.** Every Advent, the "Christ Child" (Christkind) in person opens Germany's most well known Christmas market. The products on offer are deliberately kept traditional, plastic knickknack is frowned upon.

▶ **IN THE GINGERBREAD BAKERY.** What would Christmas season be without Nürnberg gingerbread, the "original ones", as the numerous fans of the cookies assert? Back in the Middle Ages, Franconian monks created the gingerbread-forerunners, Pfefferkuchen and honey cakes, and then, in order to prevent the dough from sticking to the baking tray, put their gingerbread on a wafer base. Nürnberg was a favorable place for the gingerbread-making industry. As a center of trade, one had access to spices from distant countries, and a source of honey was to be found close by in the imperial forest, where bees were bred. Today, Nürnberg gingerbread and the particular specialty "Elisen" gingerbread are exported around the world in beautifully designed containers and boxes, which are coveted collector's items.

▶ **"DREI IM WEGGLA" (THREE IN A ROLL).** Three sausages in a roll are the most enjoyed snack in Nürnberg. And they are but a small bite, given that the Nürnberg roast sausage weighs just 25 grams. For a main meal, one takes six or twelve of the popular sausages and some side dishes. Since 1462, they have been made from defatted pork, seasoned with marjoram and are best prepared in a traditional sausage frying stall (Wurstbraterei) over a beech wood fire. Nowadays, this Nürnberg export hit is also very popular vacuum-sealed.

▶▶ **THE COSTUME GIVES AWAY THE HOME.** In tradition-conscious Franconia, wearing traditional costume is part of the active preservation of ancient customs. The liveries are different, depending on region, marital status, occasion and function. Particularly pretty and colorful is the traditional costume from the Ochsenfurt area in Lower Franconia, with frock, shawl and silk apron.

▼ A PERPETUAL MYSTERY. Ansbach, former seat of Margraves, offers prominent sights like the church St. Gumbertus, the Residence and the Orangerie in the castle gardens. However, hardly a visitor is not impressed by the mysterious saga surrounding the foundling Kaspar Hauser, who appeared 1828 in the streets of Nuremberg and came to a violent death in Ansbach in 1833. Ansbach commemorates him with a memorial in the Old Town, with a section of the Margrave Museum and with the Kaspar-Hauser-Festival.

▼▼ ERLANGEN. This cultural center and university town comprises the Old Town founded around 1367 and the New Town, which was built as a Baroque city layout for the French Huguenot refugees in 1686. The Margrave castle today houses the Friedrich-Alexander-University.

▼ DINKELSBÜHL. The medieval town on the Romantic Road features a perfectly preserved historic Old Town including fortifications and 16 towers. Worth seeing among other things are the Late Gothic St. George's Minster, the wine market and the town mill.

▼▼ WOLFRAMS-ESCHENBACH. For centuries, the town was a home to the Teutonic Order. It is due to the architecture of this knightly order that the home town of the great poet and minnesinger Wolfram von Eschenbach (around 1200), most famous for his "Parzival" epic, got its Renaissance-influenced medieval appearance.

▶ CLIFF VILLAGE TÜCHERSFELD. The most famous photo motif in Franconian Switzerland is probably the cliff village Tüchersfeld. Here also the well worth seeing Franconian Switzerland Museum can be found.

◀ **BAYREUTH — IN WAGNER'S FOOT-STEPS.** Bayreuth, the former Margravial residence, today is a modern university town and a thriving business location. Many attractive buildings, like the Margravial Opera House and the New Palace were built in the town's heyday in the 17th and 18th centuries. However, most visitors come to experience the city of Richard Wagner, who was active here from 1872. After many setbacks, he finally found his artistic completion here. The phrase he had engraved on his residence could loosely be translated as: "Here, where my illusive quest found rest, I name this house Wahnfried". Today the house "Wahnfried", which his benefactor Ludwig II had helped to fund, contains the Richard-Wagner-Museum. Back in the garden, the famous composer lies buried.

▼ **FESTIVAL THEATER ON THE GREEN HILL.** It was Richard Wagner's dream to have a festival theater. What he wanted was the concentration at one place, in a medium-sized city without competing theaters and other distractions. In Bayreuth, he was able to fulfill his life dream, as so often through the support of Ludwig II The first pageants in 1876 were opened with the opera "Rheingold". Since 1951, the artistic director of the Bayreuth Festival has been Richard Wagner's grandson Wolfgang Wagner. Together with his late brother Wieland Wagner, he is considered the pioneer of "New Bayreuth". The wooden theater building, shaped like an antique amphitheater, with its lowered orchestra pit and ascending visitors' ranks became a triumphant success.

With its distinctive architecture and its fantastic acoustics, the Festival Theater is regarded as one of the most prominent opera houses of this world. Whoever is called to attend the performance by the legendary fanfare sounds today is either a celebrity or extremely lucky, for the tickets are in great demand. The almost ritual visit to the Festival by Wagnerians and celebrities is also called "pilgrimage to the Green Hill".

◄◄ VIERZEHNHEILIGEN PILGRIMAGE CHURCH. Because of its magnificent Rococo design and the inner spatial effect, the pilgrimage church near Bad Staffelstein is considered a highlight of late Baroque. The church, which was built between 1443 and 1475, was erected on the very spot where the Christ child accompanied by 14 children is said to have appeared to a shepherd, who thought the 14 were helpers in time of need.

◄ BAMBERG – THE FRANCONIAN ROME. A thousand years of history imparted a very special atmosphere to the city of Bamberg, which locals as well as visitors to the perfectly maintained Old Town with its Gothic and Baroque buildings rave about. Since 1993, Bamberg with its three historic city centers, the hill-, island- and gardener quarters, has been listed as a World Heritage Site. In addition to the large, spectacular buildings like the Imperial Cathedral, there are many little gems to be found, for instance the fishermen's settlement on the eastern shore of the river Regnitz. The 19th century houses, which have been built on stilts, rise directly out of the water. One can even use a gondola to explore the area also known as Little-Venice.

◄ A TOWN HALL ON THE WATER. Bamberg's Old Town Hall from the 15th century stands in the middle of the river Regnitz. Its Baroque façade dates from the 18th century. Seemingly freely floating over the water is a half-timbered house attached to the town hall – Rottmeisterhaus.

◄ RESIDENCE UNDER ROSES. Not only flower fans get excited when, during the summer months, the Residence rose garden with some 4,500 rose bushes offers a glorious sight and an exhilarating scent. The gorgeous view on Bamberg's Old Town makes the experience complete.

► **COBURG.** What is it that Martin Luther, Queen Victoria and Johann Strauss have in common? All three of them left their marks in this former residence town with the beautiful half-timbered houses, the city wall and the historic ensemble. Enthroned above the city sits Veste Coburg, one of the most expansive castle grounds in the whole of Europe. On the market square with the Prince-Albert-Memorial there stands, adorned with wall paintings and façade decorations, the city villa in late Renaissance style, which was built in 1601.

► **EHRENBURG CASTLE.** The former Baroque city residence of the Coburg dukes got its Late Gothic façade, which dominates its appearance today, in the 19th century. Apart from the gigantic Baroque main hall, the building also features one of the first water closets on the European continent. It belonged to Queen Victoria.

►► **FRANCONIA'S GOLD TREASURES.** Not only wine culture has a long tradition in Franconia. Brewing has also been cultivated for centuries, mainly in the regions of Kulmbach, Bamberg and Franconian Switzerland. In the region around Brombach Lake prospers the so-called "green gold", the hop plant. In Spalt, in the Franconian Lake District, it has been cultivated since the 12th century. The main producing area for the "white gold", asparagus, is the region near Nürnberg called "Knoblauchland" (garlic country). After Southern Bavaria, Franconia produces the most asparagus in Bavaria. During the nine day asparagus market in Nürnberg, where the asparagus is sold off decorated wagons, many other culinary delights of the region are also on offer. Here the charming ambassadors of both the white and the green gold come together.

◄ WHETHER ONE RATHER wanders through wide-stretched woods, like the Bavarian or the Upper Palatinate Forest, or prefers to explore limestone rocks and stalactite caves as in the Bavarian Jura – in view of so many dream landscapes, everyone will find his personal favorite area for hiking, taking a cure, doing sports or simply watching the world go by. A journey along the mighty river Danube, the lifeline of Eastern Bavaria, inevitably leads through 2,000 years of history. There are so many things to be discovered, like the traces left by the Romans, medieval castles or their ruins, Romanesque and Gothic churches and cities with rich traditions like Passau or Regensburg, which are well aware of their historic heritage but, nevertheless, have a lively and modern air to them. The city of Regensburg, rich in history and on the UNESCO World Heritage List, by no means has the character of a museum in spite of its 1,400 historic monuments. Walking across the proud 336 meter long Stone Bridge, which, after its completion in 1146, was considered as a new wonder of the world, one relishes the magnificent view of the city and the cathedral. Then one strolls through the medieval Old Town, where numerous coffeehouse tables and beer benches beckon. Also an exceptional experience are the big historic festivals as staged by the citizens of Furth and Landshut. The preservation of old traditions is a matter of course for people here, and they are happy to give their visitors an opportunity to get to know Eastern Bavaria, its culture and its people.

▼ **Regensburg – St. Peter Cathedral.** Regensburg's most prominent church is St. Peter Cathedral, the most outstanding Gothic building in Southern Germany and sepulcher of the Regensburg bishops. Particularly pretty are the stained glass windows. The cathedral is also home to the boys' choir "Regensburger Domspatzen".

▼▼ **Old Town Hall.** At today's Kohlenmarkt (Coal Market) stands the Old Town Hall. The oldest, middle part with the tower dates from the 13th century. In its Imperial Hall, the "Perpetual Reichstag" was held between 1663 and 1806. Today the Town Hall houses the Reichstagsmuseum.

▼ **Of weighing and drinking.** At the central square Haidplatz stands the former patrician house "Neue Waag". Here the city in 1441 placed the town scale and also a "Herrentrinkstube", where the town's aldermen could have a drink after their consultations. In the Gothic vault the stone city mouse is hiding away. Whoever touches her will be coming back to Regensburg.

▼▼ **Illustrious guests.** The hotel "Goldenes Kreuz" at Haidplatz square was a guest house even in the 16th century. Emperor Karl V used to lodge here when he attended the parliamentary meetings at the Reichstag. Also King Ludwig I of Bavaria and Emperor Wilhelm I. of Prussia once stayed here.

▶ **The Germans' hall of fame.** Ten kilometers from Regensburg on the high bank of river Danube sits enthroned the Walhalla, a white marble temple. King Ludwig I had it built between 1830 and 1842 by his architect Leo von Klenze, and then had it fitted with busts of German luminaries from History and Art.

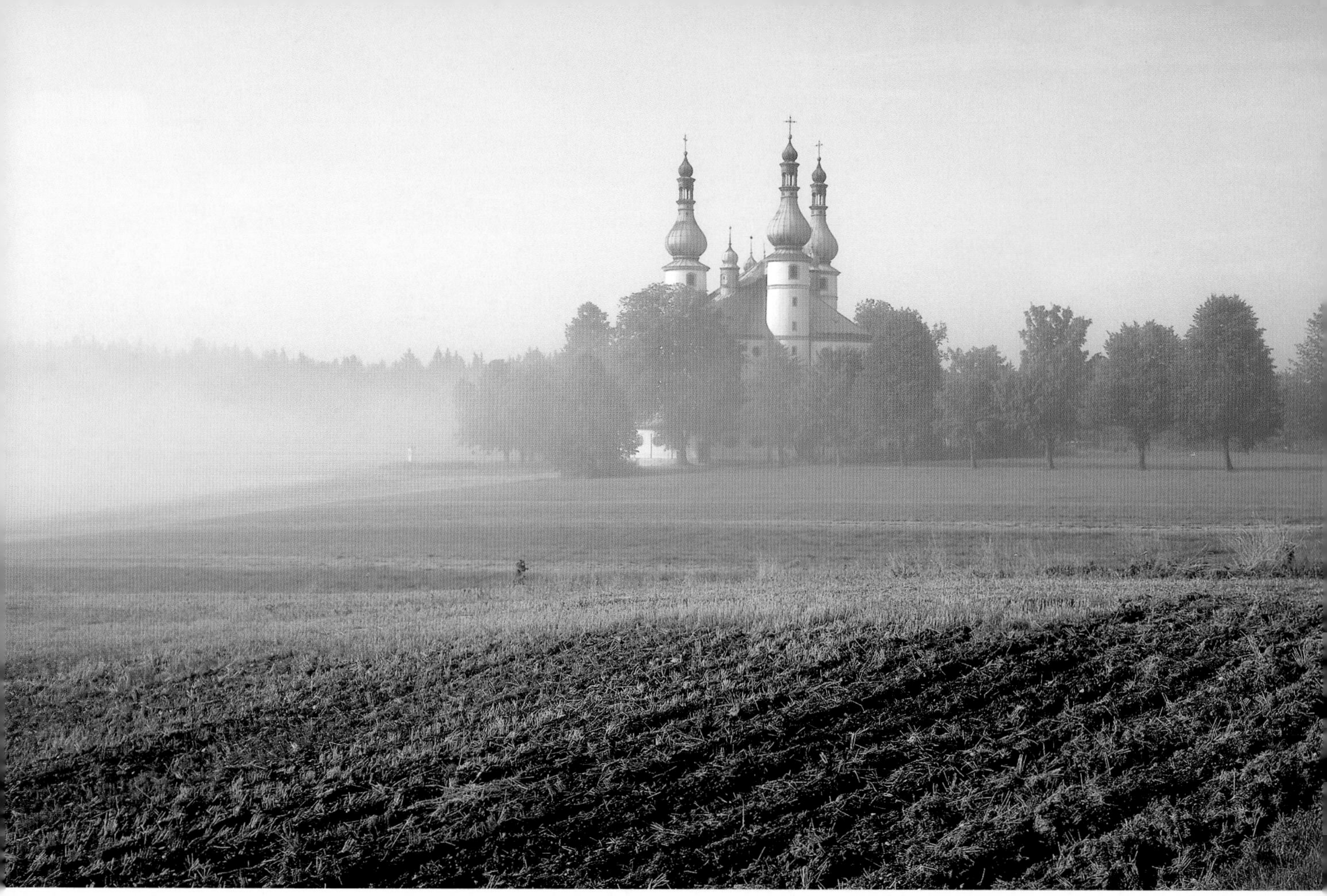

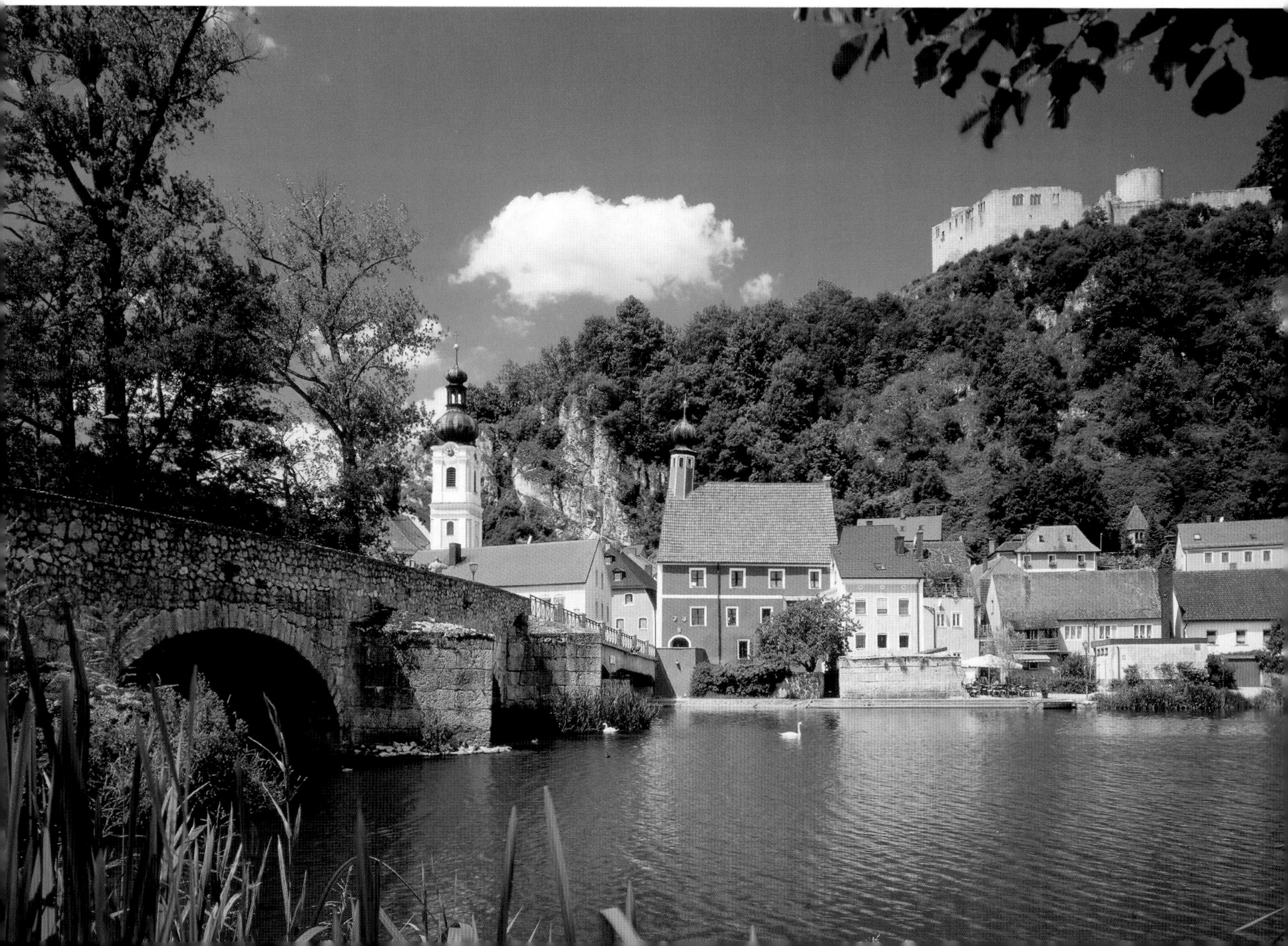

◀◀ DIE KAPPL. The little pilgrimage chapel of the Holy Trinity called "die Kappl" stands on Glasberg mountain near Waldsassen. The prominent Baroque circular church was built between 1685 and 1689. Its architecture strikingly translates the Trinity idea. There are, for example, three vaulted conches with three alcoves, three altars and also three circular towers. Inside the chapel gorgeous ceiling frescoes and stucco ornaments are to be found.

◀◀ PEARL OF NAAB VALLEY. Imbedded between Jura rocks, a stone bridge, old houses and the castle ruin dominate the medieval picture of Kallmünz on the Naab. The castle was built around 1250 in order to be able to protect the ore- and salt street between Amberg and Regensburg. Even painters like Wassily Kandinsky and Gabriele Münter were inspired here, and still today there is a small artists' colony in Kallmünz.

▲ FURTH IM WALD. Due to its beautiful surroundings, the small border town inside the Bavarian Forest Nature Park is a popular vacation spot. Especially in August, thousands travel to the place in order to watch Germany's oldest folk play "Drachenstich" (slaying of the dragon). Already for the past 500 years this enactment of good against evil is performed by the citizens of Furth.

▲ FURTH LIVES AS LONG AS THE DRAGON DIES. 18 meters long, four meters wide and weighing nine tons is the dragon, whose roaring and fire breathing is steered by four men inside.

◀ THE PAGEANT. 1500 people in historic costumes, 200 horses, bands and floats in a historical pageant bring back Furth's history and add another highlight to the "Drachenstich" weeks.

▼ BASILICA WALDSASSEN. Visible from afar is the great Baroque church, which is also considered a landmark for the Upper Palatinate. The former cloister church was built between 1682 and 1704. It features magnificent choir stalls, ceiling frescoes and stucco adornments.

▼▼ FESTIVAL FOR YOUNG AND OLD. Even the youngest participants of the Pfingstritt (Pentecostal Ride) proudly wear their traditional costume and look forward to the extensive festival program, organized around the equestrian procession.

▼ PFINGSTRITT IN BAD KÖTZTING. In 1412 the minister of Kötzting asked the local young men for an escort in order to bring the last rites to a man in Steinbühl a couple of kilometers away. Upon their safe return, they vowed to venture the ride every year anew. Thus, one of the largest equestrian processions came into being, with every year on Whit Monday 900 riders in traditional costume taking part.

▼▼ WEIDEN IN UPPER PALATINATE. The porcelain town is the gate to the Upper Palatinate Forest and starting point for hikes through diversified landscapes. Worth seeing is the market square between the upper and lower gate with its beautiful gabled houses and the old schoolhouse with town museum and archive.

▶ THE CITY IS DANCING. In the Old Town Hall, built from 1539 to 1545, not only town matters used to be decided, but also dances and theater performances were given. Since 1981 stores have also been established again on the ground floor – quite according to medieval tradition.

◄ HALL OF LIBERATION AT KELHEIM. In Altmühl valley, high above river Danube on the slopes of Michelsberg mountain, stands the Hall of Liberation. King Ludwig I. had it built in memory of the victories over Napoleon in the Wars of Liberation 1813-1815. The memorial was constructed in the years from 1842 to 1862, first under the supervision of Friedrich von Gärtner, later of Leo von Klenze. It was opened on 18 October 1863, the 50th anniversary of the Battle of Nations at Leipzig. 18 monumental statues crown the 18 buttresses that are surrounding the circular building, which is actually an 18-sided polygon. There were 18 German tribes; the battles at Leipzig and Waterloo each took place on the 18th of the month. In the interior, 34 victory goddesses form a roundel. The panorama of the Altmühl valley is also quite spectacular.

▼ WELTENBURG ABBEY. Strikingly beautiful, but at high risk of flooding, lies the oldest Bavarian monastery on a peninsula in the "Danube Gorge". The most classy way to approach the Benedictine abbey is surely by boat from Kelheim. The monastery was founded by Iro-Scottish migrant monks around the year 617. The church building, built by the famous brothers Asam in the years from 1716 until 1739, is considered a highlight of Bavarian Baroque. Today the monastery not only is a meeting and seminar place, but also a popular locale for excursions for around 500,000 visitors per year. An added appeal certainly is the picturesque beer garden where the exquisite beer from the monastery brewery is served. The Monastery Brewery Weltenburg probably is the oldest monastery brewery in the world, although the Brewery Weihenstephan in Freising also claims this title to its name. The "Weltenburger Kloster Barock Dunkel" was given the "World Beer Award" in 2004 as the best dark beer worldwide. Around the monastery there are various hiking trails; also the popular Danube-cycle path passes by Weltenburg.

◄◄ **CITY ON THREE RIVERS.** Water, wherever you look: by Passau in Lower Bavaria the three rivers Danube, Inn and Ilz meet. The present-day university town's history is long. Even the Romans appreciated the favorable situation on the rivers. In 739, Passau became a permanent bishops' see, in 1217 prince-bishopric. River navigation was the key to the city's wealth; trade and industry flourished. Italian builders gave Passau the distinct flair, which marks the Baroque city to this day. The highest point in the Old Town is St. Steven's Cathedral. It not only is the largest Baroque cathedral north of the Alps, but also features a marvelous backdrop for the Passau Christmas market.

▲ **VIEW OF PASSAU.** There is so much to see in the "Bavarian Venice", like the Old Town Hall with its 68 meter tower on the right bank of Danube river. However, the location on the water also has its price; time and again the town is afflicted by floods.

◄ **ALTMÜHL VALLEY NATURE PARK.** An exceptionally charming way to explore Altmühl Valley is a boat ride on the Main-Danube-Canal. There are also many hiking trails and cycle paths. Imbedded in fascinating landscapes lie traces of the Romans, who guarded their borders on the Limes, as well as monasteries, palaces and castles. The small, worth seeing castle Burg Brunn here is harmoniously nestled on the rocks.

◄ **"BURG" AND "BRUCK".** The market town Essing in the Altmühl Valley not only features the ruins of Burg Randeck castle, but also a 46 meter historical wooden bridge, called "die Bruck".

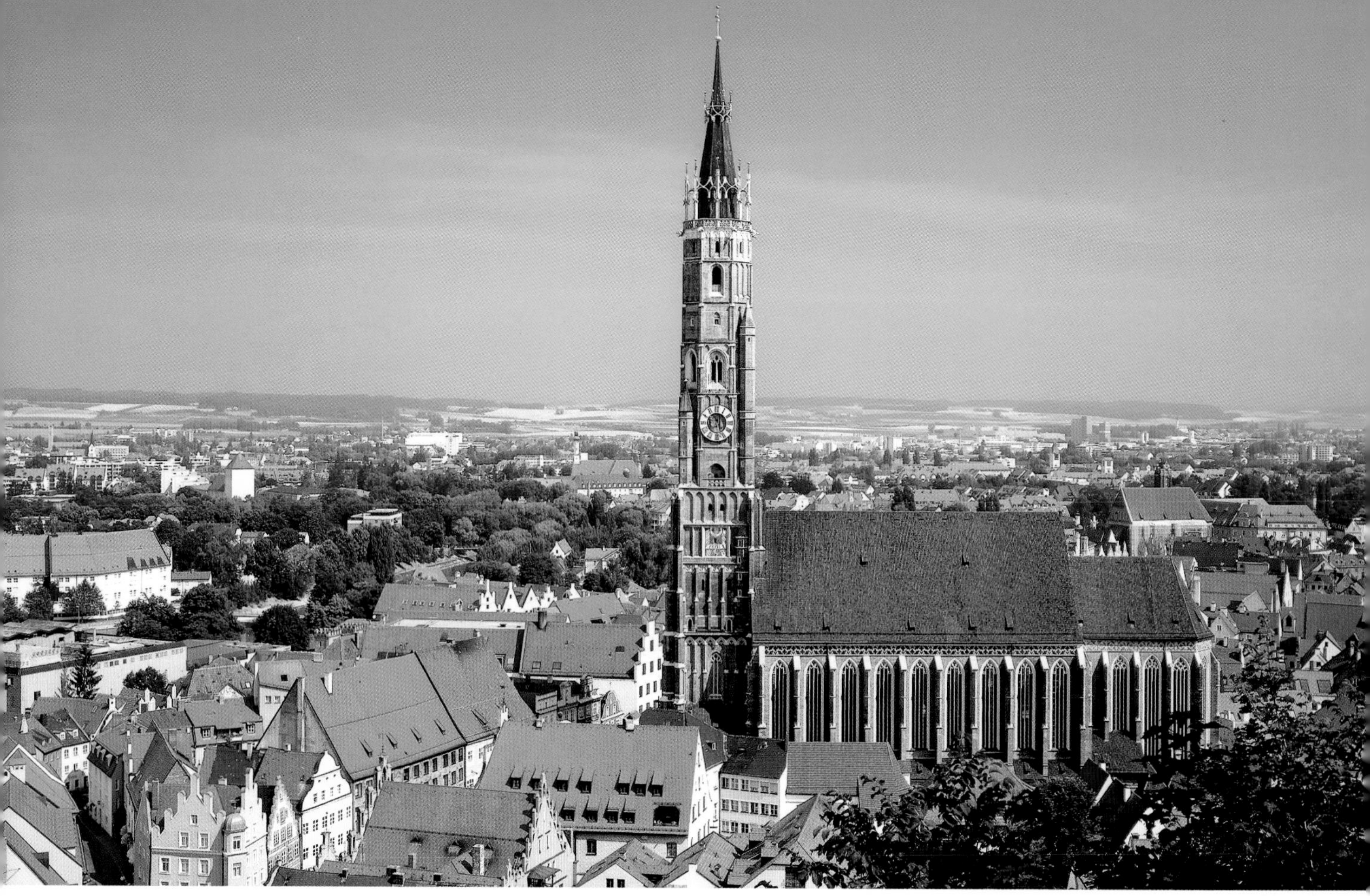

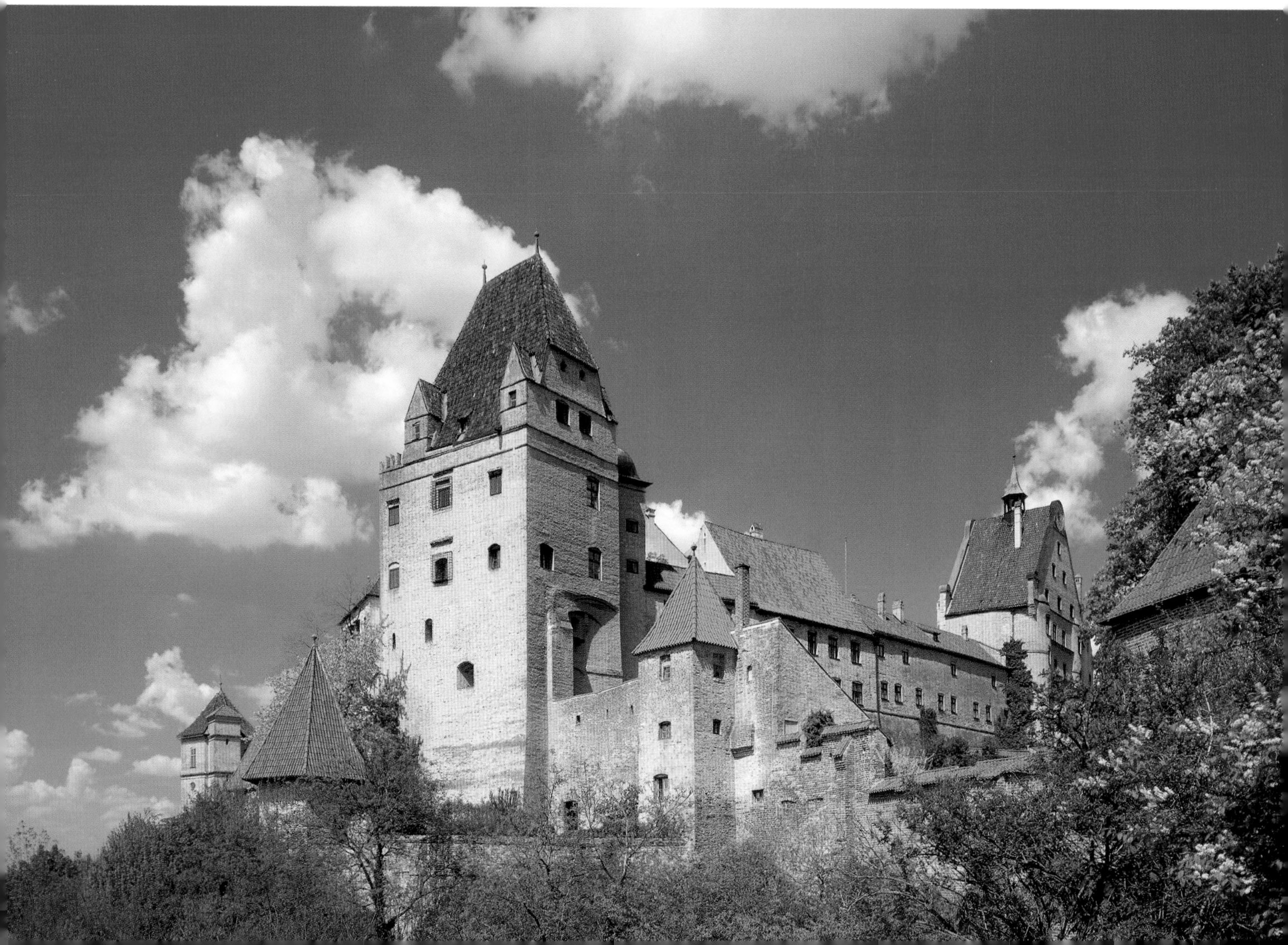

◄◄ OLD DUKE CITY ON THE ISAR. Landshut in Lower Bavaria can look back on 800 years of eventful history. The earlier main residence of the Wittelsbacher was founded in 1204 by Duke Ludwig I of Bavaria. In medieval times, Landshut was renowned as a city of the Arts; famous carvers, bronze casters, bell founders and armorers were active here. The Gothic Old Town, which consists of a wide stretch of streets with beautiful gabled houses, is dominated by the Church of St. Martin. The three nave hall church, which was built from around 1400 until 1500, features a brick tower that, with its 130.6 m/428 ft, is the highest of its kind worldwide.

◄◄ TRAUSNITZ CASTLE. The castle on a mountain above Landshut is reached via stairs or a hiking path. The fortifications, the high Wittelsbach tower and the castle chapel shape the medieval appearance of the castle. The arcades of the inner ward as well as the "Narrentreppe" (fool's stairs) with its painted figures from the Commedia dell'Arte and the interior design of the residential chambers stem from Renaissance times.

◄ WEDDING OF LANDSHUT. Every four years, next time in 2009, the biggest European historical pageant is enacted for three weeks. 2300 citizens of Landshut take part, dressed up as knights, bishops, princes, noblewomen, jugglers and gypsies. At the last wedding festivity in the year 2005, more than half a million visitors were counted. Besides the wedding procession, which moves through the city four times, there are numerous musical and dancing events, street theatre and knights' tournaments. With the festival, the wedding of Duke Georg the Rich with the Polish princess Hedwig is commemorated, which was celebrated in Landshut in the year 1475.

► **The Bavarian "Brotzeit".** Like here, on the 400 year old estate Gutshof Uttlau near Bad Griesbach, many restaurants and beer gardens serve a proper "Brotzeit". Since, in the old days the rural population had to do physically hard work, this traditional Bavarian snack is rather ample and today can easily replace lunch or dinner. It also comprises the Bavarian specialties one definitely should have tried at least once, like "Obatzt'n" (a savory cheese spread), "Kartoffelkas" (spread from potatoes, sour cream, onions and herbs) or "Presssack" (headcheese). The typical "Brotzeit" is served on a big wooden plate and some hearty sausage- and cheese slices, "Radi" (radish) and a couple of slices of bread or a pretzel must not be missing. Also a wheat beer, lager or "Radler" (shandy, mix of beer with lemonade) with the "Brotzeit" is hardly ever a mistake!

► **Deggendorf.** The city of Deggendorf on the river Danube is considered the gate to the Bavarian Forest. It features a landing stage for river cruise boats, a free-harbor, and a pear-shaped medieval Old Town with pedestrian area. In the middle of the wide street market stands the old Town Hall, built in 1535, with its Gothic tower. Attached to the southern façade are the so-called "Deggendorfer Knödel" (Deggendorf dumplings). The two stone balls connected by chains are probably a chastisement tool from the late Middle Ages.

►► **Farmstead museum.** In the spa gardens of Bad Füssing, a large spa and health resort in Passau county, an outpost of the Museum Village Bavarian Forest (Museumsdorf Bayerischer Wald) in Tittling can be found. Bruckmann house, the residential building of a farm built in 1814, houses a comprehensive exhibition depicting peasant life.

Unser komplettes Programm:

www.bruckmann.de

Product Management: Dr. Reinhard Pietsch, Susanne Caesar
Typography & Layout: Dr. Alex Klubertanz, Munich
Editing: Dr. Alex Klubertanz, Munich
Translation: Corrina Peet, Weissach; Tobias Weitmann, Munich
Text: Jasmin Seiffert, Trier
Repro: Scanner Service, Verona
Cover Design: Anna Katavic, and use of a phtograph of the Huber Picture Agency
Cartography: Astrid Fischer-Leitl, Munich
Production: Bettina Schippel, Christine Herzer
Printed in Germany by Stürtz GmbH, Würzburg

All facts contained were carefully researched by the author in consideration of the latest information available and fact-checked by the publisher. However, legal responsibility may not be inferred. We are always grateful for advice and suggestions. The address for these is:

Bruckmann Verlag
Postfach 400 209
80702 München
E-Mail: lektorat@bruckmann.de

Front Cover: St. Bartholomä
Back Cover: Neuschwanstein castle, St. Koloman, young boy in traditional costume, bavarian snack
Pages 6–7: Weltenburg, Page 93: Wellness at Bad Griesbach

All cover illustrations, as well those in the text, are by Bildagentur Huber, Garmisch-Partenkirchen.

BILDAGENTUR
HUBER

Die Deutsche Nationalbibliothek verzeichnet diese Publikation in der Deutschen Nationalbibliografie; detaillierte bibliografische Daten sind im Internet uber http://dnb.d-nb.de abrufbar.

3. unveränderte Nachauflage 2012
© 2012, 2009, 2007 Bruckmann Verlag GmbH, München
ISBN 978-3-7654-4607-8